**2nd**
*edition*

# Health and Social Care

## for Foundation GNVQ

Liam Clarke

**stanley thornes** *GNVQ*

First published in 1995 by:
Stanley Thornes (Publishers) Ltd
Ellenborough House
Wellington Street
CHELTENHAM
GL50 1YW
United Kingdom

Second edition published 2000

00  01  02  03  04  /  10  9  8  7  6  5  4  3  2  1

A catalogue record for this book is available from the British Library

ISBN 0  7487  3509  7

Line illustrations by Angela Lumley; cartoons by Shaun Williams

Typeset by Florence Production Ltd, Stoodleigh, Devon
Printed and bound in Spain by Graficas Estella S.A.

# *Contents*

| | | |
|---|---|---|
| Acknowledgements | | vi |
| Assessment for GNVQ | | vii |
| *Unit One* | Health and social care provision | 1 |
| *Unit Two* | Understanding health and well-being | 42 |
| *Unit Three* | Understanding personal development and relationships | 84 |
| *Unit Four* | Investigating common hazards and health emergencies | 128 |
| *Unit Five* | Planning diets | 173 |
| *Unit Six* | Exploring health and recreational activities | 207 |
| *Unit Seven* | Exploring physical care | 238 |
| *Unit Eight* | Preparing for employment in health and social care | 269 |
| *Unit Nine* | Working as part of a team | 305 |
| Glossary | | 335 |
| Index | | 343 |

# Acknowledgements

The author and publishers would like to acknowledge the advice of Carol Hicks and Debbie Horseman, who provided extremely useful comments on the manuscript throughout the writing process.

The author and publishers are grateful to the following for permission to reproduce material:

- Alzheimer's Disease Society – p. 38 (left).
- Association of Directors of Social Services – p. 38 (middle). © Association of Directors of Social Services, 1999.
- Gloucestershire Constabulary – p. 63.
- Health Education Authority – p. 58. © Health Education Authority.
- Her Majesty's Stationery Office – p. 36. Crown copyright material is reproduced with the permission of the Controller of Her Majesty's Stationery Office.
- National Society for the Prevention of Cruelty to Children – p. 38 (right). © NSPCC.
- Terrence Higgins Trust – p. 67.
- Kate Richards – p. 91.
- Women's Royal Voluntary Service – pp. 13 and 285.

Every attempt has been made to contact copyright holders, and we apologise if any have been overlooked. Should copyright have been unwittingly infringed in this book, the owners should contact the publishers who will make corrections at reprint.

## Photo credits

- John Birdsall (www.JohnBirdsall.co.uk) – pp. 14, 16, 20, 22, 37, 121, 124, 227, 242, 258, 262, 274, 278 and 330.
- Girl Guide Association – p. 220.
- Angela Hampton – Family Life Picture Library – pp. 113, 123, 219 and 307.
- National Osteoporosis Society – p. 53.
- Osprey RMA – p. 255.

# Assessment for GNVQ

## What is a General National Vocational Qualification (GNVQ)?

GNVQs are alternative qualifications to A levels or GCSEs and can be taken at three levels:

*Foundation*
- **Part One GNVQ (Foundation)** – equivalent to two GCSEs at grades D–G
- **Foundation GNVQ** – equivalent to four GCSEs at grades D–G; these normally take one year of full-time study

*Intermediate*
- **Part One GNVQ (Intermediate)** – equivalent to two GCSEs at grades A–C
- **Intermediate GNVQ** – equivalent to four GCSEs at grades A–C; these normally take one year of full-time study

*Advanced*
- **Advanced GNVQ (called 'vocational A levels')**
  - **Full award (12 units)** – equivalent to two A levels; these are normally taken over a two-year period of full-time study
  - **Single award (6 units)** – equivalent to one A level; these are normally taken over a one-year period of full-time study
  - **Three-unit awards** – these have been designed to encourage students to study GNVQs alongside other qualifications such as A levels, AS levels or GCSEs

## How is a GNVQ structured?

All GNVQ courses are made up of units:

- **Mandatory units** – these are units you must study
- **Optional units** – these are units you choose to study

## What is in a GNVQ unit?

All Foundation GNVQ units are of equal size and value and are organised in the same way.

You will be provided with a set of specifications from your awarding body. **Section 1** tells you about the unit and gives you brief headings of what you will learn about. For example:

---

### Unit 1: Health and social care provision

*About this unit*

You will learn

- about health and social care services and how people gain access to and use them
- how services are organised in your local area
- about the main job roles of people who work in those services, in particular those involving direct contact with clients
- the importance of the care value base.

---

It will also tell you how the unit will be assessed, for example:

---

This unit will help you with optional Foundation Unit 8 (Preparing for employment in health and social care). It will also provide the knowledge needed to help you with Intermediate Unit 1 (Health, social care and early years provision). This unit is assessed through your portfolio work. The grade on that assessment will be your grade for the unit.

---

**Section 2** tells you in more detail what you will need to learn. For example:

---

The main types of service

You will need to find out about local organisations that deliver health and/or social care. You will need to identify where local organisations are and the main types of service that they offer. The organisations may be described as:

- health services
- personal social services
- support groups and voluntary groups
- early years education services.

You should also know that some organisations might be described in more than one way depending on the services they offer.

---

**Section 3** is called Assessment Evidence. This section will tell you what you have to do to gain a pass, merit or distinction. For example:

---

You need to produce a report on local health and social care services. It must include:

- information about the health care, social care and early years services (health, personal social services, support and education services) in your local area
- identification of the main jobs in the services
- description of different jobs of people in these services
- description of access to the services.

**To achieve a pass you must show you can:**

- identify the main local health, social care and early years provision in your locality
- clearly locate these services on a map of the area
- give basic descriptions of job roles in each of the services
- describe two ways in which people are referred to in the health, social care and early years providers shown on the map.

**To achieve a merit you must show you can:**

- demonstrate the ability to work on your own in collecting some of the information you need
- accurately describe the principles of the care value base
- clearly explain the barriers that people might have to overcome to gain access to services.

**To achieve a distinction you must also show you can:**

- demonstrate an understanding of the care value base by describing clearly how it is applied by workers in the health, social care and early years services
- give relevant examples of what the services could do to overcome the barriers.

---

## What is the Foundation GNVQ in Health and Social Care?

The Foundation GNVQ is made up of:

- Three **mandatory vocational units** (these are the units you must do)
  - Unit 1: **Investigating health and social care**
  - Unit 2: **Understanding health and well-being**
  - Unit 3: **Understanding personal development and relationships**.

This unit is externally tested. This means that an external body, such as BTEC, City & Guilds or RSA, sets a test paper that you must pass to gain the unit. The grade that you get for the test will be the grade that you will get for the unit. No other assessment will take place for this unit.

- **Optional units,** which are devised by the individual awarding bodies. The range of optional units offered by each awarding body is the same.

Foundation Units can be studied separately and can be passed one at a time. If you leave a course or transfer to a school or college in another part of the country you will be credited with the units that you have already passed. This means that you will only have to complete the units that you have not already passed to gain the GNVQ. You do not have to do the whole qualification over again.

## How are GNVQs assessed?

Assessment for GNVQs focuses on what you have actually achieved. This is called outcome-based assessment. Your assessors (teachers) will assess your work after you have given them evidence that you have achieved what they have asked you to do. For example, in Unit 1 you will be asked to :

- identify the main local health, social care and early years provision in your locality
- clearly locate these services on a map of the area
- give basic descriptions of job roles in each of the services
- describe two ways in which people are referred to in the health, social care and early years providers shown on the map.

When you have done this and provided enough evidence, usually in writing, then your assessors will judge your work against national standards to see if you have met them. If you have provided enough evidence at the right standard then you will gain a pass. When you have:

- demonstrated the ability to work on your own in collecting some of the information you need
- accurately described the principles of the care value base
- clearly explained the barriers that people might have to overcome to gain access to services

you will gain a merit, and when you have:

- demonstrated an understanding of the care value base by describing clearly how it is applied by workers in the health, social care and early years services
- given relevant examples of what the services could do to overcome the barriers

you will gain a distinction.

Your written work is checked by your teacher (assessor) and if it is not up to standard the assessor will discuss with you how you can obtain the missing evidence. Remember, you can try as many times as you like to reach the required standard. No time limits can be put on you to complete the work. GNVQs are designed so that each student can work at their own pace. Some may gather evidence in a short period; others may take longer.

Your assessor will judge the evidence you have presented for each unit and ensure that your completed work meets the required national standard.

## Internal assessment

This is the assessment that takes place within your school or college. We will look a little later at what a portfolio of evidence is and what should go into it. Your teacher will support you in preparing your portfolio. Assessors have to be qualified and have adequate knowledge of the area they are working in. Their work is checked (verified) by another experienced teacher (assessor) called an internal verifier. The internal verifier selects some of your work and checks that it has met the national standards. Verification will also ensure that all the assessment within a school or college is consistent with the national standards. The work of the internal verifier is also checked by an external verifier, who is appointed by BTEC, City & Guilds or RSA to ensure that assessors and internal verifiers are working consistently to national standards. The external verifier will visit your school or college at least twice a year and will usually see some of your work and talk to you about it.

## External assessment

This will consist of written tests set by external bodies, such as BTEC, for roughly one-third of your total GNVQ. The written tests will assess the skills and knowledge that you have gained during the time you have been studying the unit content. Each GNVQ written test paper lasts about one hour; the pass mark is usually 70%.

All the awarding bodies (BTEC, City & Guilds, RSA) must ensure that assessment can be undertaken by all students, including those with learning difficulties.

## *Preparing for assessment*

Your portfolio of evidence and the external tests for the appropriate units will need to be completed and passed in order for the unit to be credited towards the full GNVQ award. Evidence may be obtained in a variety of ways, including:

- **Practical tests**. Be familiar with what you are going to be tested on and have ready all equipment and materials you will need. Do not rush, and remember to work to health and safety guidelines. Always make sure that what you are doing is safe, both for you and for any other person. Your assessor will have given you clear guidelines as to what you have to do to reach the required standard.

- **Assignments and projects**. Plan your time carefully; take time drawing up your action plan; discuss your work with your teacher or lecturer. Try to achieve all the things you set yourself to do in your action plan. Make sure your work is neat and well presented. Each assignment or project will include clear written guidelines of what you have to do to achieve a pass. These guidelines will also have been discussed with you and you will have had an opportunity to question them.

- **Observation**. You may be observed either by one of your own classmates or by a teacher. They will observe you to see how you carry out certain tasks – how you behave in groups, if you can organise other people, for instance. Try not to feel uncomfortable when being observed.

- **Oral questioning**. This is a common way to find out if you can tell your assessor why you have done certain things. What you have written or done in groups may not be clear – your assessor will ask you questions to allow you to explain and talk more about your evidence.

- **Written external tests**. Understand the process of revision – ask your teacher to explain the best way for you to revise. Start revising for written tests early. Revising is easier if you have made clear and complete notes. Always read the instructions on the test papers carefully and remember to take your time.

## Is it possible to appeal against the assessment decision of my assessor?

Each school or college **must** have an appeals procedure that will deal effectively with any complaints a student may have. This appeals procedure is different from the complaints procedure described in your college student handbook. There must be an appeals procedure for GNVQ courses. You can appeal on the grounds that an assessment procedure was not properly carried out or that an outcome (pass) was not carried out in a proper manner. Ask your teacher or lecturer for a copy of the appeals procedure – you are entitled to a copy at the beginning of the course.

# Organising a portfolio of evidence

## What is a portfolio?

Your portfolio will usually be kept in a large A4 ring binder. All your written evidence, assignments, projects, photographs, drawings, etc. will be kept in the binder. You must also keep a list (index) in the binder of other evidence, such as video tapes, sound recordings, large drawings, etc., that is kept somewhere else. This is so that the assessor, internal verifier and external verifier know that this evidence exists and can find it.

A portfolio is a convenient way to keep a record and to present evidence that you have collected. It is a permanent record of the evidence of your achievements over the year. The evidence that you have collected will allow you to demonstrate to your assessors that you have achieved the skills, knowledge and understanding to gain the Foundation GNVQ qualification.

Your portfolio should be organised into sections, each section containing evidence for one unit. The portfolio will also contain forms completed by your assessor. These forms will contain basic information about the status of your evidence for each unit.

The index to your portfolio should include:

- Name and details of class
- List of sections
  **Unit 1**: Investigating health and social care
  **Unit 2**: Understanding health and well-being
  **Unit 3**: Understanding personal development and relationships
  etc
- List of supplementary evidence
  Units that the supplementary evidence relates to.

## *Providing evidence for your portfolio*

There are two types of evidence:

- **Performance evidence**. Sometimes called direct evidence, this may consist of a report, assignment, a product (a toy, for example) or an assessor's written report of observation of something you have done.
- **Supplementary or indirect evidence**. This may consist of photographs, video tapes, audio tapes, evidence of written or oral questioning, tests or references from workplace supervisors.

Remember that work, class notes, etc. that do not provide evidence should not be kept in your portfolio.

Evidence should arise as a result of the work you have been asked to do by your assessor and you agreed to do after drawing up your action plan. How much and what evidence you require will be discussed with you. It would be helpful to have an action plan to help you organise how you are going to collect evidence.

## Example of action plan

You have been asked to find out what health and social care services are available in your locality for children with learning difficulties and when you have done this to present a verbal report to your group.

## Action plan

| Task | How | By when |
|------|-----|---------|
| Find out about services | Talk to lecturer | Now |
| | Look up Yellow Pages and telephone directory | 1st February |
| | Ring local SSD and hospital | 2nd February |
| | Visit local health centre | 5th February |
| Write report | Draft report to lecturer | 10th February |
| | Final report | 20th February |
| Prepare talk | Get OHPs from lecturer | 22nd February |
| | Prepare OHPs | 26th February |
| | Write talk | 26th February |
| Give talk | See that room is set out | 1st March |
| | Is OHP working?, etc. | |
| Review action plan | Did I meet my plans? | |

## Remember...

- Present your portfolio in a professional manner.
- All the evidence that you are providing should be sufficient (enough), authentic (your own work) and relevant (test what the performance criteria ask to be tested).
- The assessor and verifiers should find the portfolio easy to read, understand and access. The index should identify what the evidence refers to.
- The documentation should be easy to read.
- Before you present your portfolio, remember that you will be asked questions about it by the assessor and the internal and external verifier.
- You should know exactly what is in your portfolio, as you could be asked to explain the evidence to the external verifier.

# Key Skills units

- **Communication**
- **Application of number**
- **Information technology**

Key Skills units can be studied separately, but the skills in these units can be taught and tested in assignments or projects set for the Foundation Units. It is important to remember that you do not need to obtain Key Skills to pass the Foundation GNVQ in Health and Social Care. It is now a separate qualification from Key Skills.

# Health and social care provision

## What is covered in this unit

1.1 **The main types of services**
1.2 **The main jobs in the health and social care services**
1.3 **The care value base**
1.4 **How people gain access to services – referral**
1.5 **Barriers that affect the ability of a person to make use of a service**

At the end of this unit you will be asked to produce a report on local health and social care services. If you would like to see further details of the tasks you are likely to need to carry out for assessment, please refer to the end of the unit where an assignment has been set (see pages 40–41). This unit will guide you through what you need to know in order to successfully put together the report. You will be assessed on this work and awarded a grade. This grade will contribute to the overall grade you will get for Unit One.

### Materials you will need to complete this unit

- Annual reports of local health, education and social service departments, including the Annual Community Care Plan (available from local libraries)
- The Local Council for Voluntary Services usually publishes a local directory of local services
- Local telephone and trade directories
- Map of the local area
- Access to the Open Government Internet site (http://www.open.gov.uk)
- Information you have obtained from visits to organisations
- A careers database such as CID and KUDOS.

## Introduction

This unit is about the health and social care services. To help you to understand how they are organised it is important to recognise the four aspects of health and social care:

- nationally organised health care
- locally organised health care
- nationally organised social care
- locally organised social care.

Clearly, although they work together in many ways, the health services and social services are very different. It is also important to realise that the services can be provided both locally and nationally.

# 1.1 The main types of services

## The organisation of health and social care services

The 1990s saw one of the biggest changes in the organisation of the health and social care services. To understand what is happening, it is important to know something of the history and historical structure of these services. For this we can divide the discussion into four sections:

- **National Health Service** (NHS)
- **social services** of Local Authorities
- **voluntary sector** services and
- **private sector** health and social care services.

The NHS and the social services (together with the Probation Service) form the statutory sector of the health and social care services. They are called the statutory services or sector because they were set up by Acts of Parliament and are funded by public money.

The diagram on page 3 shows how these services are controlled in England and Wales. You will see that many government departments have a big say in the organisation and delivery of health and social care, even at local level.

## The National Health Service

The structure of the health services is based around the National Health Service (NHS), which was formed in 1948 by the National Health Service Act. The Act brought the health services (hospitals, hospital doctors, GPs, nurses) and, in particular, the hospitals, under the control of the Ministry of Health.

Before the Act, most of the hospitals had been run by charities or voluntary organisations. The idea behind the setting up of the NHS was

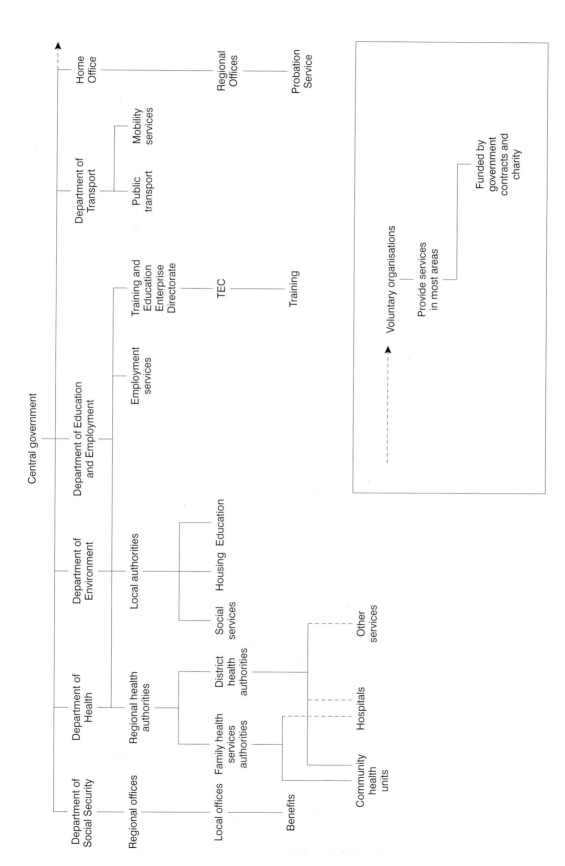

*The organisations involved in health and social care*

to provide free health care for all. The money to pay for (to fund) this health care was to come from:

- general taxation (income tax, value added tax (VAT) etc.)
- national insurance contributions and
- charges made to private patients.

The introduction of the health service was expected to reduce the amount of illness and so reduce the costs of providing the service.

Since 1948 the organisation of the NHS has changed over the years until the current structure (shown in the diagram below) was established. This structure has developed since the 1990 NHS and Community Care Act began to be implemented.

The diagram below shows the basic structure in England and Wales up to June 1999.

*Structure of the NHS up to June 1999*

There is, however, a distinctly regional flavour to the structure of the health services:

- In England there are eight **Regional Health Authorities** (1999), which are responsible for the District Health Authorities and Primary Care Groups in their region.
- Wales (1999) is rather like England except that the whole of the country can be considered as one Regional Health Authority run by a government department called the Welsh Office. Within Wales there are nine District Health Authorities.
- Northern Ireland (1999) has four Health and Social Services Boards that provide both health and personal social services under one manager.

- Scotland (1999) is like Wales. The whole of Scotland is organised like a Regional Health Authority run by the Scottish Office. Within Scotland there are 15 Health Boards that combine the roles of District Health Authorities and Primary Care Groups.

---

### Activity 1

Find out the name and address for the Regional Health Authority that is responsible for your local area. What is the name and address of your District Health Authority? If you live in Northern Ireland, find similar information for your Health and Social Services Board.

---

## Regional Health Authorities (RHAs)

These authorities are responsible for regional planning and allocating money. They also:

- identify the regional needs and priorities, such as how much specialist surgery will be provided compared with care for elderly people
- plan where any new facilities (such as a hospital) should be within the region and also identify hospitals that are regional centres for specialist treatments (e.g. heart transplant surgery is normally located in a few regional centres)
- share out the available money to the District Health Authorities and Primary Care Groups
- monitor the activities of the organisations that they fund and work to help co-operation.

## District Health Authorities (DHAs)

DHAs have responsibility for the provision of health care within their district. They:

- identify local needs
- employ staff and
- contract for health care to be provided for people living in their district.

Their role is becoming one of predicting local health care needs and contracting (entering into agreements) with health care providers, such as hospitals, Primary Care Groups and NHS Trusts, to meet the needs. These contracts are with NHS, private or voluntary sector organisations (see below).

*What do the initials DHA stand for?*

## Family Health Service Authorities (FHSAs)

FHSAs were responsible for the provision of primary care services. These were the services provided by:

*What do the initials FHSA stand for?*

- general practitioners (GPs)
- dentists – many now work exclusively in the private sector.
- opticians – who test eyesight and prescribe glasses
- pharmacists – who are responsible for providing medicines prescribed by doctors.

FHSAs were abolished in 1960.

## NHS Trusts

A careful study of the diagram on page 4 will show that there are also **NHS Trusts** involved in providing care; the government plans to change this system over the next few years. Section 1 of the **Health Act 1999** abolishes GP fundholding. The NHS and Community Care Act made it possible for units (individual hospitals, community health services or services such as the ambulance service) to become trusts.

*What responsibilities do NHS trusts have?*

NHS Trusts have responsibility for managing their own money. They employ their own staff. They compete for the contracts to provide health care alongside private and voluntary sector providers (see pages 9–10).

## Purchasers and providers

**Purchasers** are GPs, primary care groups or other organisations that buy services for clients, such as operations in hospital, etc. **Providers** are the organisations (hospitals etc.) that provide the services.

These terms were introduced by the NHS and Community Care Act 1990. You will often come across them in relation to health and social care. Their meanings are quite clear: a purchaser (such as a GP) bought

Hospital care                    Laboratory tests

*GPs could purchase (buy) a number of services for patients*

(or purchased) health or social care from a provider of that care such as a hospital. This meant that a GP and patient could often decide where to have treatment. The GP could send the patient to a hospital where the treatment was cheapest or where it was most convenient for the patient. In the health services, when a purchaser (RHA, DHA, FHSA, fundholding GP) identified a need for care for a patient (such as a home help, hip replacement, day care), any care-providing organisation (NHS, voluntary or private) could bid to provide that care. The organisation that won the bid entered into a contract with the purchaser – that is, an agreement to provide the care. The purchaser had to try to get the best care possible for the money available, so the contract to provide the service may have been given to the organisation that could provide it at the lowest cost.

So NHS patients, for example, could receive free treatment (free to the patient) in private establishments. A person needing an operation may have been sent to a private hospital and have the bill paid by the NHS. This was because the private hospital had won the contract to provide the operation. The patient still received care from the NHS, but the care was provided by a non-NHS organisation. This purchaser and provider system also exists in social care.

*What do purchasers of services do?*

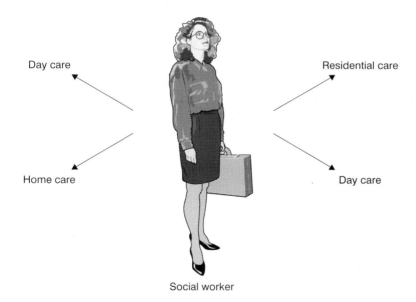

Day care

Residential care

Home care

Day care

Social worker

*Social service departments could purchase (buy) a number of services for clients*

## The health, social care and early years services: the future

### The Health Act 1999

The government in 1997 set out to change the structure of the NHS so as to provide an up-to-date, quicker and more responsive service. The government outlined its plans, in a White Paper 'The New NHS

Modern Dependable', to provide a services based on people's needs and not on their ability to pay. This new service is based on:

- making it easier and faster for people to get advice and information about health, illness and the NHS so that people can better care for themselves and their families. To help to do this the government has set up '**NHS Direct**', a 24-hour telephone advice line (0845 4647), staffed by nurses. This service is available in many areas of the country and will be available to everyone after the year 2000
- quick advice and treatment in the community in local surgeries and health centres with GPs working alongside other health care staff to provide a wide range of services
- prompt access to specialist services in hospital linked to local surgeries and health centres.

To replace the pre-June 1999 system the government has moved away from outright competition to a more collaborative approach, delivering a national service based on a set of national standards and working more closely with Local Authorities, so that what the patient needs will be at the centre of the process.

What services does NHS Direct provide?

## New Primary Health Care Groups

**Primary Health Care Groups**, made up of GPs and community nurses, work with NHS Trusts to plan the new services to deliver quick, accessible, co-ordinated care of a high standard. These groups work to set standards agreed between Health Authorities, Primary Care Groups and NHS Trusts.

### *Primary Care Groups*
Primary Care Groups are made up of all GPs in an area, together with community nurses, and take responsibility for commissioning (buying) services for the local community. All Primary Care Groups are responsible to the local Health Authority.

### *Health Authorities*
Health Authorities are relinquishing their direct commissioning (buying) roles to Primary Care Groups. Health Authorities, working with Local Authorities, NHS Trusts and Primary Care Groups, will take the lead in drawing up three-year Health Improvement Programmes that will provide the framework within which all NHS bodies will operate.

### *NHS Trusts*
NHS Trusts will provide patient care in hospital and in the community under long-term agreements with Primary Care Groups.

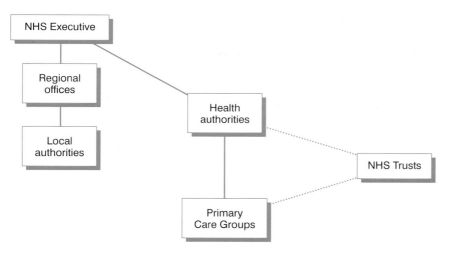

*The new NHS*

## Health Authorities

Health Authorities have a number of key jobs:

- Find out the health needs of the local population
- Develop a strategy for meeting those needs
- Decide what services are necessary to meet local needs
- Allocate resources (money) to Primary Care Groups
- Make sure that Primary Care Groups work properly.

*Who allocates (gives) money to Primary Care Groups?*

## Health Action Zones

To give priority to areas of greatest need the government has set up **Health Action Zones** to help reduce inequalities. Health Action Zones will bring together local health organisations with Local Authorities, community groups, voluntary groups and local business to provide improved health for local people.

*What will Health Action Zones do?*

## *Social services*

The origins of the social services are not as clearly defined as those of the NHS. Laws (Poor Laws for example) relating to social service-type services go back to the seventeenth century. In fact, some of the organisations, such as the NSPCC (National Society for the Prevention of Cruelty to Children), are still controlled by laws that were introduced in the early part of the twentieth century.

The organisation of Local Authority social services has changed several times. The latest changes have come about as a result of the NHS and Community Care Act 1990.

## The setting up of the social services

**1968** Social work departments established in Scotland and the Probation Service incorporated into them.

**1970** Local Authority Social Services Act set up Local Authority social services departments in England and Wales.

**1972** Health and Personal Social Services (NI) Order established the four Health and Social Services Boards in Northern Ireland.

The aim was to form an effective, family-oriented, community-based service that was available to all who needed it.

As with the health services (see above), the NHS and Community Care Act established a division between:

- the parts of the social services that purchased the care needed
- the parts that provided the care.

The purchaser could buy from both the private and voluntary sectors. The different roles will be further explained when you look in more detail at local provision.

## The voluntary care sector

The structure of a typical social services department in England and Wales

The term 'voluntary sector' refers to all the non-statutory organisations that contribute to social care. They are not set up by the government and many are charities, for example Age Concern, NSPCC, Dr Barnados.

The setting up of charitable organisations in the nineteenth century was the start of social care and social work in an organised way, with prison visiting and children's services. Many charities act as fund-raisers to provide for people with specific needs. The money is then used to purchase the equipment or care required. Others, such as Anchor, provide specific residential or sheltered accommodation for older people around the country.

The traditional image of charities is of well-meaning amateurs. This image is no longer true. While some charities work with unpaid volunteers, most are staffed almost totally by salaried staff. The term 'voluntary' refers to the status of the organisation and not to the status of the workers.

## The NSPCC

One example of a voluntary sector organisation is the NSPCC. It has the authority to take legal action on behalf of a child and has access to records such as the register of children at risk.

To carry out its work, the NSPCC employs qualified social workers and works closely with the social services departments and the police. A child may be referred to the NSPCC who then investigate the case and work with the family. If there is a need for the child to be taken into care, the case may be taken to court by the NSPCC or passed over to Local Authority social services.

The emphasis of the organisation is working with families and seeking to prevent their break-up.

Organisations within the voluntary sector can be very large, like the NSPCC, or very small local groups that are dealing with a specific need. Voluntary organisations work alongside the statutory services providing care. They can sell their services to a purchaser. This means that the voluntary organisation can be paid by the NHS or the Local Authority to provide the care.

## The Council for Voluntary Services (CVS)

Voluntary organisations are co-ordinated by the CVS. It brings together the broad range of organisations and provides a focus for discussion with government (and the European Union). On a national level, the CVS speaks to the government.

*Describe the differences between voluntary and statutory services.*

*Give an example of a small, local voluntary group.*

While the CVS is nationally based, it has local offices throughout the UK. It brings together the various local voluntary organisations to attempt to reduce the duplication of provision. It also acts as a pressure group for the member organisations. The local CVS often speaks for the voluntary sector when working with the local authority.

**Key Skills**

You can use Activity 2 to provide evidence for Key Skills Communication C1.1.

### Activity 2

Find out if you have a local office of the CVS. Try to arrange for someone from the CVS to talk to your group about voluntary sector organisations in your area.

The case study below shows how the voluntary sector supports clients in the community.

### Case study

James had suffered a serious injury and was having to relearn how to move about. Part of his therapy involved being encouraged to move his legs. To do this required one person to work with him for half an hour at a time.

James's parents were able to do this, but they were worried that they would have to give up work and that their other children would suffer. People from the local community heard about the problem and arranged a rota of volunteers to come in each day to work with James.

To make sure that they knew what was necessary, the physiotherapist working with James arranged for all the volunteers to be trained to give the specific support James needed. As a result, James received the therapy necessary. The stress on his family was reduced and, as James improved, his family's life could return to normal.

## Private organisations

There are many organisations involved in health and social care that charge for their services with the intention of making money. These organisations are part of the private sector. The private sector provides services from hospitals and residential homes to individuals working as private nurses, physiotherapists or care assistants in people's own homes.

Private organisations may bid to provide care, such as residential care for elderly people (they become a provider). The Local Authority can buy places in homes for those people in need of the care.

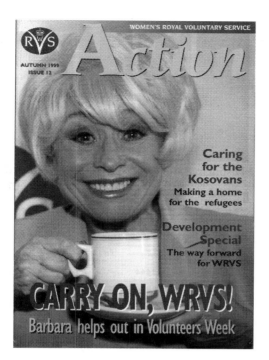

*WRVS is a voluntary organisation that provides a vast range of services, including working in hospitals and prisons, and working with families and elderly people*

## Private health care

When the NHS was formed in 1948, many health professionals, in particular doctors, were unhappy at the thought of giving up their private practices. They wanted to retain their freedom to charge for services outside the NHS. It was agreed that doctors would be allowed to work both within the NHS and in private practice. Health care is available:

- within NHS-owned institutions, with the patient paying for the services
- within totally separate private health care facilities.

*Describe the differences between purchasers and providers.*

## 1.2 The main jobs in the health and social care services

### General practitioners

The first person that we go to for health care within the community is the general practitioner (GP) or family doctor. GPs are qualified doctors who have undergone special training. Everyone permanently resident or working in the UK may be registered with a GP. They may select their own GP when they are over 16 years old from the list of GPs kept by the Local Health Authority.

The first port of call for most people requiring health care is the doctor's surgery. The GP:

- diagnoses (finds out) what is wrong with an individual
- may prescribe treatment, such as medicines, which are then obtained from a pharmacist.

GPs are specialists in general **diagnosis**; that is they try to find out what is wrong with you. They have a good knowledge of a broad range of types of ill-health. When they do not have the facilities or skills to diagnose or treat a patient, they refer the patient to a specialist doctor based in a hospital, for example if a person needs an operation.

Some doctors' surgeries dispense the medicines that the doctors prescribe. This usually happens in rural or remote areas where it is difficult for patients to get to a pharmacist.

It is now common for a group of GPs to work together in a local centre. Each of the doctors will have the general diagnostic skills, but each will also have a specialist interest or skill to contribute to the practice. The move towards group practices started in the 1960s. It is now very common for a practice to be based in a health centre.

**What does diagnose mean?**

**What do the initials GP stand for?**

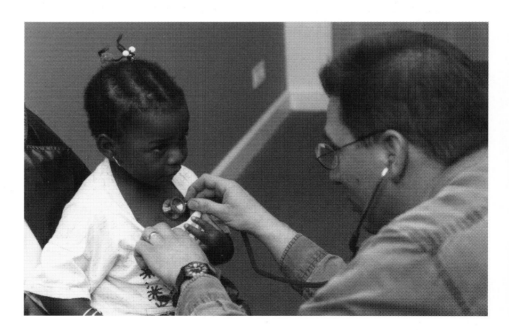

## *Health centres*

In a health centre you will find:

- GPs
- a practice nurse
- services provided by

- midwives, who work with pregnant women, may assist the mother to give birth and support the mother and child in the days after the birth
- health visitors, who take over the support of children from midwives. They have a responsibility until the child is five
- community nurses (formerly district nurses), who work with people recovering from illness who require health support in their homes. They may be involved in changing dressings on wounds or looking after patients recovering from illness.

There may also be other professionals providing services, such as:

- the school nurse
- speech therapist
- occupational therapist
- physiotherapist
- dentist.

You will also come across the following people in a GP surgery:

- receptionists
- a practice manager (someone who organises the doctors and nurses at the centre) and
- clerical staff.

Also based in the community, and developing a more important role following the NHS and Community Care Act, are:

- community psychiatric nurses
- community-based mental handicap (RNMH) nurses.

These nurses provide care for people who may have been receiving long-term hospital care and who have now returned to living in the community. They work closely with social workers. Their work is part of the community care that is planned by Local Authorities.

---

### Activity 3

Many nurses work within the community. Find out about the different types of nurse working with your own GP practice or in your health centre and find out what they do. Present your findings to your class colleagues.

---

### Key Skills

You can use Activity 3 to provide evidence for Key Skills Communication C1.2.

## *Dentists*

Dentists are part of the NHS. The services they offer include:

- preventive dentistry – advice and treatment to prevent the need for fillings and extracting teeth
- dental treatment – including fillings and extractions
- **remedial treatment** – including corrective work to ensure teeth grow in appropriate positions and the provision of crowns.

A large part of a NHS dentist's income is in the form of payment for treatment. In recent years, people have been taking better care of their teeth and payments have been reduced. So, in some cases, dentists have moved outside the NHS and work in the private sector.

Some dentists work within the schools' dental service. This service provides for dental checks and treatment for school children, although many children visit their own dentist.

There are some dentists who work in hospitals. These may be dental hospitals, where dental students also learn their skills. Dentists also work alongside doctors in providing dental treatment for people with facial injuries that have occurred as a result of an accident or because of illness and bone decay.

## People who work in hospitals

Hospitals are traditionally seen as places where people, who are too ill to be cared for at home, are taken for treatment. They are also the places where people go for operations or for help from a specialist on an out-patient basis. They are staffed by specialist doctors who each concentrate on a small area of medicine, such as surgeons and cancer specialists.

Patients are normally referred to a hospital specialist by their GP who provides details of the initial diagnosis. Most people are seen first as an out-patient following referral. This means that they attend hospital at an appointed time, when the specialist examines their situation, attempts a diagnosis and plans a course of treatment. This can involve:

- referral for further specialist information (such as an X-ray)
- admission to hospital for treatment
- treatment at home
- planned admission and treatment on a day basis (day care).

Hospitals have a range of specialist equipment and staff. These help to find out what is wrong with people and treat their illnesses.

*A hospital ward*

The staff involved include the following:

- Nurses carry out the care plan that has been developed by the doctors. Within nursing there are several specialisms, such as nursing sick children, mental health and mental disability.
- Health care assistants work closely with nurses in delivering practical care.
- Radiographers have two important roles:
  - they use X-rays and ultrasound to produce pictures of internal structures
  - they use X-rays in treatment.
- Physiotherapists help people to improve their ability to move, often helping a patient to develop full movement after breaking a bone. They also assist with breathing and treatment routines to help people with cystic fibrosis to clear their lungs.
- Occupational therapists (OTs) work to treat illness, both mental and physical, with activity. They work on a one-to-one basis, with groups and with recreational activities. Many OTs work in the community.
- Speech therapists work with people with speech disorders. These range from children with delayed speech development to older people recovering from strokes. Speech therapists work throughout the health service, often going into schools.

## People who work in residential social care

There are times when people are unable to be cared for in their own homes. These people may include:

- elders
- children
- people with disabilities.

**quick fire**

*What does a speech therapist do?*

*A physiotherapist at work*

### Residential care for elderly people

The largest group of people requiring residential care are elders. The reasons for entering residential care vary:

- they may be unable to care for themselves
- they may simply wish to live with other people, while still maintaining their independence
- they may be recovering from an illness
- it may be to give their families or carers a break.

Because the needs of people vary, the types of residential care also vary. Residential care includes:

- Nursing homes, which provide care for people needing the support and skills of a nurse. These people may be recovering from illness or in need of regular nursing treatment.
- Residential homes, which provide all the necessities for daily living. People in residential homes can be almost self-supporting or may need support for almost all activities.
- Sheltered accommodation, which is a form of residential care where individuals take a lot of responsibility for themselves, and may be almost totally independent. What it does provide is the support of other people and, in particular, the support of the organisation providing the accommodation. There may be a warden or wardens who live on site. Food, cleaning and laundry services may be provided.

*How many types of residential care are available?*

### Residential care for children

At one time many children who were not being looked after by their parents were cared for in children's homes. These varied in size, but they all provided for the needs of children and were staffed by resident and non-resident workers.

### Foster parents

Many local authorities have moved away from using children's homes and now place children in foster care. In this situation, a child or children lives with foster parent(s) as part of their family. The foster care can be for a short time, such as when a natural parent is in hospital. It can also be longer term, when the child's own family structure has broken down because of one or both parents' sickness or abuse, for example.

### Adoptive parents

In some cases children may need to become a permanent part of a new family. This process is called adoption. Many people think of adoption as involving young babies who are not wanted by their parents. In fact, most adoptions are of older children. More adoptions now also involve maintaining strong links with the children's natural family. As such, adoption is a form of residential care that gives children stability, while not denying their links with their birth families.

## Residential care for people with disabilities

There are many people who need specific support because of a disability. This includes people with mental and/or physical disabilities.

The purpose of the residential care is to provide the support necessary to enable the individuals to become as independent as possible. For example, many people who are registered blind spend some time in residential care. There they learn the skills necessary to live safely and with confidence in a society of mostly sighted people.

For some people the disability may be so great that they would find it difficult to cope outside their residential care. Their care is planned to enable them to be as independent as possible. In some instances, the residential care may be in a **therapeutic community**, where individuals are supported with specialist psychiatric help to enable them to fulfil their full potential.

In the past, people who were termed 'mentally handicapped' or 'mentally sub-normal' were placed in mental hospitals. These terms are no longer used and such hospitals are closing down. The residents are, in many cases, moving into community-based care and sheltered accommodation. This is a recognition of their rights to be treated as members of society and not shut away from it.

## *Community-based personal social care*

The aim of a lot of social care is to support a person living in their own home. The range of workers who provide this support includes the following people:

* Social workers may make home visits to support a child and family in conflict. This may prevent the later need for the child to move into foster care.
* Home helps offer domiciliary support (home help) for people unable to do things for themselves. This includes home help support for elderly people who need someone to do their housework and shopping. But, most important of all, it provides regular company.
* Day-care workers work in day-care centres. Many people who can be supported at home also benefit from the opportunity of being with others by regularly attending a day-care centre. The day care may be to provide the home-based carer with time to themselves or to go to work. Day nurseries and child-minders are included in this category.
* Supervisory workers in sheltered workshops provide a halfway stage for some people with disabilities. They provide an opportunity for disabled people to learn and develop skills. These

What is the main role
of nurses in a hospital
and what are their
specialisms?

may be the skills of daily living or they may be skills associated
with employment. Employment in sheltered workshops provides
both an income and builds self-confidence in the people working
there.

*A home carer with a client*

## Support groups and voluntary groups

This covers a range of organisations from major voluntary organisations,
such as the WRVS (Women's Royal Voluntary Service), to
neighbourhood groups that are formed to support an individual in need
of care. Support groups can also be for people who have had a specific
crisis, such as victim support groups and rape crisis centres.

The case study on page 12 gives an example of a small support group
forming to meet a specific need. It is often the case that a group of
people, or even an individual, identifies a care need and does something
about it. From this small development, many national voluntary
organisations have been formed. For example, Oxfam started in 1942 as
the Oxford Committee for Famine Relief, with the aim of helping
hungry civilians in Nazi-occupied Greece. It is now the UK's largest
overseas development agency.

## Indirect care

The following workers provide **indirect care** to clients – they do not provide direct services such as a social worker or nurse:

- medical receptionist
- hospital cleaner
- hospital porter
- hospital reception staff
- hospital manager
- security staff
- GP health centre manager
- clerical staff.

Name two types of workers who provide indirect care.

## Early years services for children

Early years services for children includes pre-school education, such as nurseries and playgroups, which provide important support for young children.

The delivery of any services for children should be based upon the following principles:

- parents and professionals (teachers, nursery nurses etc.) should be involved in the organisation of these services
- the needs and welfare of the children must come first
- all children should be protected and allowed to play in a safe environment
- services should not discriminate.

Early years services should be developed working in partnership with the voluntary and private organisations so that parents have a wide and varied choice of services.

### Services available for children under eight years of age

#### Day nurseries (private, voluntary and local authority)
Day nurseries look after children under five. Many are run by Social Service Departments or Education Departments, but voluntary groups, private companies or individuals also provide these services.

#### Playgroups
Playgroups provide care for children aged between three and five. Some playgroups may take children at age two-and-a-half years. Playgroups allow children to learn through playing. Many of the groups are run with the support of parents with one or two paid staff. A few playgroups are run by Local Authorities and some look after children with special needs, such as physical disabilities. Most playgroup sessions last for a morning or afternoon.

#### Child-minders
Child-minders look after children up to the age of four during the working day. Parents and child-minders decide on payment between themselves.

Describe the differences between a playgroup and a day nursery.

**21**

*Day nurseries for children between 6 months and 5 years are staffed by workers with qualifications in childcare*

### Out of school clubs

Out of school clubs provide support for children before and after school. Holiday clubs provide care all day during school holidays.

### Family centres

Family centres provide a range of facilities for children such as play sessions, toy libraries, out of school activities. These centres can be attended by children of any age and their families.

## 1.3 The care value base

### Value judgements

Much of our relationships with clients is guided by our personal values and attitudes. What we think is right and many of our ideas are based on what we were told as children and later on what we have seen and heard on television or read about.

In the past and even now services for people have been developed without any discussion with the people most likely to use the service, the clients themselves. Many services were planned on the basis of prejudice and hearsay. They were planned around what the person could not do rather than on what they could do.

The **care value base** describes the standards and qualities we consider worth while when working with people. Professions such as health and social care and education require that much attention is paid to these care values.

Care values involve respect for:

- individual rights, for example the client should be able to refuse to accept the help we offer
- personal beliefs such as religion – food, dress etc.
- race
- **confidentiality** – not to divulge anything the client tells you without their permission
- the way we communicate with people.

People who work in social care should:

- identify and question their own values and prejudices
- respect and value individuality in people
- promote people's rights to choice, privacy and confidentiality
- assist people to gain control of, and improve the quality of, their lives
- identify and take action to deal with **discrimination**, racism, disadvantage, inequality and injustice
- carry out their job in a way that does not disadvantage either individuals, groups or communities.

## Confidentiality

Confidentiality is a principle common to all health, social care and early years services. Before any information you have gained is shared with other people you must get the client's permission. You must never divulge anything a client tells you.

## Individual rights – treat each person as an individual

Unless you treat each person as an individual you are likely to make judgements about them based on something you may have seen or read. This judgement may be wrong but it affects the way you work with that person, as we may make the person fit the image we have of them (for example, thinking that all elderly people are dependent or all people with a disability are also dependent), rather than accepting them for what they are. These stereotypes can act as barriers to good communication.

Good carers try to be aware of the attitudes they may have about the person they are trying to help. The client may be from a different social class background, a different ethnic background or the opposite gender. Here are some examples of how we can easily misjudge people and get the wrong message.

You can use Activity 4 to provide evidence for Key Skills Communication C1.1.

---

### Activity 4

Write down the gender that you think is best suited to the following occupations/careers:

**a**  nanny
**b**  nurse
**c**  engineer
**d**  home help
**e**  builder
**f**  joiner
**g**  counsellor
**h**  footballer
**i**  car mechanic
**j**  nursery nurse
**k**  electrician
**l**  plumber
**m**  cook
**n**  soldier

Now discuss your responses with someone else in your group.

---

## The ways in which individuals may be stereotyped

### *Age*
Older people may be seen by others as disabled, slow or inefficient.

### *Disability*
Often the way we think about disabled people is based on misunderstandings. Access and opportunities are very significant to disabled people. If they are denied access to a building or the opportunity to do a job, then they cannot demonstrate the capabilities they have.

The possible effects of discrimination are so wide-ranging that it is impossible to explain or describe them with accuracy. Also, most people have never experienced discrimination.

The possible effects of not seeing people as individuals can be as follows:

- People with disabilities may never achieve full physical involvement. For example, they may not be allowed to play particular sports or get work in certain occupations.
- People may be considered as intellectually less capable in some areas and therefore not given opportunities educationally. In the past many families did not think it was worth educating girls for example.
- Physical access is often denied to disabled people so life becomes more difficult.
- People may be regarded as intellectually weak even if their disability is physical.

- Emotional dependence may have been encouraged from childhood. This is usually well intentioned, but can create a situation where the person feels dependent on others and fails to develop independence, even over matters like choice of clothes or hairstyle.
- Disabled people may have been subtly dissuaded from visiting holiday centres, clubs, pubs and cinemas, thus depriving them socially.
- People from ethnic groups may be discriminated against in terms of access to health care.
- In classrooms, racist tensions among staff and pupils can affect students' learning.

*Explain the term 'stereotype' by providing an example.*

## Having a non-judgemental attitude

Everyone stereotypes to a certain extent. For example, if you met a young male wearing sports clothes you might assume he enjoyed playing sport. If you met a teenage girl wearing trendy clothes you might assume she liked listening to music and socialising. You might be very wrong in both cases.

The following four statements make judgemental attitudes about people or groups:

- 'A woman's place is in the home.'
- 'People with AIDS have got what they deserve.'
- 'Disabled people shouldn't have children – it's not fair to the children.'
- 'Men should not be nursery nurses.'

*You can be prejudiced against someone wearing the wrong scarf!*

## Non-discriminatory attitude

While prejudice is what a person thinks, discrimination is what a person does. A person who discriminates treats another person or group unfairly.

## What kinds of discrimination are there?

The following are assumptions that you might make about a person by looking at them:

| | | |
|---|---|---|
| nationality | married or single | sexual orientation |
| age | overweight, obese | social class or status |
| skin colour | disability/ability | occupation |

### Activity 5

Think of other words for:

businessman
man hours
manhole
manpower
man-made
fireman
salesgirl
headmaster

housewife
chairman
matron
ice-cream man
salesman
newsman
dustman

*Give an example of direct discrimination.*

### Behaviours indicating discrimination

Using offensive language, denying people rights or being rude is discriminating behaviour. Here is an example: an elderly black woman was sitting on the inside seat of a bus. Her white friend sitting beside her stood up to let a person with a physical disability sit down. The disabled person refused the seat, saying she would rather stand than sit next to 'one of them'. The elderly black woman was the victim of direct discrimination.

Indirect discrimination could be not taking a person seriously or not respecting what they say. Indirect discrimination is hard to do something about because it is expressed through attitudes. We use words to identify people, for example 'the elderly' instead of 'elderly people' or 'the disabled' instead of 'people with disabilities'.

*How does indirect discrimination differ from direct discrimination?*

## Sexual discrimination

Ask the people in your group, 'Which would you rather be – male or female?' Ask someone to keep a record. Then ask, 'Would you, or your partner, rather have a boy or a girl baby?' Again, keep a note.

Some research shows that more people actually want to have boy rather than girl children. Why do you think this may be true?

Think about the moment a child is born – Is it all right? Is it a boy or girl? The pink or the blue blanket covers the little body. The cards arrive conveying good wishes for the bouncing boy or the darling daughter. Soon, room decoration, clothes, toys, language, attitudes and responses all work to reinforce male or female roles. Later, books, films, television programmes and expectations of relatives, parents and teachers may further confirm these roles. There may not seem anything wrong with this, but consider the following questions.

### Activity 6

Tape your answers to these questions or write them down.

**a** Why are there so few male nurses, secretaries, childminders and nursery teachers? What difficulties would a man have if he tried to do any of these jobs?
**b** What happens if a girl wants to follow a traditionally male-dominated career such as train driving or airline pilot?
**c** Why are there so few women MPs?

**Key Skills**

You can use Activity 6 to provide evidence for Key Skills Communication C1.3.

When you answer these questions it becomes clear that by pre-judging people on the basis of gender, we are actually discriminating against them. We are not allowing them to develop in the way they wish to. We stereotype people and put them into a box in our minds which may say 'She is a woman who should take care of her family before she thinks about her career'. This limits development and, in some cases, stops people aspiring, or going on to, jobs or promotion.

# 1.4 How people gain access to services – referral

It is easy to describe the different services but, in order to use them, people need to know about them and also make contact with them. In this section you will find out how people can be referred to different care services. But, first, it is important to recognise that people have different requirements for care. Individuals may have different requirements from the same care service. Needs include:

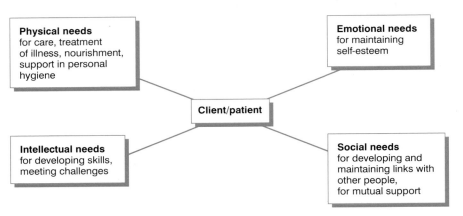

All four areas affect both physical and psychological health. It is essential that any care planned meets the individual's needs.

## How do we gain access to services?

It is important to look at how people can make use of the services offered. There are three ways that a person can be referred to the care services. These are:

- self-referral, where people seek help themselves, perhaps with support from family members
- referral through a professional, where a doctor, social worker, nurse, teacher or other professional may assist the person to request care
- compulsory referral, where some people who are a danger to themselves or who are mentally ill may be compulsory referred to hospital for care.

### Self-referral

This is often the first route for most people receiving health and social care. Within the health service, this may be by simply turning up at the GP's or dentist's surgery. Within social care, referral may be to an area office, or direct to a care facility, such as a day-care centre or a nursery.

In all cases, the person requiring care (or a friend or relative) makes the first contact. For example, a mother of a child would enquire about a place in a day nursery.

## Referral through a professional

Planned access to hospital care is usually through referral by a GP. Where a GP suspects ill-health that requires specialist treatment, the patient is referred to an out-patient clinic or, in more urgent cases, direct admission to a ward may be arranged.

In social care, an example of referral by professionals would be when a teacher in a school suspects child abuse and refers the case to the duty social worker in the social services department. Under the Children Act 1990, all schools should have a named person who makes this type of referral. Another example would be when the police have given a warning to a child who has committed an offence and they feel he or she should be referred to social services.

### Activity 7

As a group, discuss different situations that might lead to people seeking care. Identify the workers who might assist them.

## Compulsory referral

There are some cases where a person can be compulsorily referred into care. This may involve either a doctor or a social worker who identifies a person unable to make a decision for themselves. This may be because the person is too young, or unable to make a decision because of mental ill-health.

## Case study

Alice had been a teacher. Soon after she retired, her family noticed that her behaviour had altered. She was forgetting things that had just happened, but she was able to talk about her teaching as if it was still happening. Her GP noticed a little increase in her confusion, but he always asked basic questions requiring only yes or no answers.

Eventually Alice became so confused that her husband, John, was becoming very concerned. He spent a lot of time looking after her and could not easily approach social services in the nearest town which was seven miles away.

The situation changed when John developed a chest infection. The doctor wanted to refer John to hospital but was surprised when he asked, Who will look after Alice? This was the first time that the GP had realised that Alice was becoming seriously ill with Alzheimer's disease.

The doctor contacted the hospital to arrange for John to be admitted. At the same time, he contacted social services to arrange for Alice to move temporarily into residential care.

@ *What type of referral was John's referral to the doctor?*

@ *What type of referral was John's referral to hospital?*

@ *What type of referral was Alice's referral to residential care?*

@ *From the local services identify where John and Alice might have received their care.*

# 1.5 Barriers that affect the ability of a person to make use of a service

## Lack of information

The first barrier to receiving care is lack of knowledge. If you do not know what is available or how to ask for support, your chances of meeting your needs are low.

To ensure that people know what is available, the health and social services provide publicity about what they do. This is available in a wide variety of places that are regularly visited by the public, including:

- health centres
- doctors' surgeries
- libraries
- colleges and schools
- Citizens' Advice Bureaux
- post offices
- council information offices
- Thomson directories, Yellow Pages and the Phone Book.

Not all sources contain all the information, but most can guide people as to where more information is available.

For more about communicating information about health and social care services, see pages 35–39.

## Difficult physical access

Have you ever considered why new buildings are allowed to have steps up to the main entrance? A major difficulty of gaining access to buildings can be the steps at the front door. If all new buildings had to have ramps instead of steps then many access problems would be solved!

Caring services are aware of the difficulties that many people have in walking into buildings. It is not only people with physical disabilities who have problems.

Parents with children in prams or buggies can also find physical access difficult.

*Worries about theft or loss can provide barriers to access*

### Activity 8

This activity asks you to identify two local clients with different needs and to investigate how they gained access to health and social care services. You will need to:

a identify the referral methods used
b identify the barriers to access experienced
c suggest how access could be improved.

Alternatively, you might make up two imaginary clients. For example, if you choose to look at maternity services, compare how easy access would be for a pregnant woman who is physically fit and a one who uses a wheelchair. You will need to consider the following:

a How were each referred to the service (in this example, it would probably be self-referral)?
b Where are the antenatal classes held?
c Where are the maternity hospital/wards?
d What are the car parking facilities like for pregnant women?
e What public transport is available, and what areas are not served by it?
f What transport can be provided by the service (ambulance?)?
g How easy it is to physically get into the building (are there ramps, lifts, steps)?
h Are the doors easy to open?
i Are there areas to rest before a journey home?
j Is there easy access to toilets?
k Is the lighting near the entrance appropriate?
l Are there areas where a person might feel vulnerable to being approached by strangers?

Write a short report about what you have found out and suggest how you could improve access to the service. When you have considered your chosen service, compare your conclusions with those of the rest of your group.

## Who pays for health and social care?

Care today is not free. Even when it is a friend or unpaid volunteer providing the care, they are still paying with their time.

In the UK much of the statutory health care is not charged for at the point of delivery (that is, when it is received). It is paid for by all of us through general taxation and National Insurance contributions.

There are some services for which a client still has to pay all or part of the costs. The payments may be affected by the client's age or ability to pay. If you are under eighteen, for example, you may not have had to pay yet. Generally, people over the national retirement age do not have to pay for basic services.

Common NHS services that require contributions to the costs from the clients include:

- prescriptions for medicines
- prescriptions for appliances, such as surgical corsets
- dental checks
- dental treatment
- eyesight tests
- glasses and contact lenses
- transport to and from hospital (in some cases)
- the costs of transport and treatment following a road accident★
- some medical checks and vaccinations for business purposes.

★ The Road Traffic Act makes the vehicle owner responsible for the costs. Car insurance normally covers this.

## Paying for social care

Local authority social care often requires some payment to be made. Generally payment levels are assessed on the basis of income. Here, age is not a factor and so elders with savings are not exempt from the payments. Some care services that normally require some contribution from the client include:

- day nurseries
- residential care (although not for children)
- day care
- domiciliary care (home helps/home carers)
- meals on wheels.

## Paying for care in the private sector

Private sector care requires payment. This payment can be:

- by the client
- by an insurance company
- by the statutory services (where the care has been bought by the GP for instance).

Private health care is often paid for by insurance companies where the client pays regular contributions to the company to insure against treatment costs.

### *Residential and nursing homes*

As we have already mentioned, there are very many residential and nursing homes in the private sector. Until recently, the fees for residents who could not pay for their care were often met by the Department of Social Security (DSS). However, the increasing number of people requiring residential care means that there will not be enough money to pay for all who need care. People are now being advised to take out

*List six services provided by the health authority that many people have to pay for.*

insurance to pay for future residential care. This is because it is unlikely that the statutory sector will be able to provide sufficient care for those who cannot pay in the future.

## Cost of the service

There are two aspects to this:

- If the client has to pay for care, can he or she afford it?
- Do the services have enough money to provide the care needed by everyone?

### Can the client afford the care?

Where a service has to be paid for by a client, there are often times when the cost is difficult to meet. For people who receive social security benefits, there may be no charges. People with low wages may find the costs too great.

## Case study

Tom is a pensioner. He and his wife have, until now, been able to live at home quite comfortably on the money from their two pensions. His wife's pension is much higher than his.

However, Tom's wife has recently had a stroke and become paralysed down her left side. After she left hospital, Tom tried to look after her at home but found it very difficult. Eventually he decided that he needed to consider residential care for her.

When Tom asked about the care, he found out that for his wife to go into a nearby nursing home they would have to pay part of the cost. If they did this, then Tom would not have enough money to pay all the household bills and provide for himself. He has a problem. He cannot look after his wife. He cannot afford for her to go into the local nursing home.

Ⓠ *Read the case study above. In your group, discuss how you might feel in Tom's position. Suggest who Tom might go to for advice in your local area.*

## Has the service enough money to provide all the care needed?

When the NHS was established it was thought that health would improve and the costs of the service would drop. They didn't. There is always a demand for caring services that cannot be met immediately. There are also problems about deciding who is first in the queue for the available money.

There are more older people in the UK than ever before. The number of people who pay national insurance and income tax is not going to be sufficient to pay for all the services that are needed. The people who manage the caring services have to make decisions about the amount of care available. They also have to decide which care is most important.

When the decisions are made there are bound to be some people who do not get the care they need.

---

**Activity 9**

Imagine that your group has to make a decision about care funding. You have enough money for just one of the following:

- an incubator that will help to keep premature babies alive
- a kidney transplant that will keep a teenager alive
- physiotherapy to help five accident victims walk and work normally again.

In your group, think about the things that the manager might take into consideration. Is it easy to choose how to spend the money?

---

**Key Skills**

You can use Activity 9 to provide evidence for Key Skills Communication C1.1.

---

The problem of funding care is recognised by the NHS and Community Care Act. The Act states that people can expect to have their care needs assessed, but that they have no right for the needs to be met. For example, a person may have been assessed as needing a home help every day, but may be offered help on just two days a week because there are not enough home helps to go around.

## Communicating information in health and social care

You have already looked at where information about your local health and social care services is available.

In general this information will be in the form of printed leaflets, possibly illustrated with diagrams to make them look more interesting. Their aim is to tell you about the services available. Other information about health and social care frequently appears in newspapers. For example, there are annual reports of how different services are meeting charter standards (see below).

There are two other major sources of information about services. These are:

- the people who work in a particular service
- people who have already used a particular service.

It is often the first source of information that is the most difficult to find. But once a client has gained access to care, he or she has access to a network of information about caring services. The first source can very often be someone who has already received care or the carers themselves.

When a person makes use of a health or care service, the people delivering the care are able to pass on information about other services available.

### Charters

Since 1990, caring organisations have produced charters, such as The Patient's Charter, to explain the standards of service that a client can expect. The individual services also publish figures to show how well they are meeting the standards set down in these charters (standards such as waiting list times, how many people have been treated etc.). The statistics can be used by clients and care professionals to help them to choose which organisation to use.

## Key Skills

You can use Activity 10 to provide evidence for Key Skills Communication C1.2.

### Activity 10

Ask a health or social care service of your choice whether they have a charter. Obtain a copy of it, if you can. Find out what information the service publishes about how it meets the charter standards.

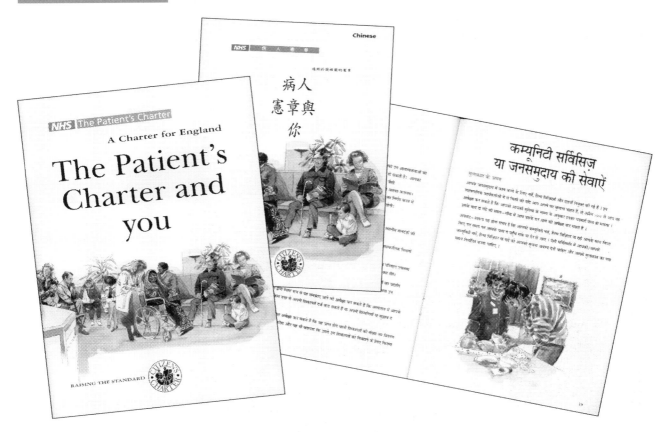

*The Patient's Charter is available (free of charge) in 12 languages, and also in braille, in large print, as an audio cassette and as a sign language video*

*Some trusts produce newsletters to inform people in the area about existing, new and improved services*

## Adapting communication to meet client needs

Most of the information that you have found about services available will have been written down. What did you find that was written in a language other than English? How do you think a person with little or no sight would be able to find out about services available?

Most caring services recognise that they need to adapt communication to meet the needs of different groups of people. Most leaflets are available in the major languages spoken by people living in the area. Where people do not speak English well, many services employ translators.

There are two other languages that are important in providing care information:

- Braille
- sign language.

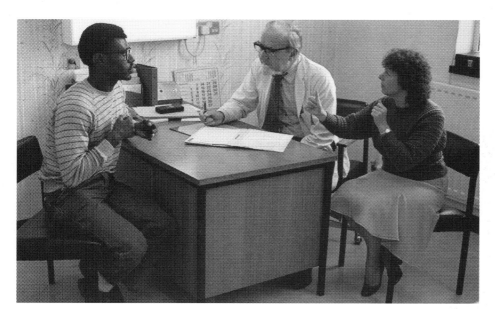

*Sometimes interpreters are needed to assist communication*

### Braille

Some visually impaired people are able to read words written as a code of raised dots. This language is called Braille. Many leaflets are translated into Braille so that information is available. Often information about these leaflets is broadcast on the radio during programmes for visually impaired people such as *In Touch*.

Written information for visually impaired people who have some vision is also available in large print.

### Sign language

People with hearing difficulties are normally able to read information leaflets. When it comes to receiving care, it is important to ensure that the person involved understands as much as possible. In many cases, communication can involve using a standard sign language such as the British Sign Language.

Other adaptations are available to hearing-impaired people once they are in contact with the services. These includes an electronic phonic ear hearing aid linked to a microphone that is worn by the carer.

*Where would be the best places to put each of these posters and leaflets?*

## Location of publicity

Sometimes it might be necessary to place posters and leaflets in specific places in order to reach particular groups of people. For example, it might be more effective to place a poster advertising a new clinic for drug users in a place where they are likely go. Some styles or designs of leaflets or posters may also be found to be effective with different groups of people.

### Activity 11

If you have the opportunity to talk to a health or care service provider (such as a visiting speaker to your class), ask how communication is adapted to meet client needs.

## Key terms

After reading this unit you should be able to understand the following words and phrases. If you do not, go back through the unit and find out, or look them up in the Glossary.

| | |
|---|---|
| *National Health Service* | *Primary Health Care Groups* |
| *Social services* | *Health Action Zones* |
| *Voluntary sector* | *Diagnosis* |
| *Private sector* | *Remedial treatment* |
| *Regional Health Authorities* | *Therapeutic community* |
| *NHS Trusts* | *Indirect care* |
| *Health Act 1999* | *The care value base* |
| *Purchasers and providers* | *Confidentiality* |
| *NHS Direct* | *Discrimination* |

## Test yourself

1 What groups of staff support doctors in hospitals to look after patients?
2 What training is now available for social workers?
3 What are the main responsibilities of the Local Authority Social Services Committee?
4 What does a Primary Care Group do?
5 What are the main responsibilities of the Regional Health Authority?
6 What is the difference between a purchaser and provider?
7 What are the main provisions of the NHS and Community Care Act?
8 List four issues covered by the care value base.
9 What does it mean when it is said that you have a non-judgemental attitude?
10 List three ways in which a person can gain access to health services.

# Assignment for Unit One

### REPORT: Produce a booklet for your local volunteer centre

You have been placed for work experience with the local volunteer centre. The first job they have asked you to do is to produce a booklet for local people which includes the following tasks.

### Tasks

1. Identify the main local health, social care and early years services and also identify at least six of these services on a map.

2. So as to give people an idea of what to expect of these services, you are also asked to write a basic description of the work of at least two staff who work in the services.

3. To help local people gain access to the services you are also asked to describe at least two ways that people can be referred to the services you have identified on your map.

4. Identify and explain the barriers that people might have to overcome to gain access to the services.

5. You should also accurately write a short account or description of the care value base that is essential to all care workers.

6. To gain a merit it is essential that you collect some of the information you need on your own.

7. To get a distinction you must describe clearly how the care value base is applied by workers in the services by giving examples.

8. Give examples of what the services you have described could do to overcome the barriers to access that you have identified.

## Get the grade

To achieve a **PASS** you must complete tasks 1–3.

To achieve a **MERIT** you must complete tasks 1–6.

To achieve a **DISTINCTION** you must complete tasks 1–8.

# Key Skills

## Opportunity

**You can use this opportunity to provide evidence for the following key skills**

| | |
|---|---|
| Application of Number N1.1 | List the main local health, social care and early years services and locate them on a map. |
| Information Technology IT1.1 | Use a computer database for investigating job roles. |
| Information Technology IT1.2 | Word process basic descriptions of job roles of different workers and a description of how people are referred to services. |
| Communication C1.1 | Take part in a one-to-one discussion and a group discussion about identifying the local health, social care and early years services. |
| Communication C1.2 | Read and obtain information from documents about the jobs and roles of health, social care and early years workers. |
| Communication C1.3 | Describe the different ways that people are referred to different services. |

# *Understanding health and well-being*

## *What is covered in this unit*

**2.1** *What is meant by health and well-being and by good health*

**2.2** *What can cause ill-health*

**2.3** *How to explore risks to health*

**2.4** *How people can stay healthy*

At the end of this unit you will be asked to produce a **health plan** for improving one person's physical health and well-being. You may base the plan on yourself. If you would like to see further details of the tasks you are likely to need to carry out for assessment, please refer to the end of the unit where an assignment has been set (see pages 81–83). This unit will guide you through what you need to know in order to successfully put together the plan. You will be assessed on this work and awarded a grade. This grade will contribute to the overall grade you will get for Unit Two.

### *Materials you will need to complete this unit*

- The Health Education Authority – the Internet site
- Local health promotion units – pamphlets and leaflets
- Appendix 6 Manual of nutrition (Department of Health and MAFF)
- Extract from the report, The Dietary and Nutritional Needs of British Adults and the summary of The National Diet and Nutrition Survey available at http://www.doh.gov.uk/HPSS/INDEX
- The NHS – A Force for Health, Department of Health, 1998.

You will need to read Unit Five on Planning Diets and Unit Six on Exploring Health and Recreational Activities.

## Introduction

The first part of this unit focuses on the factors which contribute to good health. You will look at your own health and well-being, the food you eat, the exercise you take, and the recreational activities you enjoy. You will then present a plan of how to improve your health and well-being. This information will also allow you to prepare a plan to improve to improve a person health and well-being.

The second half of the unit looks at:

* **basic health needs**
* the main **risks to health** and how to reduce them
* the effect that **major life changes** may have on health and well-being and how people cope with these changes.

# 2.1 What is meant by health and well-being and by good health

People in the UK are living longer but, if you look at the numbers of people who die from preventable causes, it is clear that the situation could be better.

## What contributes to good health and well-being?

The World Health Organisation describes health as: 'A state of complete physical, mental and social well-being and not merely the absence of disease or infirmity.'

Health is not just being free of illness or disability (physical health). It also includes mental and social well-being.

But what is well-being? It is not easy to define. It describes how you feel about yourself and it includes your relationships with other people that contribute to your own 'feel good' factor.

### Activity 1

**a** Spend a few minutes with members of your group trying to define what health and well-being mean to you.
**b** Check how your ideas match up to the World Health Organisation's description of health above.

We will consider the following three main factors that contribute to health and well-being:

*Which of these people is not healthy?*

All the people above could be healthy. There is nothing in the pictures to prove that they are not. It is important for you to realise that health and well-being is not about being super-fit, never eating junk food or never drinking alcohol. It is about maintaining a balance to meet your individual needs.

*Why do you need to consider all aspects of your health now?*

## But why do I need to think about it now?

Most of you reading this will be teenagers and may not be too worried now about ill-health that shows up later, in middle age. However, it is important to consider all aspects of your health now in order to prevent later problems.

## Diet

One of the most common problems in the UK is a poor diet. This can be from over-eating and not getting the balance of nutrients right. You should monitor your diet now because:

- the damage caused by a poor diet may not be obvious, but it builds up to cause ill-health in later years
- your current eating habits are just that – habits. You have a pattern of eating that may or may not be a good one. If you educate yourself into good eating habits now, they should stay with you into middle age.

A good diet now can be very beneficial in your later life.

Good diet is not just about physical dangers. There are also risks to a person's self-image (how they see themselves). People who are overweight, underweight, anaemic or have rotten teeth may well feel unhappy about themselves and the way they look. This may affect their behaviour and also their general health.

Unit Five provides more information about the role of diet in health and well-being.

*Why do you need to monitor your diet?*

## Recreational activities

What you do as a break from work is important to your health and well-being. Recreational activities can be classified as those involving:

- physical exercise
- other people in a social setting
- intellectual activity.

*Recreation can overlap different classes of activity. Dancing involves exercise as well as being a social activity*

Some activities may fall into more than one of these groups. For example:

- dancing is a physical activity in a social setting
- a quiz night is an intellectual activity in a social setting.

The activities are all linked because they involve the development and maintenance of physical, social and intellectual well-being.

We will spend some time looking at physical activities. It is also important to consider social and intellectual activities. All three have an effect on reducing stress and increasing your mental well-being. The role of recreational activities is covered in greater detail in Unit Six.

## *Relaxation and sleep*

Whether these can be considered as recreational activities may be open to debate. However, they are both vital to health and well-being:

- During sleep and deep relaxation the body repairs itself.
- It is a time for growth to occur.
- Sleep involves dreaming. Even if you cannot remember your dreams, you do dream. This is a time when your brain appears to be processing information, and possibly supporting memory and learning. This is not really well understood. However, it is known that people deprived of dreaming sleep become physically and mentally ill.
- Sleep and relaxation also enable your muscles to be re-supplied with nutrients to enable them to take on further exercise.
- Relaxation also helps to reduce stress. Stress is exhausting. It is important to deal with this exhaustion by making sure you get enough sleep and undertaking relaxing activities. For more about stress, see page 73.

### What is enough sleep?

There is no precise answer to this question. Everyone's needs are different. Your need for sleep is determined by:

- your internal body clock
- your emotional state
- your level of stress
- your general well-being.

It is easier to say what amount of sleep is too little. This can be shown by the effect that lack of sleep has on you. It affects your ability to concentrate and, as a result, your ability to cope with the demands of the day.

Often you may find yourself in the situation where you feel physically tired, but cannot sleep because you are mentally alert. This is often an indication of your level of stress. To correct this you should try to reduce your stress levels and re-establish your correct sleep patterns.

*Parents have to adapt to a new baby's sleep patterns*

Sleep patterns vary throughout life:

- Babies and young children need a lot of sleep but do so for short periods at a time and then wake.
- As children grow up into adulthood, they need less sleep and soon a regular sleep pattern is established – they sleep for an average of about eight hours at night, and remain awake during the day. However, some adults still have a sleep pattern of 'cat napping' during the day, and need little sleep at night.
- In old age, the pattern of early childhood can return – short periods of sleep followed by periods of being awake. This is normal and should be recognised by those working in caring situations.

## Developing a plan to improve health and well-being

If you have worked through the unit this far, you will already have started to look at your own health and well-being. You will also have thought about some of the ways in which you can improve your current health.

Before you undertake any **health plan**, you should understand the benefits of improving it. These can be summarised as:

- Increased mobility as a result of increased exercise and an improved diet. Weight loss may improve your flexibility and mobility, while weight gain (if you are underweight) may increase your general energy level and again improve your mobility.
- Improved **self-esteem**. If you do something about the phrase, 'I'm too (fat/thin/unfit/etc.)', you will feel better about yourself.

**What are the benefits of a health plan?**

- Reduced risks to health, particularly those that show up in later life. The big killers of middle age – heart disease and smoking-related diseases – often come from poor habits in earlier years. Changes to your diet, exercise routines and other habits now will be beneficial to you in later life.

Monitoring your recreational activities may help you to identify possible dangers to your well-being that can be addressed now. Habits are easier to establish than they are to get rid of.

## Aspects of health and well-being relating to different groups

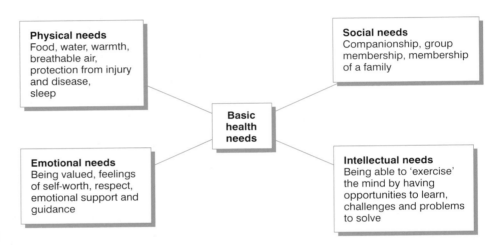

**Physical needs**
Food, water, warmth, breathable air, protection from injury and disease, sleep

**Social needs**
Companionship, group membership, membership of a family

**Basic health needs**

**Emotional needs**
Being valued, feelings of self-worth, respect, emotional support and guidance

**Intellectual needs**
Being able to 'exercise' the mind by having opportunities to learn, challenges and problems to solve

*Basic health needs*

How are basic health needs expressed and met in different groups of people? The table opposite explains. Basic needs do not change. The differences are in the ability of an individual to provide for his or her own needs. Put another way, people need different amounts and types of support to meet their needs throughout life.

Different needs also have differing importance:

- Food, shelter and water are essential to stay alive.
- The next important need is for safety.
- Having achieved the first two, a person is in need of emotional and social support.
- Further needs which follow on are the need for self-respect and self-esteem.
- Finally there is a need for what you want.

For example, if you consider people who are starving, they may take risks or degrade themselves by doing things that they would not do if they were fully-fed. Their primary need is for food and only later can they consider their own self-respect. This 'hierarchy of needs' was described by a researcher called Abraham Maslow (see Unit Three, page 104).

## How basic health needs are expressed and met in different age groups

| Life stage | Basic health need | How the need is expressed and met |
|---|---|---|
| Infant 0–2 | Physical | Food, warmth, water from parents. Medical support/vaccination for long-term protection. |
| | Social | Very solitary, relying on carers, brothers and sisters for social roles. |
| | Emotional | Very reliant on primary carers for emotional support. |
| | Intellectual | Learning to play and learn from new situation. |
| Child 2–10 | Physical | Walking gives access to a range of areas. Food and warmth and protection from carers. |
| | Social | Developing circle of friends. Greater range of social contacts. |
| | Emotional | Very reliant on primary carers for emotional support and as models for beliefs. |
| | Intellectual | Learning through play. Formal education. |
| Adolescent 10–18 | Physical | Rapid growth at puberty linked to taking more personal control of supplying physical needs. |
| | Social | Peer group (people of same age and interests) becomes very important. Group membership provides support beyond the family. |
| | Emotional | A time of mixed emotions needing careful support. Starts to move away from parents to peers for support. |
| | Intellectual | Formal education. More learning from experience as new situations are met in peer groups. |
| Adult 18–65 | Physical | Becoming self-reliant and a provider of physical support for others (becoming a parent). |
| | Social | Develops through a variety of stages including marriage, starting a family and children leaving home. |
| | Emotional | Developing strong attachments to a partner. Being a model for and supplying support for others in family. |
| | Intellectual | Formal education reduces. Challenges come from work roles. |
| Older adult 65+ | Physical | Senses become less efficient. General wear and tear means support from others or artificial aids (e.g. spectacles) may be needed. |
| | Social | Family will have left home. One partner may die before the other. Movement difficulties increase isolation. Organised activities support social well-being. |
| | Emotional | Friends and relatives get older and die. Children become independent, emotional support needs to come from other people. Often a time where reduced ability means self-esteem and self-worth are at a low ebb. Carers need to promote these. |
| | Intellectual | Mental activity often outstrips physical ability leading to some frustration. Intellectual activities are very important. |

# 2.2 What can cause ill-health

So far you have studied yourself and some of the factors that help promote your health and well-being. We now need to look at risks to the health of people in general. By identifying the risks we hope you will be able to avoid them and also help people you work with avoid the dangers.

Risks to health and well-being may be associated with the normal activities of daily living, including:

- diet
- exercise
- personal hygiene.

| Health need | Risks |
|---|---|
| Physical | Risk of accidents<br>Risks associated with poor diet<br>Risks associated with poor exercise<br>Risks associated with personal abuse, e.g. alcohol, drug abuse<br>Risks associated with ill-health and disease |
| Social | Risks associated with loss and bereavement<br>Risks associated with divorce<br>Risks associated with changes in circumstances: employment, moving house, changing schools |
| Emotional | Risks associated with loss and bereavement, divorce, changing jobs, moving house or changing school |
| Intellectual | Risks associated with change and allied to all other areas |

There are also risks associated with activities that people choose to undertake. These include:

- drug abuse (including alcohol and tobacco)
- unsafe sexual practices.

We all need to eat, exercise and practise good hygiene. But it is not essential to smoke, drink, take drugs or practise unsafe sex. However, in your group you will find people who risk their health with one or more of these activities.

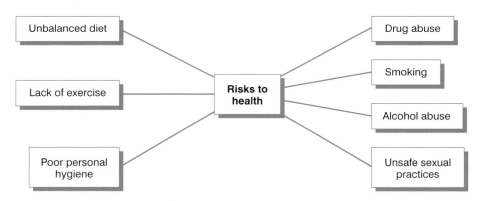

## Risk and diet

Unit Five describes what constitutes a balanced diet. It also describes some of the effects (risks) of an unbalanced diet.

We will consider the following two questions about diet here:

- Who controls the food a person eats?
- What are the effects of the amount of money available to spend on food?

# Who controls the food a person eats?

The answer to this question varies for different groups of people.

### Babies
A baby is totally reliant on others for its food. Both breast milk and formula foods supply dietary needs. Even at this stage the diet can become unbalanced if formula food is not made up correctly.

### Children
With children the control is still mainly with parents and carers. Children have access to a wider range of foods. For many, this will include sweets and biscuits. Eating these in excess can lead to tooth decay and becoming overweight. There is also a temptation to eat foods containing a lot of fat (chips, pizzas and crisps), that again leads to increased risks from overweight and heart disease in later life. Habits set up in childhood often last into later life.

### Adolescents
Adolescents have even more control over their food intake. Many schools run cafeterias with a range of foods, and tuck shops selling sweets and snacks. Adolescence can also be a time of major changes in food intake as individuals choose new dietary patterns. Many people choose to become vegetarian during their teenage years. In itself this is not a problem, but there is a risk of an unbalanced diet if meals are not carefully planned. (This is particularly so if only one member of a group is vegetarian.)

*Many adolescent people develop poor eating habits that can be encouraged in schools and colleges*

In adults, what is the result of reducing physical activity without reducing energy intake?

### Adults

Adults tend to be in charge of their own nutrition. They have access to more money, and diets change. There is a wide range of food available in ready-prepared forms. Lifestyles often dictate regular consumption of 'fast' foods. These are often high in fat and carbohydrate. Care needs to be taken to avoid obesity. Many adults reduce their physical activity without reducing their energy intake, leading to overweight.

### Older adults

Older adults have lower energy requirements and need to reduce their food intake. They also tend to take less exercise. The cost of food can also be an issue and so there are greater risks of an unbalanced diet.

## What are the effects of the amount of money available?

For many people living on a limited budget, planning meals becomes difficult. It is possible to provide a well-balanced diet on a limited income, but there is a risk that the types of food will become boring.

Lentils and brown rice followed by fresh fruit may well be nutritious, but they may not be appetising on a regular basis. Foods that are easier to prepare are normally more expensive. Lack of money can, therefore, often mean that more time has to be taken to prepare meals. Fillet steak and shin beef may be equally nutritious, but the fillet can be cooked in minutes, while the shin takes longer. The style of cooking is also limited by income.

## Other risks linked to diet

Different groups of people can be exposed to other dangers from diet. In particular, two are worth considering here. Both of them are common, even with people who have otherwise eaten a balanced diet:

- anaemia in adolescent women
- calcium and vitamin imbalance in older women.

### Anaemia in adolescent women

Many adolescent women suffer from anaemia. This is linked to the start of menstruation and its associated blood loss. The iron lost needs to be replaced by iron in food, but often the diet does not supply this.

While before puberty there was sufficient iron, the demands for iron caused by rapid growth and menstruation are often not met. Awareness of this potential problem, and action, will help stop anaemia in this group of people.

### Calcium and vitamin D imbalance in older women

Women going through the menopause (see page 98) have a greater need for calcium than they did before that time. Changes in hormones during the menopause mean that bone regrowth is not efficient and calcium is lost. This can lead to a bone-weakening disorder called osteoporosis.

*Mrs L. has the typical 'stoop' of osteoporosis. She has lost 6 inches in height*

Vitamin D is needed to assist the absorption of calcium in the diet. It is important for women to ensure they have a diet containing both vitamin D and calcium in order to reduce these risks during the menopause.

## *Exercise*

### Does exercise really matter?

Watch any international athletics meeting and you will see some people who look very muscular. Others are thin and appear to have little muscle, yet they are able to run long distance races. In both cases the athletes are very fit and exercise regularly. The types of exercise they do depend on their choice of sport: for example, the training that a shot-putter does is quite different to that of a distance runner.

Most of us will never become international athletes and we will never have to exercise as much as they do. But even if we do not desire to be extremely fit, it is still important to exercise. If you exercise regularly, it helps to keep your body in efficient working order.

### How to exercise

It is important to consider the best way to exercise so that you can devise a programme for other people. The first thing to recognise is that the type and pattern of exercise needs to fit in with a person's lifestyle. Many people fail to maintain an exercise programme because they are not prepared to make a major change in their lifestyle.

To be really effective, exercise has to be taken regularly. This is very important because:

- increased fitness takes time to develop
- exercising only occasionally puts an unfair strain on the body and does not give it time to adapt to the increased exercise and activity.

Exercise has to be planned so that there is a build-up to a maximum level. To attempt to jog five miles on the first day is asking for failure. To build up to five miles over several weeks causes less physical and mental strain.

The mental strain is something that we all face when starting any new routine. By exercising regularly a person will fall into a pattern where they are mentally ready for the exercise. It becomes a pleasurable activity as fitness increases. This is where it is easier to plan exercise that fits into the person's lifestyle.

It is often easier for people to plan to exercise together, as each person can support the others with encouragement to continue. It is also more enjoyable to exercise with friends.

### The 'quick fix' exercise routine

It seems that every year there is a new trend in exercise routines. Another new, miracle method of exercising is developed that will get you fit in half the time! Often the adverts will be supported by people who say the routine or equipment worked for them. These systems all prey on our own desires to get fit without having to work at it.

There are no ways of exercising that do not involve effort from you. Every new system is likely to work for some people who find the routine acceptable and can adapt their lifestyles to the activity. For others, who want the cure without the work, the new routine is a failure.

### Activity 3

**a** There are more exercise bikes stored in cupboards and cellars than are ever used regularly. Why do you think this is?

**b** Aerobics groups have been very successful in helping people to maintain regular exercise. What do you think are the risks and benefits of aerobics groups?

### Types of exercise

There are many exercise programmes and equipment advertised. But exercise does not necessarily require specific equipment. What exercise does involve is increasing muscle activity with the associated improvements in the respiratory and circulatory systems (lungs and heart).

There are two basic types of exercise:

- Aerobic exercise: 'aerobic' means 'with oxygen'. This type of exercise works the heart, lungs and muscles in such a way that there is sufficient oxygen supplied to meet the needs of the muscles. The aim is to work at 90 per cent efficiency. In other words, the exercise should not go to a stage where muscles are not receiving enough oxygen. Aerobic exercise includes:
  - walking briskly
  - swimming
  - running
  - cycling and, of course,
  - aerobics.
- Anaerobic exercise: 'anaerobic' means 'without oxygen'. This involves stretching and contracting muscles in a slow, controlled way. When a muscle is being held in a contracted form, the blood supply is temporarily reduced. In such situations energy is generated without using oxygen. As soon as the blood supply returns oxygen is again available. Anaerobic exercise includes:
  - yoga
  - general stretch work
  - isometric routines (contracting muscles without causing movement).

Anaerobic situations also occur during aerobic exercise when the activity continues beyond the ability of the heart and lungs to supply oxygen. Being out of breath and needing to breathe deeply for several minutes after stopping exercise is an indication that anaerobic conditions have occurred.

*What is the difference between aerobic and anaerobic exercise?*

## Different exercise strategies

International athletes provide good models for the benefits of different exercise strategies. A weight-lifter, for example, needs great strength, while a marathon runner needs stamina and a gymnast needs suppleness. Each needs to exercise regularly but in a different way.

If you want to become fitter without concentrating on any particular sport, it is useful to exercise to develop:

- stamina
- strength
- suppleness.

The table below lists some activities and their importance in developing stamina, strength and suppleness:

## The benefits of various physical activities

| Activity | Stamina rating | Suppleness rating | Strength rating |
| --- | --- | --- | --- |
| Badminton | 2 | 3 | 2 |
| Canoeing | 3 | 2 | 3 |
| Climbing stairs | 3 | 1 | 2 |
| Cricket | 1 | 2 | 1 |
| Cycling (hard) | 4 | 2 | 3 |
| Dancing (ballroom) | 1 | 3 | 1 |
| Dancing (disco) | 3 | 4 | 1 |
| Football | 3 | 3 | 3 |
| Golf | 1 | 2 | 1 |
| Gymnastics | 2 | 4 | 3 |
| Hillwalking | 3 | 1 | 2 |
| Jogging | 4 | 2 | 2 |
| Judo | 2 | 4 | 2 |
| Rowing | 4 | 2 | 4 |
| Sailing | 1 | 2 | 2 |
| Squash | 3 | 3 | 2 |
| Swimming (hard) | 4 | 4 | 4 |
| Tennis | 2 | 3 | 2 |
| Walking (briskly) | 2 | 1 | 1 |
| Weightlifting | 1 | 1 | 4 |
| Yoga | 1 | 4 | 1 |

Key   1 = no real effect   2 = beneficial effect   3 = very good effect   4 = excellent effect

**Head**
Increased blood flow and oxygen supply to the brain means a person is more alert.

**Heart**
Exercise causes the heart to beat faster and increases the amount of blood pumped with each beat. This increases the efficiency of the heart and reduces the resting heart rate.

**Circulation**
- The flow of blood to the body increases and stretches the blood vessel walls, helping to keep them elastic and flexible.
- While blood pressure increases during exercise, the resting blood pressure drops and so there is less strain on the heart.

**Lungs**
Exercise increases the rate and depth of breathing. This means that the lungs maintain their flexibility and efficiency in supplying oxygen to the body.

**Muscles**
- Improved blood circulation and oxygen supply means the muscles use energy efficiently.
- Exercise promotes muscle formation and increased strength.
- Posture is improved and risk of injury is reduced.

**Joints**
The flexibility of joints is maintained and improved.

**General**
- Exercise increases energy usage and may help use up excess fat.
- Increased physical fitness helps improve the repair systems of the body.
- There is greater resistance to disease and wounds heal faster.

*The benefits of exercise*

## Starting an exercise regime

It is best to start exercising slowly. This helps to:

- ensure that the exercise is aerobic
- reduce the risk of any strain injuries.

Aim to exercise for 20 minutes, three or four times a week. The exercise should be enough to increase the heart rate, but not so much that it does not return to its resting rate within about five minutes of stopping exercise.

Whatever you do, try to make it enjoyable and to fit in with your lifestyle. For example, you could make it part of your routine to get off the bus to school or college two stops earlier than usual and walk briskly. It is easy to do and helps to build up stamina.

| Remember... |
| --- |

When starting to exercise:

- warm up thoroughly
- start with gentle stretching to ensure that the muscles to be used are ready for the exercise
- avoid sudden changes of direction or jerky movements
- avoid exercises that put a strain on the lower back, such as sit-ups and double-leg raises. These may form part of a stricter exercise regime.

*Exercise is good for you*

# 2.3 How to explore risks to health

## Risk and exercise

### Children

Young children are always exploring their surroundings. Their work is play and by 'working' they take plenty of exercise.

However, children can also be at risk where exercise is not encouraged by their parents/carers. Some circumstances, particularly at school, may discourage a child from taking part in physical activities. There is always the child who is last to be chosen for team games or who is never chosen. The child then becomes isolated from organised exercise and has low self-esteem because of rejection. The desire to be part of a group activity is denied and any exercise has to be solitary.

Rejection from team games is often as a result of poor fitness. The failure to exercise makes later rejection more likely and a vicious cycle starts. As individuals it is important that we value and encourage colleagues. There should be a commitment to assist friends to join in activities that support their health.

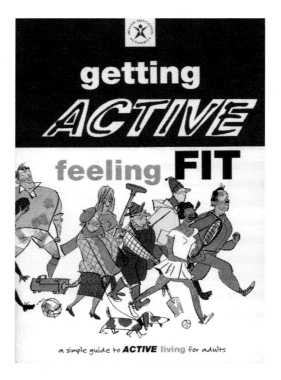

### Adults

As people get older they have a greater choice of activities and work. There is a risk that exercise levels do not match needs. This is particularly important with adults.

The change in lifestyle brought about by starting work often means that exercise levels drop. Therefore levels of fitness drop and the risk of heart disease increases.

People at risk from lack of exercise tend to be those whose work roles involve minimal exercise and who choose not to undertake any exercise routine. Such people may also be at risk from a poor diet and overweight. It should be possible, however, for them to develop an exercise routine to fit with their lifestyle (see page 55).

## Older adults

Many elderly people do not feel able to exercise. They may have been fit in earlier years but are unable to continue their activity. Exercise routines can be developed to meet their individual lifestyle needs.

## *Risk and personal hygiene*

Poor personal hygiene causes the spread of more diseases than anything else. The common cold and influenza (flu) are spread by droplets coughed or sneezed out by an infected person. They are also breathed out but do not spread as far. Failure to use handkerchiefs (preferably disposable) increases the spread.

Personal hygiene is important and is a way of maintaining good health. Use of soap and hot water in washing removes many bacteria from skin. It also removes dead skin cells and oils that provide a food source for bacteria and fungi. Hopefully, you are fully aware of your own responsibilities regarding personal hygiene.

*It is important to keep babies' feeding bottles clean. Babies may suffer damage from even mild doses of food poisoning*

However, if we consider different groups of people, hygiene issues become more important:

- Young babies are less resistant to disease than most other people and may suffer serious damage from even mild doses of food poisoning. Older adults are in a similar situation. In both cases hygiene levels need to be higher than you might have in your own home.
- For older people who are reliant on others for care, other issues of personal hygiene are important. Ensuring that they are clean is not sufficient. Carers must look after other aspects of grooming such as hair and nail care. Shaving is important for men without beards. By paying attention to personal hygiene for these people, and supporting its achievement, you not only maintain physical health but you also promote emotional well-being.

## Risk and the breakdown in normal daily activities

So far we have looked at health risks to people who, to a large extent, have their health under their own control. We have been talking about stereotypes of 'average' people. For most of these people diet, exercise and hygiene are a matter of choice.

However, some people in society have little choice about what they eat or what exercise they take. Personal hygiene may also be affected. People in this situation include:

- those who are physically or mentally unable to look after themselves, such as elderly people (see below)
- those who do not have a regular access to resources to meet their basic needs, including people who are unable to obtain social security benefits (such as homeless people, see below) and also many who do receive benefits, but who have difficulty meeting all their family's needs. People unable to care for themselves, for whatever reason, are often cared for by others. The carers are responsible for helping the individuals to obtain food and exercise (and in many cases exercise is not seen as a priority) and ensuring that they have access to the things they need. Such people include:
  - those who for mental reasons cannot support themselves
  - those with physical disabilities that mean they need support. The support required can vary from guidance in carrying out the activities to total dependence on the carer.

### Elderly people

The number of elderly people in the UK is increasing. People are living longer and more people develop some form of dementia (such as Alzheimer's disease). (Dementia can occur in younger people but the incidence is greatest in elders.) In the later stages of dementia the person becomes totally dependent on others. In fact they return to the situation of babies in their requirement for total support.

## Homeless people

It is an unfortunate fact that many people in the UK today are living rough. Most of these people have no choice about their situation. Some, because of disability, may be ill-equipped to look after themselves. These people have little access to money and cannot plan their diet. Their primary concerns are for the basics of food and shelter. The poor diet and lack of shelter exposes them to increased risk of illness. Tuberculosis is increasing in the UK because of the rising number of people living below the 'poverty line'. They are also at risk of deficiency diseases – diseases that occur because particular nutrients are missing from the diet.

### Activity 4

Imagine you have no home to go back to and no regular income. Everything you need has to be carried around.

**a** How would you get food, and what food might you get?
**b** How would you ensure that the food was 'hygienic' and safe to eat?
**c** How might you cope with food poisoning?
**d** How might you cope without easy access to clean toilets or washing facilities?
**e** How much would you be able to exercise, if you had barely enough food to survive?

Discuss your answers with your class colleagues.

### Key Skills

You can use this opportunity to provide evidence for Key Skills for Communication C1.1

*Some people in society have little real choice about diet, exercise and sleep*

## Risk and smoking

**Key Skills**

You can use Activity 5 to provide evidence for Key Skills Application of Number N1.1, N1.3 and Information Technology IT1.2.

**Activity 5**

Conduct a small survey, asking people the following questions:

**a** Do you smoke?
**b** Why do you (or do you not) smoke?
**c** Do you know of any dangers from smoking?

Present the results of your survey as pie charts. Use a computer if you can.

The results of such a survey are predictable. Many people smoke even though they know some of the risks. Almost everybody will know that smoking causes lung cancer and also that it is a cause of heart disease. The reasons why people smoke vary but, for whatever reason, they took up the habit and are now addicted.

Nicotine (from tobacco) is an addictive drug. People who smoke, while they may give all sorts of reasons, do so because they are drug addicts.

### The risks of smoking

The following risks have been identified with smoking:

* Chemicals in tobacco are known to cause cancer (particularly lung cancer).
* Lung tissues are damaged irreversibly by smoking. (Ninety per cent of emphysema cases have smoking as one of the causes.)
* Smoking leads to an increased risk of heart disease.
* Smoking leads to an increased risk of chest and throat infections.
* Bronchitis, the inflammation of the lungs and tubes to the lungs, is caused by smoking.
* Carbon monoxide in tobacco smoke reduces the ability of the blood to carry oxygen.
* Pregnant women who smoke may suffer a miscarriage.
* There is a greater risk of premature birth, stillbirth and low birth-weight in babies of smokers.
* The risks are not just to the smoker, but also to people nearby who inhale the smoke (passive smoking).

In hygiene terms, smoking literally stinks. Clothing, hair and skin become impregnated with the smell of smoke.

## Risk and alcohol

The situation with alcohol is more complex than that of tobacco. While it is addictive and can kill, it can also have a beneficial effect – in moderate quantities it can help prevent heart disease.

7mg TAR 0·7mg NICOTINE
SMOKING CAUSES HEART DISEASE
Health Departments' Chief Medical Officers

*Group pressure often leads people to become addicted to drugs like tobacco, even though they know the dangers*

However, alcohol is a drug. In moderate amounts, it can make a person feel good about themselves (like a tranquilliser). But when it is taken in large amounts it can make the drinker depressed. This can eventually lead to alcoholism (addiction to alcohol).

Alcohol also has the effect of removing inhibitions. People who have had a drink often say or do things that they would not normally do and that they later regret. It's easy to say 'sorry' to someone you may have insulted when you were drunk. However, it's not so easy to say 'sorry' to the relatives of a person killed by a driver who has been drinking.

*What is alcoholism?*

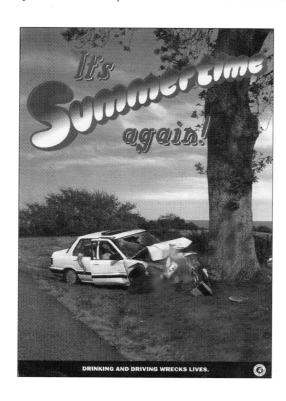

It's Summertime again!

DRINKING AND DRIVING WRECKS LIVES.

Some of the consequences of drinking alcohol:

- Reaction times become slower, leading to increased risk of road accidents.
- Removal of inhibitions:
    - you may do things that you would not normally do, such as having sex with a friend (more likely to be unprotected)
    - you may say things you later wish you hadn't
    - you may generally do things without thinking.
- Damage to your stomach lining and liver:
    - moderate to heavy drinking damages the stomach lining
    - there is an increased risk of stomach ulcers
    - the liver becomes damaged leading to cirrhosis.
- Overweight/poor diet: alcoholic drinks have high energy values and so lead to obesity. Your diet can be affected. Heavy drinkers often spend money on alcohol and not food. As a consequence they may suffer from malnutrition.
- In small quantities it is thought that alcohol can help prevent heart disease.

List five consequences of drinking

## How much alcohol is safe?

The answer to this question varies. If you are driving then the answer should be that no alcohol is safe (although the law allows 80mg/100ml blood = 4 units). If you are at home, in a relatively safe environment, it is not unreasonable to drink several units of alcohol. For an alcoholic (who is addicted to alcohol), any alcohol can be positively dangerous.

How much alcohol is safe if you are driving?

The Health Education Authority has produced guidelines on alcohol consumption. These indicate maximum recommended amounts and recognise the importance of not drinking every day (see the table below).

### Recommended alcohol consumption

| | Maximum recommended (units per week) | Increased risk | Harmful | Recommended number of alcohol-free days |
|---|---|---|---|---|
| Men | 21 | 50 | 50+ | 2–3 |
| Women | 14 | 35 | 35+ | 2–3 |
| Pregnant women | Ideally no alcohol, at most, 4 units | – | – | 5–6 |

What is a unit?
1 unit = ½ pint of beer or lager
1 small glass of wine
1 small glass of sherry
1 measure of vermouth or aperitif
1 standard measure of spirits (UK)

**Note:** 1 pint of extra-strong beer or lager = 5 units

## The risks of other drug abuse

Tobacco and alcohol are legal drugs. However, there are several drugs that are illegal to own, sell or use. These range from so-called 'soft' drugs, such as cannabis, to the 'hard', addictive drugs, such as crack cocaine. The table on page 66 describes some of these drugs and their dangers.

There are some dangers that are general to illegal drugs:

- Criminal conviction – the use or sale of all of the materials listed in the table is controlled by law. A criminal record will reduce employment opportunities. Also, many abusers steal to get the money for drugs.
- Diseases – most drugs are taken by people in groups. They share the required materials. Where drugs are injected, shared needles could transmit the Human Immunodeficiency Virus (HIV).
- Cost – the cost of drugs means that there is less money for other things, such as food. This means that many drug abusers suffer from malnutrition.
- Relationships – there are knock-on effects to families and friends as a result of a drug abuser's mood changes, lack of money, crime or illness.
- Increased risks – it is thought that many drug abusers go on to try different, 'harder' drugs with the increased risk to health.
- Death – drug abuse exposes users to hazards that increase the risk of death. This may be increased risk of lung cancer for cannabis users or risk of HIV infection and AIDS for people injecting drugs.

### Activity 6

You have been working in a community centre for a few weeks. The organiser realises that you know something about health needs and health risks.

As part of your work you have been asked to prepare a short report that describes the factors that affect the health and well-being of people. You are not expected to go into great detail, but you should prepare a short report with the following headings:

- Physical needs
- Emotional needs
- Social needs
- Intellectual needs.

You may find it easiest to produce this part as a table. If you can, use a word processor to write your report and produce your table.

**Key Skills**

You can use Activity 6 to provide evidence for Key Skills Communication C1.2 and, if you use a computer to prepare your report, Information Technology IT1.2.

## Illegal drugs: their effects and dangers

| Drug | Form | How taken | Effects | Dangers |
|------|------|-----------|---------|---------|
| Cannabis | Resin (hash) or leaf | Smoked, often with tobacco in a pipe or cigarette | Relaxation, talkativeness, increased intensity of colour or sound | As for smoking tobacco. Using machinery or driving while under the influence is dangerous |
| Amphetamine | Powder or tablets | Inhaled or swallowed | Stimulates the nervous system, produces feelings of alertness | Developing tolerance and need for larger doses Loss of sleep, loss of appetite, anxiety attacks |
| Cocaine and crack cocaine | Powder (cocaine), crystals (crack) | Powder is usually sniffed, but can be injected. Crack is smoked or heated and vapours inhaled | As for amphetamines | May cause respiratory problems, damage to nasal bones. Otherwise as for amphetamines |
| Ecstasy | Tablets (various types) | Swallowed | Calming, heightened awareness of colour and sound, co-ordination may be affected | Similar to amphetamines. Damage to kidneys can occur if used without drinking plenty of water. (Particular problem at raves where overheating and sweating are likely) |
| LSD | Impregnated on to blotting paper | Dissolved on to the tongue | Powerful hallucinogen – visions vary from joy and beauty to nightmares | May trigger psychotic responses. Actions during a 'trip' may put individual in danger |
| Heroin | Powder | Injected, sniffed or smoked | Produces 'pleasant' drowsiness, nausea and vomiting depending on user. Addictive | Constipation, disrupted menstrual cycle. Dangers associated with method of use (HIV from shared needles) |
| Anabolic steroids | Tablets or injectable solution | Swallowed or injected | Promotes muscle growth | Drugs stimulate aggression. Growth restriction in young people. Reduced sex drive in men. Masculinisation of women. Many effects not reversible |
| Organic solvents | Liquid as a component of some glues and aerosols | Inhaled, often breathing exhaled air | Similar to drunkenness, including hallucinations | Serious brain damage, suffocation related to method of use, liver damage |

## *Risk and sexual practice*

A loving relationship could involve sexual intercourse. Some people may only ever have one sexual partner, while others may have many partners. Whatever the situation it is important to recognise the risks involved in sexual activity.

## Pregnancy

At its basic level, sexual intercourse has evolved as a way of men and women producing more men and women. The sex act has the purpose of enabling sperm and an ovum (egg cell) to get together to start the process of producing other human beings. This is fine, so long as both people involved want the responsibility for the third person they create.

Many people, for whatever reason, do not wish to start a pregnancy but do want to have sex. The answer in this case is to practise some form of contraception. The safest form for stopping a pregnancy is the contraceptive pill, closely followed by using a condom with a spermicidal cream. The safest form for reducing the risks of catching diseases is the use of a condom (rubber, johnny, Durex).

## Other risks associated with sex

There are several diseases specifically associated with sexual activity. All of these present dangers varying from:

- infertility (gonorrhoea)
- cervical cancer (genital warts)
- death (HIV/AIDS).

*What risks are associated with sex?*

These diseases are known as sexually transmitted diseases, or STDs.

The spread of these diseases is preventable by using safe sexual practice. All of the disease-causing organisms can be trapped by using a condom. If either partner is infected, the condom provides a barrier and stops the infection spreading. However, for condoms to work they must be used before any sexual contact has been made.

## Activity 7

In the early 1980s there was a big campaign advising people to use condoms to prevent the spread of HIV and AIDS. The success of the campaign can be seen in the reduced number of cases of gonorrhoea and syphilis. The table below gives some statistics.

### New cases of STDs reported in England, 1980–90

| Year | Gonorrhoea | | | Syphilis | | |
| | Men | Women | Total | Men | Women | Total |
|------|--------|--------|--------|------|-------|-------|
| 1980 | 34 087 | 20 346 | 54 433 | 3134 | 925 | 4059 |
| 1981 | 33 454 | 18 746 | 52 200 | 2963 | 847 | 3810 |
| 1982 | 33 058 | 19 098 | 52 156 | 2739 | 825 | 3564 |
| 1983 | 30 464 | 17 929 | 48 393 | 2662 | 665 | 3327 |
| 1984 | 29 791 | 17 871 | 47 662 | 2315 | 618 | 2933 |
| 1985 | 28 759 | 17 555 | 46 314 | 1819 | 585 | 2404 |
| 1986 | 24 450 | 16 255 | 40 705 | 1387 | 545 | 1932 |
| 1987 | 14 888 | 10 377 | 25 265 | 1029 | 509 | 1538 |
| 1988 | 10 487 | 7 891 | 18 378 | 846 | 396 | 1242 |
| 1989 | 11 346 | 8 415 | 19 761 | 923 | 488 | 1411 |
| 1990 | 11 757 | 7 329 | 19 086 | 810 | 495 | 1305 |

**a** What happens to the number of cases between 1980 and 1988?

**b** What happens in 1989 and 1990?

**c** Why do you think these changes occurred?

**d** Use more recent figures to see if the 1989 and 1990 results are the start of a trend.

The results of Activity 7 should show that the 'safe sex' message got across. They will also show that some people may now be ignoring the message.

The message for you must be that barrier methods (condoms) help prevent disease transmission, but that they only work if they are used. It is each individual's responsibility to make sure that any sexual activity is safe. Gonorrhoea is curable; HIV/AIDS is not – it can kill! Treat all sexual partners as potentially infected.

## *Accidents*

Living is a hazardous activity!

- Hazards or dangers are all around us.
- At different stages in our lives we are more vulnerable to certain hazards. The old and young are most vulnerable.
- It is important that we can recognise potential hazards.
- More accidents occur at times of peak activity in the day.
- Seasonal factors affect a number of types of accidents.
- Accidents don't just happen. They are usually the result of human, environmental or material factors.

## Unsafe practices in the home

Every year thousands of people are injured in the home. The most common types of accident are:

- falls down stairs, and from ladders and buildings
- bites – from animals or insects
- cuts
- blows – being struck by an object or by a person
- burns, scalds
- foreign bodies
- inhaling poisons
- swallowing poisons
- suffocation
- choking
- electric current.

---

### Activity 8

**a** Draw a plan of a house.
**b** Divide it into kitchen, lounge/dining room, stairs, bedrooms, bathroom/toilet.
**c** On your drawing, note the potential hazards in each room.
**d** What are the most common types of accident?

---

**Key Skills**

You can use Activity 8 to provide evidence for Key Skills Communication C1.3.

## Poisonous plants

Berries and flowers look attractive, so they can be a danger to children who may put them in their mouths.

## *Personal hygiene*

## Skin

Remember that the skin has pores that need to be kept clean as the body rids itself of grease and sweat. If skin is left unwashed, then the smell is obvious and the growth of germs is encouraged. Summer weather, hectic sports and certain clothing can necessitate frequent baths or showers. Extra care must be given to areas where sweat is trapped in the folds of the skin. Most people try to prevent stale odours by using deodorants. Check what the difference is between a deodorant and an anti-perspirant next time you buy one. Think of reasons why people may not perform personal hygiene routines. For instance, practically it may be difficult for them if they are living in poor housing which may be cold, damp and difficult to keep clean.

Adolescents may feel self-conscious about using a deodorant or taking a shower after games at school, and because of body changes and hormones working overtime, they actually need showers more than ever.

Young children may have difficult situations at home so their personal care routines are not taught or encouraged. There are many reasons why they may arrive at school unwashed.

People who live rough because they are homeless have obvious difficulties. Hostels for homeless people provide washing facilities and often clean clothing.

## Hair

Most people know how often their hair needs washing and conditioning. Some people need to wash their hair more frequently than others because their skin and scalp are naturally more oily. Things like taking exercise, cooking or being in a smoky environment also affect how often the hair needs washing.

## Teeth

Clean teeth means healthy teeth and less chance of bad breath. It is far better for your teeth if you eat healthy foods at meal times and then avoid eating between meals. Every time you eat, a harmful substance called plaque starts to build up on your teeth. Sugar is particularly hard on teeth, so long-lasting boiled sweets may be nice at the time but too many could cause pain later.

## Nails

If you work in health and social care then clean and short is probably the best habit.

## Feet

If you work in health and social care you will probably be on your feet a lot, so keeping them fresh, clean and comfortable is sensible. Keep toe-nails short and remove hard skin, but anything more major like athlete's foot, bunions or corns should be seen by a doctor or a chiropodist.

It's tempting to squeeze your feet into fashionable shoes at times, but this can cause deformities later. Children's feet are particularly vulnerable in this way and it is best to have their feet measured and shoes properly fitted.

# 2.4 How people can stay healthy

It is easy to say don't smoke, drink, do drugs or practise unsafe sex. We can also advise on appropriate diets and levels of exercise. In all of these cases, you have choices. You can choose to follow guidance or to ignore it. What is important is for you to make informed decisions and think about them before you do anything.

If you think about where you might be exposed to risk, you can identify ways of dealing with situations:

*   At home you are subject to pressures from members of your family to conform to their ways of doing things. You may have no control over your diet, or over other people smoking.
*   Away from home you are subject to different pressures. At school or college your teachers will impose rules and provide pressure for their ideas about risks. You will also be influenced by your friends and colleagues.
*   When you are away from both home and school, participating in leisure activities or at parties, different pressures will be on you again. Drinking alcohol may reduce your inhibitions and you may be tempted to do things that are unsafe or that you would not normally do. At such times, you need to have thought about issues beforehand and stick to any decisions you have made.

### Activity 9

As a group, think of situations where you may be pressured to do things that you don't want to do or would not normally do. How might you deal with such situations? What might you feel like if you gave in to the pressure?

In all these situations it is for you to make an informed choice. This book only provides an outline in terms of guidance. You need to develop your own plans for dealing with risks to your own health.

## The effects of major changes in circumstances on health

Throughout life we all have to face up to changes. Sometimes the changes are planned, while others are unexpected. The types of change we need to consider are:

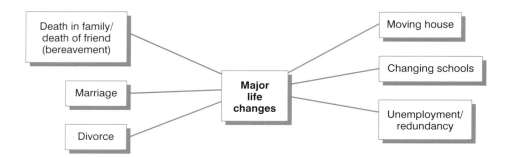

These all have similar effects. They are all a source of stress and all involve loss. This may be:

- loss of a partner, family member or friend
- loss of a lifestyle.

With loss comes a need to grieve and it is this process that is important.

## Activity 10

Reflect upon changes in your own life. For some of you there may have been major upheavals, such as a divorce in your family or a death. For all of you there will have been changes of school.

**a** What things changed?
**b** How did you feel about the change?
**c** What effect did the change have on your health?

Your answer to the last question may be 'I don't know' or 'I don't think it had any effect'. Let's now look at some of the things that can happen.

## Grieving

Grieving is your response to loss. The process may involve:

- tiredness
- anxiety
- loss of appetite or change in eating habits
- becoming withdrawn
- depression
- guilt
- change in sleep patterns.

It can also include:

- suicidal thoughts
- panic
- increased risk of physical illness.

If you now look back at your response to change, you may be able to identify some of the indicators of your grieving processes.

## Stress

In physical terms many of the responses to change are related to stress. Stress occurs when a person is unable to respond to all the demands made upon him or her.

Stress involves the release of adrenaline. This is the same hormone that causes the 'butterflies in the stomach' feelings when you are frightened. The purpose of adrenaline is to prepare your body for fighting or running from danger. The low levels released as a result of stress do not cause the 'butterflies', but do mean that your body is constantly 'geared for action'. The release of adrenaline can have long-term effects on health, including increased risk of heart attacks.

The amount of stress involved in different life events has been given a points score (see the table on page 75). The significance of this table is that anyone who scores 300 points or more in a 12-month period is at risk of becoming ill.

## Social effects of change

When your life goes through a change it is likely that your social activities will change. Moving school means that you lose contact with some friends. Getting married means that your activities are more likely to focus around you 'as a couple' than previously. The death of a partner means that the survivor can no longer do things as a couple. Friends may find it difficult to cope with the grief and so the survivor becomes isolated.

*Short-term effects of stress*

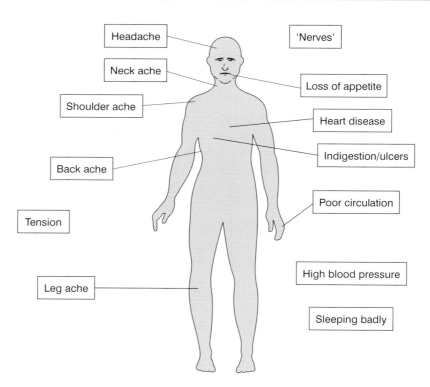

Headache

'Nerves'

Neck ache

Loss of appetite

Shoulder ache

Heart disease

Indigestion/ulcers

Back ache

Poor circulation

Tension

High blood pressure

Leg ache

Sleeping badly

*Long-term effects of stress*

In many situations eating habits change. Some people take to comfort eating and put on weight. Others may feel they 'cannot be bothered' to prepare food and so may eat an unbalanced diet. Eating is generally a social activity and so social changes affect eating habits.

For some people the loss is of income and status. Loss of status can mean that social activities have to change. Loss of income means reduced opportunities to spend money on social activities. It can also involve changes in eating habits and lifestyle.

## Emotional changes

We identified depression as a 'symptom of grief'. Depression leads to a lowering of self-esteem. It means a person feels devalued (feels unimportant, has a low opinion of him or herself). There are also increases in anxiety. When a person is depressed, they feel unable to cope and, at the same time, feel anxious about the inability to cope. It is a vicious circle.

All of these indicate a lack of emotional well-being. They can have a increasingly negative effect on health and can even lead to death.

| Stress scale | |
|---|---|
| Key life events | Points |
| Death of husband or wife | 100 |
| Divorce | 73 |
| Marital separation | 65 |
| Death or serious illness of close family member | 63 |
| Jail sentence | 63 |
| Illness or injury | 53 |
| Marriage | 50 |
| Loss of job | 47 |
| Retirement | 45 |
| Pregnancy | 40 |
| Sex problem | 39 |
| Major change of work | 39 |
| Large mortgage taken on | 31 |
| Starting a new school | 26 |
| Leaving school | 26 |
| Change in residence | 20 |
| Change in sleeping habits | 16 |
| Major change in eating pattern | 15 |
| Holiday | 13 |
| Christmas | 12 |
| Minor violation of law | 11 |

**Activity 11**

**a** For men of the same age, a greater proportion of widowers die than married men. Why do you think this might be?
**b** There are often stories of a person dying soon after a partner. Why might this be?

## Coping with major changes

Some of the resistance to change is caused by fear of the unknown and a feeling of security in what has happened in the past. Knowing this helps us to face change ourselves or help others to cope with change.

### *Relaxation*

The physical effects of change in lifestyle can be minimised by learning to relax. This is easy to say, but difficult to do. It is often best done by setting aside a time to do something not associated with the cause of the change. It could be reading a favourite book or sitting listening to music. It can even be carrying out specific techniques designed to assist relaxation. Yoga, for example, encourages controlled deep breathing to help relaxation.

*Diet*

A second way of dealing with the physical effects of change is to be aware of any alterations in dietary habits and to try to control or avoid them. This may not be easy for an individual, but groups of people (families) can be supportive.

*Exercise and hygiene*

It is also important to maintain physical health by maintaining exercise and hygiene levels. Taking care about how you look increases your self-esteem and reduces the effects of stress on emotional development.

*Support*

Perhaps the most important way of coping with change is to acknowledge any problems and seek support. This can be from friends, family or from trained professionals.

When helping a person pass through a change in life events it is important to recognise the three phases of response to change:

- denial that anything has happened, trying to carry on as if nothing has happened
- shock – feeling the pain of the change. People may cry, be angry or guilty. They may also feel rejected by others because of the change
- acceptance – a stage where the change is acknowledged and the individual starts to live his or her own life again. It often involves learning new skills and making new friends.

Don't forget that key life events include planned, happy experiences as well as unplanned, sad ones. If we consider a couple getting married the phases could be expressed as:

- denial – some marriages never happen because one partner fails to turn up or calls it off
- shock – many couples argue very soon after getting married. This may be an expression of the anger associated with the change
- acceptance – settling down to married life and learning the skills of living with another person.

## Some indicators of good physical health

**Warning**

Do not attempt to carry out Activity 12 if you know you have any breathing difficulties or heart disease. The activities are not dangerous, but it would be best to get medical advice about exercise routines.

### Activity 12

There are many tests that have been devised to determine physical fitness. Many involve detailed measurements and calculations. This activity will give you some idea of the level of exercise that will help you to improve your health.

a  Work with a partner so that you can measure each other's pulse rate. You will need a watch with a second hand. Together decide what you consider to be gentle exercise. (This may be as simple as walking steadily upstairs.)

▶▶

**b** Before you start, measure your resting heartbeat by counting the heartbeats for 15 seconds using the pulse found in your wrist. Multiply the answer by four to get the beats per minute. Record this figure as resting pulse.

**c** Carry out your gentle exercise for 1 minute. Then record your heartbeat at 1-minute intervals until it gets back to the resting rate.

**d** Repeat the activity for longer periods of 2, 5 and 10 minutes (or possibly longer), until it takes more than 5 minutes for your pulse to return to its resting rate.

**Key Skills**

You can use Activity 12 to provide evidence for Key Skills Application of Number N1.1, N1.2 and N1.3.

### Activity 13

The heart rate is a guide to fitness and also a guide as to the level you should work to.

**a** Using the results from the previous activity as a guide, plan a programme of exercises three or four times a week. At the end of each exercise session, measure your maximum heart rate and the time taken to return to the resting rate.

**b** Increase the amount of exercise to reach your maximum pulse that still returns to normal after 5 minutes' rest. You should find that you are able to exercise more as you get fitter.

**Key Skills**

You can use Activity 13 to provide evidence for Key Skills Application of Number N1.1, N1.2 and N1.3.

#### Note

The maximum heart rate that you should not exceed is calculated by subtracting your age from 220:

220 – your age = maximum heartbeats per minute

It is unlikely that you will approach this rate with the gentle exercises, but you should try to double your heartbeat during exercise.

## Height and weight

We are all familiar with our own body size and shape. Looking around we can see there is an immense variation in others' sizes and shapes. We are all individuals.

### Average or normal?

What do we mean by average and normal? Always remember, it is possible to be different from the average height, weight, length etc., but still be within normal limits.

The following measurements are used as a guide to an individual's health and well-being (body mass index):

- height
- body fat
- weight.

### Weight

The average weight for a newborn baby is 3.5kg. The largest recorded live-born baby weighed in at 9.3kg! Babies should be weighed regularly, as weight gain and contentment are signs that they are being fed adequately.

Suggested times for weighing:

- months 1 and 2 – weigh once a week;
- months 3 to 12 – weigh once a month;
- over 12 months – weigh at 6-monthly intervals.

A baby can be expected to double his or her birth weight in the first six months, and treble it by the end of the first year.

Too fat? Children will become fat if they over-eat and do not have enough exercise. Both children and adults can tend to over-eat if they are worried, bored or insecure. It is unwise to give a small child excessive quantities of sweets or fattening foods. Excessive weight gain in the early months makes it more likely that a child will be overweight in later life.

### Height

The average length of a new baby is 50cm. By the second birthday, a child is likely to have reached half his or her eventual adult height. The table below shows height and weight from birth to five years.

### Average heights and weights – birth to 5 years

| Age | Weight | | Height | |
|-----|--------|-----|--------|-----|
| | kg | lb | cm | in |
| *Girls* | | | | |
| Birth | 3.4 | 7.5 | 53.0 | 20.9 |
| 3 months | 5.6 | 12.3 | – | – |
| 6 months | 6.9 | 15.2 | – | – |
| 9 months | 8.7 | 19.2 | – | – |
| 1 year | 9.7 | 21.4 | 74.2 | 29.2 |
| 2 years | 12.2 | 26.9 | 85.6 | 33.7 |
| 3 years | 14.3 | 31.5 | 93.0 | 36.6 |
| 4 years | 16.3 | 35.9 | 100.4 | 39.5 |
| 5 years | 18.3 | 40.3 | 107.2 | 42.4 |
| | | | | |
| *Boys* | | | | |
| Birth | 3.5 | 7.7 | 54.0 | 21.3 |
| 3 months | 5.9 | 13.1 | – | – |
| 6 months | 7.9 | 17.4 | – | – |
| 9 months | 9.2 | 20.3 | – | – |
| 1 year | 10.2 | 22.5 | 76.3 | 30.0 |
| 2 years | 12.7 | 28.0 | 86.9 | 34.2 |
| 3 years | 14.7 | 32.4 | 94.2 | 37.1 |
| 4 years | 16.6 | 36.6 | 101.6 | 40.0 |
| 5 years | 18.5 | 40.7 | 108.3 | 42.6 |

It can be dangerous for parents or carers to become too preoccupied with a child's size. If a child is happy, contented, growing and energetic there is nothing to worry about.

---

### Activity 14

**a** Within your group, ask everyone to find out what their birth weight was. Work out the average birth weight for the group.

**b** Ask your parent(s) or guardian what length you were when you were born (perhaps you still have a record). Compare your length at birth with your height now.

**c** What is your present height and weight? Compare them with the graph below. Are you the appropriate weight for your height?

**d** Within your group, calculate the average heights and weights.

You can use Activity 14 to provide evidence for Key Skills Application of Number N1.1, N1.2 and N1.3.

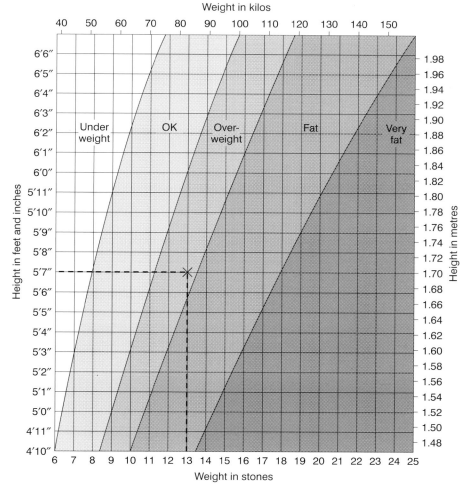

– – – – For example, a person who is 5′7″ tall and weighs 13 stones is overweight

*This is a graph showing the heights and weights of adults. To find out whether you need to lose or gain weight, draw a line up from your weight and across from your height. Put a cross where the two lines meet*

## Measuring the pulse

Each time the heart beats to pump blood, a wave passes along the walls of the arteries. This wave is the pulse. Each time the heart beats to pump blood, a wave passes along the walls of the arteries. This wave is the pulse and it can be felt at any point in the body where a large artery crosses a bone just beneath the skin.

The pulse is usually counted at the radial artery in the wrist or the carotid artery in the neck.

To take a pulse, the fingertips (but not the thumb tips) are placed over the site where the pulse is being taken. The beats are counted for a full minute and then recorded. Normally the rhythm is regular and the volume is sufficient to make the pulse easily felt.

The three main observations that are made on the pulse are:

- rate
- rhythm
- strength.

*What are the main observations that are made on the pulse?*

The average adult pulse rate varies between 60 and 80 beats per minute, while a young baby has a heart rate of about 140 beats per minute.

An increased pulse rate may indicate recent exercise, emotion, infection, blood or fluid loss, shock and heart disease.

### Key Skills

You can use Activity 15 to provide evidence for Key Skills Application of Number N1.1, N1.2.

### Activity 15

**a** In your group, practise taking pulse rates.
**b** Make an accurate recording of each group member's pulse rate.
**c** Calculate the average pulse rate for your group.

### Key terms

After reading this unit you should be able to understand the following words and phrases. If you do not, go back through the unit and find out, or look them up in the Glossary.

Health plan
Risks to health
Major life changes

Diet
Self-esteem
Basic health needs

## Test yourself

1 What are the three main factors that contribute to good health and well-being?
2 Give three reasons for improving health and well-being.
3 List three ways in which smoking can damage a smoker.
4 Who, besides a smoker, is at risk from smoking?
5 How might setting targets help a person planning to improve his or her health?
6 What are the four basic health needs of all individuals?
7 How do the basic health needs change as a child gets older?
8 How many units of alcohol can be drunk before it is illegal to drive? How many units is it safest to have consumed before driving?
9 List two major life changes that are predictable and two that are unpredictable.
10 Give two effects that major life changes may have on a person's health.

# Assignment for Unit Two

***Produce a health plan for improving or maintaining one person's physical health and well-being. (You can do this exercise on yourself.)***

### Tasks

1 Describe your state of health and well-being. You will need to make use of Units Five and Six.

Spend time checking out your current state of health and well-being.

(a) Look up your height and weight on the graph (page 79) to see your weight status.

(b) Review your diet to see if it is well balanced. (Remember to consider the snacks as well as the main meals.)

(c) Record your current exercise activities and check your fitness.

(d) Note down your leisure and recreational activities.

(e) Draw a picture of yourself like the one overleaf. Label one side 'Me now' and the other 'Future me'.

(f) Use the information about your current state of health to complete the 'now' part of the picture. We have given you some examples on this picture to show you what we mean.

### Get the grade

To achieve a **PASS** you must complete tasks 1–4.

To achieve a **MERIT** you must complete tasks 1–7.

To achieve a **DISTINCTION** you must complete tasks 1–9.

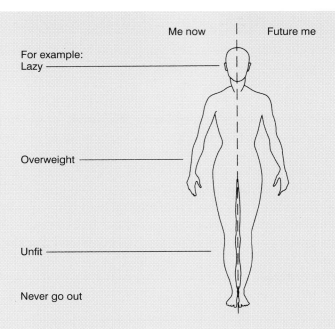

2   List factors that cause potential risk to your health and well-being.

3   Use correctly at least one measure of health

4   Study the 'now' diagram and think carefully about an area that you may want to change. These may be because of either your current state of health and well-being or possible future issues. Make a list of the thing(s) that you wish to change. For the area of change fill in a table like the one below (use a computer if you can). Fill in the second half of the diagram with details of the 'Future me'.

| Aspect to change | Long-term target | How will I know I've got there? | Short-term target | Medium-term target |
|---|---|---|---|---|
|  |  |  |  |  |
| Reward for reaching target |  |  |  |  |

5   Identify short-term and long-term targets for the area in your life that you have chosen to change.

6   Correctly interpret two physical measures of health and use them correctly in your plan.

7   Develop your plan using a variety of sources – also think about who wrote the information and why.

**8** Produce your plan in an appropriate form (remember who you are writing it for – a child, elderly person etc).

**9** Justify the usefulness of your plan. Check the potential physical, emotional and social effects upon your health. You now need to think about how you will check that your plan is working and how you will reward yourself when you reach any intermediate and final targets. Prepare a detailed plan for one week. This should include:

- what you have identified as needing changes/improving

- what you want to gain from the change

- how you plan to introduce the diet, exercise etc., in the first week, making sure with exercise that you start slowly

- what your target is for the end of the first week, for example, for a weight-reducing diet, it could be not eating chocolate biscuits between meals.

**Key Skills** | **Opportunity**
--- | ---
| You can use this opportunity to provide evidence for the following key skills
Communication C1.2 | Develop the plan using information from a number of sources.
Communication C1.3 | Describe health and well-being. Communicate the basic ideas for health maintenance or improvement.
Application of Number N1.1 | Use measures of health.
Application of Number N1.2 | Calculate measures of health.

# Understanding personal development and relationships

## What is covered in this unit

*3.1* **The stages of personal growth and development**
*3.2* **What social and economic factors are and how social and economic factors affect people**
*3.3* **How relationships change over time and their effects on personal development**

At the end of this unit you will be asked to produce a case study of the personal development and relationships of one person. If you would like to see further details of the tasks you are likely to need to carry out for assessment, please refer to the end of the unit where an assignment has been set (see pages 125–126). This unit will guide you through what you need to know in order to successfully put together this case study. You will be assessed on this work and awarded a grade. This grade will contribute to the overall grade you will get for Unit Three.

### Materials you will need to complete this unit

- Development charts and tests
- Information provided by professionals who have visited you in school or college or people you have interviewed.

## Introduction

This chapter will focus on:

- how people develop during their lifetime and the things that influence how they develop, such as the size of family they were brought up in, the groups they have belonged to or the type of housing or neighbourhoods they have lived in
- the personal relationships (friendships, working relationships, parents) that people form at various times in their lives and how these affect how people behave
- the kinds of relationship that may build up between clients (the people we help) and their carers or helpers.

# 3.1 The stages of personal growth and development

One useful way to study human development is to use the following headings:

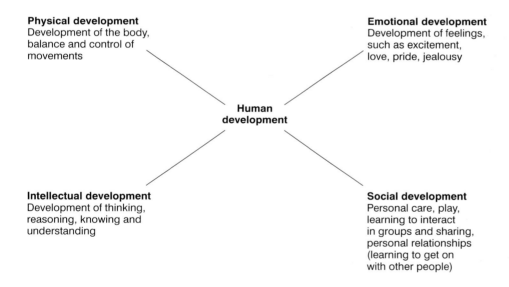

**Physical development**
Development of the body, balance and control of movements

**Emotional development**
Development of feelings, such as excitement, love, pride, jealousy

**Human development**

**Intellectual development**
Development of thinking, reasoning, knowing and understanding

**Social development**
Personal care, play, learning to interact in groups and sharing, personal relationships (learning to get on with other people)

Remember that 'growth' and 'development' are different things:

- growth refers to an increase in actual size
- development means an increase in complexity, for example the child's ability to walk, talk or manipulate things with their fingers.

For example, becoming taller is an obvious growth, while a baby's ability to reach for objects or transfer them from one hand to another shows a development of complex skills.

When looking at personal development we must also consider certain basic needs, which are both physical and emotional.

*Make a list of things you consider to be basic human needs.*

*Development is an increase in complexity of skills*

*Growth is an increase in size*

Does your list of needs look something like this?

| Physical needs | Emotional needs |
|---|---|
| Shelter | Affection |
| Protection | Continuous individual care |
| Fresh air and sunlight | Personal identity |
| Security and rest | Dignity and self-respect |
| Prevention of illness or injury | Opportunity to learn from |
| Training in life skills | experience |

You will find more about needs on pages 103–104.

We will look at the following stages of human development:

- infancy
- childhood
- adolescence
- adulthood
- old age.

## *Infancy*

### Birth to three years

Personal development begins at birth. The sequence of development is roughly the same for all children, but the rate of development will vary from child to child. Parts of the body near the brain develop first. For example, active use of the mouth, eyes and hearing come before sitting, walking and the use of fingers.

Knowing what the average baby or child might be expected to do helps the family and carers to recognise possible problems. If necessary, suitable care or activities can be planned to correct these problems.

When a baby is born, one of the first questions a mother may well ask is 'Is my baby normal?'. To check that all is well, a number of tests are carried out on the baby:

- the airway, palate and colour are examined
- a test, called the Apgar score, is carried out to assess the baby's heart rate, breathing, reflexes and colour
- the baby's hips are checked to see that they are not dislocated
- head size and birth weight are recorded
- skin colour is observed – new babies may be jaundiced and they appear yellow in colour.

| Features of a new-born baby | |
|---|---|
| Average weight | 3.5kg |
| Average length | 50cm |
| Head size | 33–35cm |

Compared with other animals, the human baby is the most helpless and its growth is very slow. The new baby cries to attract its mother's attention and after a few weeks will smile and show pleasure when its mother or father appears. The table on pages 88–89 summarises human development in the first three years.

Children are generally referred to as infants in their first year and as toddlers in their second and third years.

| List of actions | |
|---|---|
| Eyes followed a moving light | Reached for a toy |
| Smiled | Slept through night |
| Sat without support | Crawled |
| Spoke first word | Put two or three words together |
| Used a spoon and fork | Dry during the day |
| Dry during the night | Achieved bowel movement |
| Built a tower of three bricks | Drew a circle |
| Began to understand sharing | Recognised parents |

## Development: birth to 3 years

| Age | Physical development | Intellectual development | Emotional development | Social development |
|---|---|---|---|---|
| 1 month | Holds head erect for a few seconds. Eyes follow a moving light. | Interested in sounds. | Cries in response to pain, hunger and thirst. | May sleep up to 20 hours in a 24-hour period. Stops crying when picked up and spoken to. |
| 3 months | Eyes follow a person moving. Kicks vigorously. | Recognises carer's face. Shows excitement. Listens, smiles, holds rattle. | Enjoys being cuddled and played with. Misses carer and cries for him/her to return. | Responds happily to carer. Becomes excited at prospect of a feed or bath. |
| 6 months | Able to lift head and chest up supported by wrists. Turns to a person who is speaking. Listens to sound. | Responds to speech. Vocalises. Uses eyes a lot. Holds toys. Explores using hands. | Can be anxious in presence of strangers. Can show anger and frustration. Shows a clear preference for mother's company. | Puts everything in mouth. Plays with hands and feet. Tries to hold bottle when feeding. |
| 9 months | Stands when supported. May crawl. Gazes at self in mirror. Tries to hold drinking cup. Sits without support. | Tries to talk, babbling. May say 'Mama' and 'Dada'. Shouts for attention. Understands 'No'. | Can recognise individuals – mother, father, siblings. Still anxious about strangers. Sometimes irritable if routine is altered. | Plays 'Peek-a-boo'. Imitates hand clapping. Puts hands round cup when feeding. |
| 12 months | Pulls self up to standing position. Uses pincer grip. Feeds self using fingers. May walk without assistance. | Knows own name. Obeys simple instructions. Says about three words. | Shows affection. Gives kisses and cuddles. Likes to see familiar faces but less worried by strangers. | Drinks from a cup without assistance. Holds a spoon but cannot feed him/herself. Plays 'Pat-a-cake'. Quickly finds hidden toys. |
| 1.5 years | Walks well, feet apart. Runs carefully. Pushes and pulls large toys. Walks upstairs. Creeps backwards downstairs. | Uses 6–20 recognisable words. Repeats last word of short sentences. Enjoys and tries to join in with nursery rhymes Picks up named toys. Enjoys looking at simple picture books. Builds a tower of 3–4 bricks. Scribbles and makes dots. Preference for right or left hand shown. | Affectionate, but may still be reserved with strangers. Likes to see familiar faces. | Able to hold spoon and to get food into mouth. Holds drinking cup and hands it back when finished. Can take off shoes and socks. Bowel control may have been achieved. Remembers where objects belong. |

## Development: birth to 3 years continued

| Age | Physical development | Intellectual development | Emotional development | Social development |
|---|---|---|---|---|
| 2 years | Runs on whole foot. Squats steadily. Climbs on furniture. Throws a small ball. Sits on a small tricycle and moves vehicle with feet. | Uses 50 or more recognisable words; understands many more words; puts 2 or 3 words together to form simple sentences. Refers to self by name. Asks names of objects and people. Scribbles in circles. Can build a tower of 6 or 7 cubes. Hand preference is obvious. | Can display negative behaviour and resistance. May have temper tantrums if thwarted. Plays contentedly beside other children but not with them. Constantly demands mother's attention. | Asks for food and drink. Spoon feeds without spilling Puts on shoes. |
| 2.5 years | All locomotive skills now improving. Runs and climbs. Able to jump from a low step with feet together. Kicks a large ball. | May use 200 or more words. Knows full name. Continually asking questions, likes stories and recognises details in picture books. Recognises self in photographs. Builds a tower of 7 or more cubes. | Usually active and restless. Emotionally still very dependent on adults. Tends not to want to share playthings. | Eats skilfully with a spoon and may sometimes use a fork. Active and restless. Often dry through the day. |
| 3 years | Sits with feet crossed at ankles. Walks upstairs using alternating feet. | Able to state full name, sex and sometimes age. Carries on simple conversations and constantly questioning. Demands favourite story over and over again. Can count to 10 by rote. Can thread wooden beads on string. Can copy a circle and a cross. Names colours. Cuts with scissors. Paints with a large brush. | Becomes less prone to temper tantrums. Affectionate and confiding, showing affection for younger siblings. Begins to understand sharing. | Eats with a fork and spoon. May be dry through the night. |

**Key Skills**

You can use Activity 1 to provide evidence for Key Skills Communication C1.1, C1.3 and Information Technology IT1.2.

| Activity 1 |

Read the list of actions on pages 88–89 above and on the following pages.

**a** Arrange to interview a parent of a child under the age of 4 to find out when the child was first observed carrying out these actions.

**b** Make your own chart displaying:
- the actions
- the average age when the actions would be accomplished
- the age when the child was actually observed carrying out the actions.

Use a computer to produce the chart, if you have access to one.

## Childhood

### Between 3 and 5 years of age

A child between the ages of 3 and 5 is referred to as a **pre-school child**. At this age a child is increasingly active and communicative.

#### Physical development

During this period in his or her life, a child continues to develop and perfect many of the physical skills that have been acquired since birth. Skills include:

*What is a child between the ages of 3 and 5 called?*

- running
- walking
- climbing
- riding a tricycle
- sitting cross-legged
- moving in time with music
- playing ball games.

#### Intellectual development

Between the ages of 3 and 5, a child will begin to speak grammatically (using words in their proper place), recount recent events accurately, enjoy jokes and be able to state their name, address, age and usually their birthday.

The child will also be gaining control in writing and drawing. A recognisable person may be drawn, such as father or mother, also a house with doors, windows and a roof. Pictures are coloured neatly and four or more colours can be named.

#### Emotional and social development

By the age of 5, a child is able to use a fork, spoon and knife. They can dress and undress themselves, although they may have some difficulty with fastenings. They indulge in make-believe play and in general are

*'Kate and Tom' by Kate, aged 3 ¾*

more sensitive. They relate clock time to daily programmes of events. They will know when they have their dinner or tea and the time they usually go to bed.

Children of this age need the companionship of other children and begin to develop personal relationships. They gradually become more independent from their parents. They will play with other children and also by themselves. They will comfort playmates who are upset, choose their own friends, begin to understand the rules of games and understand what is fair play.

## Between 5 and 10 years of age

For children of this age, life revolves around the family, school and the community. Independence is increasing and variations in children's abilities to do different things become more obvious. At about 5 years of age, a child will usually start to attend school. What do we expect from a child of this age?

### Physical development

The 5-year-old child appears taller and slimmer than the toddler and his or her features have a more adult look. Movements are well co-ordinated and physical skill increases. The growth rate follows a steady, but slower, pattern until puberty ends at about 18 years of age. Girls tend to develop more quickly than boys, physically and intellectually.

### Intellectual development

The child begins to develop a greater capacity for **directed thinking** (to concentrate on one thing) – he or she can concentrate on one task and finish it. When you work with children of this age group in school, you will see how they learn a range of activities. These activities are designed by teachers to help the children gain knowledge and skills.

Children who have never been separated from their parents before may experience problems of adjustment when they start school. They may be unable to settle, cry, become aggressive or angry. Carers working with

*What does directed thinking mean?*

children of this age should be sensitive to this situation. Think about your own first day at school and your feelings at that time. Discuss with your parents what your reactions were then.

**You can use Activity 2 to provide evidence for Key Skills for Information Technology IT1.2.**

## Activity 2

Starting school for the first time may be a difficult experience for a 4 or 5 year old. Produce an advice sheet to help parents prepare their child for starting school. Carry out some research by talking to teachers, care staff, parents and your friends first. Use a computer to produce the sheet, if you can.

### Social development

A child first relates to his or her mother and then to the father, brothers, sisters and other relations.

The range of contacts grows when school starts. In school, the teacher may take on the role of parent in the child's eyes, but the teacher cannot give undivided attention to every child. Sometimes, therefore, a child who is used to a lot of individual attention from his or her parents may find it difficult to adjust to school at first.

Between the ages of 5 and 10 girls tend to develop more rapidly than boys, both physically and intellectually. Boys tend not to play or develop relationships with girls – you may have noticed this during your work experience. Boys will tend to play football, 'rough and tumble' games and other activities in groups, while girls will have their own activities and games.

*Between the ages of 7 and 10 special friendships develop between children of the same sex. Some children are excluded*

By the time a child is 9, special friendships will have been developed. However, 9 year olds can be very critical of each other and may exclude certain individuals from their games. You will see this in any school playground.

### *Emotional development*

Boys and girls continue their emotional development. They experience the growth of feelings about themselves and others. They also begin to develop their self-image and **identity** (how they see themselves).

By the age of 10, childhood is nearly finished and puberty is beginning. The skills of the 10 year old bring together all that has been experienced and learned in childhood.

## Adolescence

**Adolescence** is the name given to the period of life between the onset of **puberty** at about 11 to the beginning of adult life at 18.

In western society, adolescence coincides with a growth spurt. It is a time of social and biological change. In Victorian times children left school and were sent out to work at about the age of 6 or 7. They didn't have the opportunity that adolescents have today to gain experience and education. Today, the tendency is to prolong adolescence, and people now stay on at school until 16 or 18.

## Physical development

Puberty means 'age of manhood'. Physical changes occur because of increased production of sex hormones:

- **oestrogen** in girls
- **testosterone** in boys.

### *Puberty in girls*

Changes in girls tend to start at 10 to 12 years of age, sometimes even earlier. These include:

- a growth spurt
- breast development
- appearance of pubic and armpit hair
- broadening of the hips
- a redistribution of fat
- menstruation.

### *Puberty in boys*

In boys, the changes associated with puberty usually start at 12 to 14 years. These include:

- a growth spurt
- facial hair
- deepening of the voice
- enlargement of the penis, scrotum and testes

Name the sex hormones that cause physical changes in adolescent boys and girls.

*Puberty in girls*       *Puberty in boys*

- appearance of pubic, chest and armpit hair
- the limbs lengthen and shoulders become broader
- the ability to ejaculate.

Physical changes can lead adolescent boys and girls to develop spots. While this is common and can develop into acne, it is a normal part of growing up and is treatable.

Adolescence is a period when a lot of social, intellectual and emotional changes occur. Adolescents have to grow physically into a new body, as we have already seen. They also have to come to terms with new feelings and attitudes.

## Social development

In western society adolescence is a time when a person is neither a child nor an adult. However, it is also a period when interest in the opposite sex begins.

Many of the issues associated to adolescence are **psycho-social** in nature. For example, spots are physical things, but they may also cause psycho-social problems such as depression, shyness, embarrassment, and prevent a person socialising and developing personal relationships.

It is also a time when a person's individual identity (their own **personality**) becomes established. Moral (right and wrong), social and personal responsibilities are also developed. Adolescents often do this by challenging accepted ways of behaving. By rebelling against their parents or teachers, they are testing and developing their own ideas of what is right and wrong.

## Emotional development

Adolescents experience mood swings and feelings of ambivalence. For example, sometimes they may co-operate with their parents, but at other times they may 'dig their heels in' and not co-operate. Parents and friends may be confused by such behaviour. They may not understand what adolescents are thinking or feeling. This is a very difficult time for most parents and children.

## Intellectual development

Adolescents begin to think about themselves and what others think about them. They begin to compare the ideal world with what they experience in reality, in terms of families, politics and religion.

*What do adolescents say about this period in their life?*

Adolescents will experiment with different identities. For example, they may try being a punk, a hippie or even a delinquent. Many of these may be the opposite of what their parents are or want for them. This role-playing may not be a bad thing as it allows adolescents to achieve their personal identity.

Adolescence is also a time when a person is starting to think about the future – a possible career or going on to university, for example.

---

**Activity 3**

Prepare a 'problem page' as it might appear in a teenage magazine. Design the page using a computer, if you can.

**a** Start by finding out as much as you can about the problems associated with adolescence.

**b** Write a selection of letters asking for advice on a range of adolescent issues.

**c** From your reading and research, prepare clear answers for each letter.

---

## Adulthood

Adult life begins at 18 years of age and ends at death. We will look at the years 18 to 64 here and the years 65+ on pages 99–102.

During adulthood most people reach the peak of their performance. Skeletal growth ends in the late teens or early twenties, and a person is at their peak at this time. From the age of 30 or so signs of ageing begin to show.

During childhood and adolescence the individual is dependent upon others. During adulthood, however, the individual is expected take responsibility for his or her own self, for their children, for their own old age and perhaps for the care of older people.

### The 18 to 25 year olds

Who are this group? They are young people at the beginning of adult life, who may still be involved in education or training. Perhaps they are at university or college and still receiving financial support in the form of grants, loans or assistance from parents.

In addition, they may have left the family home and be living in a different part of the country. They may be considering home ownership.

They may be employed or unemployed and receiving state benefits. This can be a time of freedom, providing financial stability has been achieved.

People may also be considering settling down as couples and starting families. The process of becoming a 'couple' will tend to follow a certain path:

- First, there is the single-sex group within which social activities occur.
- Then mixed groups start to form.
- Girls and boys begin to take an interest in forming relationships with each other. For girls, the approval of boys becomes more important than acceptance by their girlfriends.

- Mixed groups of couples appear, but later individual couples dominate the social scene.
- Couples may develop an interest in sexual relationships, hopefully within a framework of respect and caring.

---

**Activity 4**

**a** What do you think it means to be a 'couple'?

**b** What qualities do you think you will look for when choosing a partner?

**c** Complete the quiz below, writing your response on a sheet of paper.

**d** Discuss the responses with your fellow students.

| Quiz | | | | | | | | | | |
|---|---|---|---|---|---|---|---|---|---|---|
| Qualities | Score | | | | | | | | | |
| | 1 | 2 | 3 | 4 | 5 | 6 | 7 | 8 | 9 | 10 |
| Good wage earner | | | | | | | | | | |
| Good-looking | | | | | | | | | | |
| Good sense of humour | | | | | | | | | | |
| Handyman/woman | | | | | | | | | | |
| Good with children | | | | | | | | | | |
| Likes a good social life | | | | | | | | | | |
| Rich | | | | | | | | | | |
| Hardworking | | | | | | | | | | |
| Manages money well | | | | | | | | | | |
| Dresses well | | | | | | | | | | |

Give each quality a score out of ten, the higher score showing the importance you attach to each quality.

## The 25 to 40 year olds

This group is made up of men and women who may be married or single, with or without children. They may live as couples or single people.

If employed, they will usually be concentrating on their career, hoping to do well and improve their position and looking for promotion. Look at job adverts in magazines and newspapers – many employers are looking for people in this age group, because they have some experience yet are still energetic and ambitious.

Often by the time people are in their late twenties they have formed a steady relationship. They may get engaged, get married or decide to live together as a couple in a stable relationship. However, many relationships end in separation or divorce.

During this stage, couples and single parents will be bringing up families, with the need for a reasonable income, housing and community facilities to help them to do so.

## The 40 to 64 year olds

People in this age group (often called 'middle age') may have experienced a career change, may have taken early retirement or may have been made redundant.

Children of people in this age group will probably be growing up and starting their own families and careers. The parents of this age group will be becoming elderly and possibly dependent on others.

Middle age can be a time of greater security in life. People will have brought up their own children, have greater financial security and will have achieved some, if not all, of their career goals. It should be a time to feel confident, relaxed and able to enjoy life.

However, people sometimes feel negative during this life stage. They may feel, perhaps, that they have lost the main role in their life – bringing up children. They may be faced with the prospect of caring for elderly relatives just when they would like to enjoy some independence. Dissatisfaction with achievements or lack of recognition at work can also cause concern.

People in this age group may experience some of the early symptoms of ageing, such as grey hair, long-sightedness and dental problems. Ill-health is also more common. People are more likely to die as a result of heart disease, cancer and respiratory disorders.

Women begin to experience the **menopause** (the 'change of life') any time after 40. This involves a series of changes in hormones, which eventually means the end of a woman's ability to have children.

**You can use Activity 5 to provide evidence for Key Skills Communication C1.1.**

---

### Activity 5

Arrange to interview a person in this age group. Find out how they feel about their age and stage in life and what social and economic factors affected their life. You could ask your parents or grandparents or a neighbour.

Before you start, write down the questions you want to ask under these headings:

* Work/career
* Home life
* Relationships with parents/children
* Social life
* Physical state.

---

## Old age

Old age is often viewed in a negative way – as a stage of life that just brings problems, such as the need for residential accommodation or health and social care. But people do not change simply because they have reached old age. They continue with their lives in the same way they have always done. Many remain independent for most, if not all, of their lives.

The poet Robert Browning expressed an optimistic view of old age:

> Grow old along with me
> The best is yet to be
> The last of life for which the first was made.

Another poet, Dylan Thomas, felt that 'Old age should burn and rage at close of day'. Do you agree with this sentiment? What do you think these two poets meant?

Old age can be divided into two stages:

* early old age (up to 75 years old) and
* late old age (beyond 75 years).

Today, people are living longer than ever before. About 18 per cent of the population are now over retirement age. Women tend to outlive men by about five years on average. The length of time a person can expect to live in years is known as his or her **life expectancy**. Things that can affect life expectancy include:

*Do men tend to outlive women?*

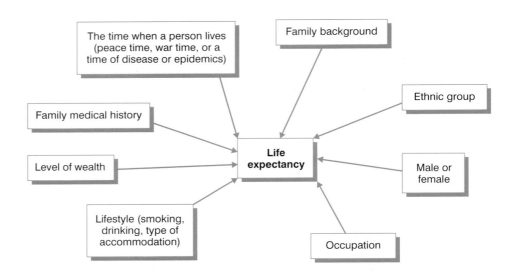

## Physical changes in old age

Some of the physical changes that are happening throughout life and that may become more obvious in old age include the following:

- Skin – dryness, wrinkling and loss of elasticity may occur.
- Hair – growth slows, thinning occurs, men may go bald and all body hair goes grey.
- Eyesight – long-sightedness may develop. People find it harder to distinguish colours. Changing from bright light to dark becomes a problem. Side vision becomes more narrow. Cataracts and glaucoma can lead to blindness if left untreated.
- Hearing – the ability to hear deteriorates. Appreciation of high-pitch frequencies is lost first.
- Smell and taste – these senses deteriorate, sometimes causing loss of appetite.
- Teeth – may deteriorate quite early in life. Gum disease and decay are major problems. Carers need to be sensitive to this when providing food and attending to oral hygiene.
- The lungs and respiratory system – the lungs become less elastic and respiratory muscles weaken. Older people are more likely to be affected by physical disorders.
- The heart and blood vessels – the efficiency of the heart decreases. Blood vessels become less elastic and blood pressure may be raised.
- The digestive system – secretions of saliva and digestive juices decrease with age. Food takes much longer to pass through the body as muscles become weaker and less effective. Constipation can then become a problem.
- The urinary system – the kidneys become less efficient at filtering out waste products effectively.

- The reproductive system – in women the menopause will have marked the end of reproductive life.
- The skeleton and muscles – between the ages of 20 and 70 a person can lose 5cm in height. Total bone mass is reduced and muscles become less flexible. Posture and mobility are likely to be altered considerably.

This all sounds negative. There is no denying that certain aspects of the ageing process can be very troublesome to some individuals, but not to everyone.

## Psychological changes in old age

### Personality
It is often said that old people do not like change. Like most of us, elderly people find familiar surroundings and situations a comfort. They are less likely to make mistakes in their own homes than when in hospital or residential care.

### Memory
You may notice that some elderly people easily forget what has happened recently, but clearly remember things that happened several decades ago. This may be because of the way the memory works – earlier events are imprinted on the brain by repetition (the person may have experienced a particular event a number of times). The brain remembers these earlier events rather than more recent events.

### Learning and intelligence
Older people do tend to take longer to absorb new information than younger people, but they do not become less **intelligent**. Many older people take Open University degrees or enrol in classes in local colleges.

## Social aspects of ageing

The main social aspects of ageing are:

- retirement
- family changes
- loneliness
- changing roles.

### Retirement
Retirement ages vary around the world – from 55 in Japan to 70 in the USA. When people leave work they feel that they lose their status in society. For example, a bank manager is no longer a bank manager or a teacher a teacher. People may lose their friendships, their income drops and their lifestyle changes.

Reduced income can give rise to problems. A retired person needs between 65 and 80 per cent of their previous income to maintain their standard of living at the same level. Most people's incomes drop by half and many drop by a lot more.

### Family changes

When their children have grown up, many elderly people will become grandparents and great-grandparents. Older people do have a considerable role to play in looking after their grandchildren, often in the form of child care and sometimes even giving financial help.

*Adapting after losing a partner*

Drastic changes are brought about when one partner dies. The remaining partner may have little experience of managing financial matters. They may not drive or feel confident to attend functions by themselves or they may lack the ability to cook and care for themselves and their home.

### Loneliness

This may occur for a variety of reasons. People can be isolated in their own homes because of poor mobility or because they do not have many visitors or friends. It is also possible for people to feel extremely lonely when they live in residential homes. They may have difficulty in forming relationships with other residents and staff. Many people in residential care or hospital miss their own homes and familiar possessions.

### Changing roles

Many elderly people worry that their declining health may cause them to be a burden to other people. An elderly person may become totally dependent on one of their children – the roles have been reversed.

**Activity 6**

Describe the main characteristics of the following types of personal relationship:

**a** friendships
**b** sexual relationships
**c** working relationships
**d** family relationships

at each of the following life stages:

* adolescent
* adult.

# 3.2 What social and economic factors are and how social and economic factors affect people

## The needs of clients

We also build relationships with clients by showing them that we have up-to-date knowledge about the services that are available and how these services can help them.

Before you can give any advice, however, you need to find out what a client's needs are. How do you do this? First you have to carry out an assessment of the client's situation – his or her abilities, expectations and aspirations. You do this by looking at the client's needs under the following headings:

* physical needs
* emotional needs
* intellectual needs
* social and cultural needs.

## How are a client's needs assessed?

### Maslow's theory of human needs

This theory is a useful starting point. Maslow suggests that human needs are arranged in a series of five levels as shown in the diagram overleaf.

The needs at Level 1, such as shelter, food and water, are the basic, essential requirements for any individual to live. The more complex needs shown from the middle of the pyramid upwards are only considered when the basic needs have been taken care of. For example, a homeless, hungry person needs shelter and food before they might worry about their social needs.

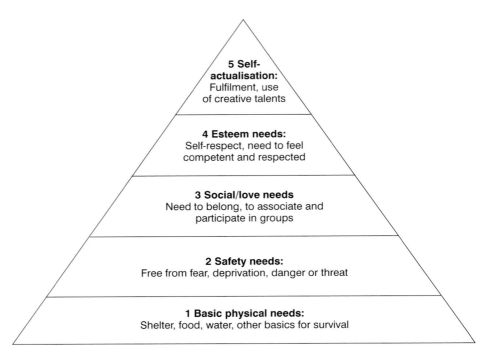

*Maslow's hierarchy of needs*

*Level 1 Basic physical needs:* These include the need to satisfy hunger and thirst, the need for oxygen and the need to maintain temperature regulation. These also include the need for sleep, sensory pleasures, maternal behaviour and sexual desire. If people are denied any of these needs, they may spend long periods of time looking for them. For example, if water or food is not readily available, most people's energies will be spent trying to obtain a supply.

### Activity 7

Mrs Jones is elderly and confused. She has been missing for twenty-four hours. She is found in a local wood, very tired, hungry and thirsty. What would you say are her most pressing needs?

*Level 2 Safety needs:* Once basic physical needs have been met, a person's next concern is usually for safety and security, freedom from pain, threat of physical attack and protection from danger.

*Level 3 Love and social needs:* These include affection, a sense of belonging, the need for social activities, friendships, and the giving and receiving of love.

**Key Skills**

You can use Activity 8 to provide evidence for Key Skills Communication C1.1

### Activity 8

Discuss with your class how children might have their economic and social needs met. In what situations might these needs occur?

*Level 4 Self-esteem needs:* These include the need to have self-respect and to have the esteem of others. Self-respect involves the desire to have confidence, strength, independence, freedom and achievement. The esteem of others involves having prestige, status, recognition, attention, reputation and appreciation from other people.

**Key Skills**

You can use Activity 9 to provide evidence for Key Skills Communication C1.3

### Activity 9

List as many situations as you can where a person's social needs might not be recognised in a residential care setting. Examples might be not allowing residents to choose when to eat or to have friends in their own room.

*Level 5 Self-actualisation/self-fulfilment needs:* This is the development and realisation of your full potential. All the other needs in the pyramid have to be achieved before you can reach this stage.

### Activities of daily living

Another way to assess a client's needs is by using the 'activities of daily living' model. The assessor looks at the client's situation in relation to the everyday activities that people need to carry out. The activities include:

- safe environment – freedom from pain, comfort
- body functions – breathing comfortably, passing urine and faeces regularly, maintaining body temperature etc.
- nutrition – a healthy diet, ability to eat, adequate and suitable fluids
- personal cleaning and dressing – mouth, teeth, eyes, ears, skin, suitable clothing, ability to dress and undress
- mobility – can the client get out of bed or exercise?
- sleep – sleep pattern, does the client wake during the night or sleep during the day?
- sexuality – is the client able to express their feelings? do they have the ability to enter into meaningful sexual relationships?
- religion – are the cultural needs of client being met? do they have the freedom to worship?
- communication – is the client able to communicate verbally, express emotions, use smell, touch?

You can use
Activity 10 to
provide evidence
for Key Skills
Communication
C1.1.

---

**Activity 10**

**a** Decide what you think might be examples of the following needs:
- religious needs
- sexual needs
- nutritional needs
- physical needs.

**b** With your class colleagues, discuss and decide at which levels of Maslow's pyramid these needs could be met, in a residential establishment.

---

## How social and economic factors affect people

### How are people's needs met?

*Physical needs*

These may be met by:

- the provision of appropriate food and drink. For example, babies and people who are ill (such as someone suffering from diabetes) need different diets to a healthy adult
- attending to personal hygiene. This is essential to prevent infection and spread of disease.

*Intellectual and emotional needs*

These may be more difficult to meet. It is important to:

- treat people as individuals
- respect people's individuality and opinions
- allow people to be as independent as possible.

For example, in a residential home for elderly people these needs may be met by allowing residents to:

- be independent
- choose their own meals
- make decisions about their own meal times, bed times, visiting times
- participate in social and educational activities in the establishment and outside of it.

Emotional needs are not separate from physical needs. People often feel better after a bath or a visit to the hairdresser. If they feel clean, they feel more secure when interacting with others. For example, someone who smells of urine will not feel emotionally secure when talking to relatives or friends. By meeting their physical need, their emotional need may also be met.

## Social and cultural needs

These are an important aspect of a person's life. Social needs can be met by:

- encouraging people to socialise
- encouraging people to keep in touch with relatives and friends
- arranging for volunteers to visit them in their own homes if they are housebound.

Cultural needs are recognised when people are allowed to practise their cultural rituals and traditions. They can be met by recognising that people:

- need to practise their religion
- have cultural food preferences
- relate to individuals in their family according to their cultural practices.

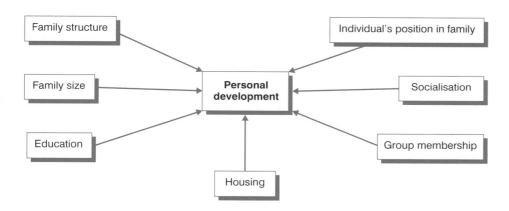

## The family

### Family structure

The image we see of families in magazines and on television is that they all live in beautifully decorated homes, that mothers are always glamorous, patient and perfectly groomed, and that fathers are well-built, smart and friendly. These parents are shown with their new car and their two 'designer' children. The reality may be something quite different.

Most people understand that the word 'family' refers to a group of people who may be related to each other by blood and by marriage. Everyone knows what a family is – a mum, a dad, sisters, brothers, grandparents.

Look around at your own family and compare it with those of your friends. It is clear that some families are large, some are small, some have two parents and others only one.

---

### Activity 11

**a** Write down what you think a 'family' was over 100 years ago and is in the year 2000.

**b** Compare what you have written with other members of your group.

---

You may find that you have written down many similar points. Marriage or a partnership may have featured in some of your definitions, but of course there are many single-parent families.

Traditional marriage is declining and more people are living alone. In 1971 only 4 per cent of women were still unmarried by age 50. By 1987 this had risen to 17 per cent.

Today, more than one in four children are born to unmarried mothers. Most of these mothers are not lone parents, however. They live with partners, usually the father of the child.

However, the majority of people in the UK are married and living as a family unit, with or without children.

There are many ways in which the family can be organised and still carry out basic tasks. In some societies, the family structure is very different from that in the UK. For example, in the UK it is customary for one wife to have one husband. This is termed **monogamy**. In Tibet, however, one woman may have several husbands – **polyandry**. In other countries, one husband may have several wives – **polygamy**.

> ## Remember
>
> A family is a group with relationships, created on the basis of blood relationship.
>
> A family household consists of family members who live together.

---

### Activity 12

**a** Write down what you think are the positive and negative effects of living in a one-parent family.

**b** Discuss what you have written down with your class colleagues.

---

### Family size

Families are now smaller than they used to be. In Victorian times the average family would have about six children. Today, the average is approximately two children.

---

### Activity 13

**a** Write down what you think are the reasons for the fall in the average size of the family over the past hundred years.

**b** Compare a child living in a family of two children with a child living in a family of ten children. How do you think the size of the family affects a child's ability to develop personal relationships?

---

## An individual's position in the family

A child's position in the family may affect how he or she behaves. Here are some examples:

- A younger child may feel inferior. This may be because they have been looked after by older siblings (brother or sister). The younger child may feel that the older child is superior to them or more like their parents.
- A younger child may have to work hard to get their views or wishes heard in a family with older children.
- An older child does not have to 'fight' to establish their place in the family.
- An older child, particularly the first-born, is more curious and interested in new situations and things. They tend to be less aggressive and show more responsibility than their younger siblings.

## The family and emotional security

Some people stress the importance of the family in providing emotional satisfaction and security for its members. The family home is a place where people can relax and be themselves, and test out relationships with confidence.

Other people argue that the family can restrict a person's ability to build relationships. They say that the family stifles personal development, causing strain, tension and discontent.

# Socialisation and education

A society needs its new members to be socialised into its patterns of behaviour, its values and its rules, such as:

- how to behave in public
- how to relate to older people
- what is 'right' and 'wrong'.

**Socialisation** means to become part of society, to make social. It begins with our families, especially our parents. Later, playgroup staff, nursery staff and teachers will also play a part in this process. Gradually, and unconsciously, children learn the 'rules' of the society they live in.

The process is never-ending – it continues throughout life as we meet new experiences. However, the part our families play is very important.

The intellectual needs of children are partly met by their time at school. There a child not only improves the skills learned at home, such as eating and drinking, but also learns how to relate to others and develop intellectual skills.

Schools offer linguistic (**language**) and intellectual stimulation. Children learn how to play and take part in creative activities. These activities will become more ordered as the child gets older, and the child will learn to read and use numbers (numeracy).

Those who stay at school until they are 16 will have the opportunity to obtain qualifications such as GCSEs and GNVQs. Staying at school or college until the age of 18 allows a student to gain vocational qualifications, BTEC or City & Guilds qualifications, or A levels. These will allow a young person to enter higher education.

When a child is at school, he or she will be influenced by teachers. Think back to your days at primary school. Was there a teacher you liked? Did you work harder for this teacher? If you did, why do you think this was so?

Parents also play a part in the education of their children. Early stimulation and the availability of opportunities for personal development provided by parents can make a great difference to a child's academic performance and ability to make personal relationships.

Children also learn how to behave and interact with other children and adults in a nursery, playgroup or school. (See also 'Peer groups' on page 113.)

/ **Activity 14** /

In pairs or small groups, think about the skills that a child may not develop between birth and 5 years if he or she is denied all social contact. Make a list and discuss it with your colleagues.

*What games do girls play? Are they different in any way from the games played by boys?*

## Stereotyping

Socialisation gives us our first lessons in **stereotyping**. As part of the socialisation process, we copy what our parents do. They decide the way we dress, the games and toys we play with and they tell us which roles are appropriate in different social situations. Have you noticed that in many cases boys will tend to play with guns, and girls with dolls? Do they do this naturally or do they learn it from their parents and friends?

## Housing

For many people, home is not only a place of accommodation, but also a source of their physical and mental well-being. As we saw when looking at 'The family', above, home should be a place where you can relax away from the tensions and pressures of the workplace. A person's house is regarded as their territory. People talk of 'home sickness' when they miss being at home.

People may be judged because of where they live, the type of house they live in, whether it is owned or rented. So housing is much more than bricks and mortar.

## *How can housing affect personal development?*

During the Second World War, when many thousands of homes were damaged or destroyed, local authorities took the opportunity to clear away the slums and build new homes. In many instances, they replaced this poor housing with high-rise blocks of flats. The flats were generally of a higher standard than the housing they replaced. For the first time people had good sanitation, bathrooms and hot and cold water.

However, rehousing and slum clearances also meant destroying whole neighbourhoods and the feeling of community that existed in them. People who were moved often felt isolated, lonely and missed the support of the extended family – their brothers, sisters, grandparents or aunts or uncles.

The problems associated with high-rise flats caused mental and emotional stress to many people living in them. Lack of social facilities caused frustration, which in a number of areas led to violence and vandalism. Many local authorities later realised that high-rise flats were a mistake. In recent years, therefore, authorities such as Sheffield, Leeds and Liverpool have demolished these flats and built conventional housing.

### Activity 15

What disadvantages can be associated with living in high-rise flats? You might like to consider some of the following:

**a** problems of noise
**b** lack of privacy
**c** access problems
**d** lack of play facilities
**e** lack of community spirit
**f** difficulties with stairs or lifts.

*People who live in high-rise blocks often feel isolated and miss the support of friends, neighbours and extended families*

**111**

## Activity 16

How would living in a high-rise flat help or hinder a person's ability to develop personal relationships? Examine:

a  teenagers
b  adults
c  elderly people.

### Sheltered housing

Sheltered housing was developed during the 1920s and 1930s. It can be described as housing that has:

- a resident warden
- an alarm system fitted to each dwelling
- occupancy restricted to elderly people only
- accommodation all on one site.

Sheltered housing fulfils many housing needs:

- it meets the special needs of many elderly or disabled people
- it reduces the possibility of emergencies occurring, as it has a resident warden
- it offers more choice to people, as it is an alternative to residential care
- it also helps to combat loneliness by offering the possibility of wide social contact, which also fosters independence.

## Group membership

Most of us have been or are members of a group at some times in our lives. We form groups for many reasons, some of which might be:

- for security
- to share common ideas and pleasures, for example to play football or basketball
- to help others, for example as a volunteer at a youth club
- to get things done, for example if you feel that the food is not up to standard at your college, you may form an action group to try to improve it
- to enjoy the companionship of others.

We feel safe and confident as one of a group, sharing so much in common with other members.

### Primary groups

Primary groups are small groups of people. They allow the members to establish close personal relationships with one another. As a result, the group forms a strong sense of togetherness. The members are able to rely on each other. Examples of primary groups are a family, a peer group (see below) or a football team.

### Secondary groups

In secondary groups, the members do not have such close personal relationships. Examples of secondary groups are the National Union of Students, a football supporters' club.

### Peer groups

Peer groups are groups of people who are about the same age, share similar interests or circumstances and value each other's opinions, such as:

- children at school
- students in college
- groups of professionals at work, for example teachers, social workers, doctors or nurses
- elderly people in a day centre.

Peer groups have a strong influence on how we behave. When you are at school, for example, peer groups are likely to influence your attitudes towards school work, the music you like, the way you dress and even the way you express yourself. They are an important part of the socialisation process (see pages 109 and 110).

*A group of 3 and 4 year olds at a playgroup – a peer group*

---

**Activity 17**

**a** Make a list of the peer groups that you belong to.
**b** Note down how you think the groups influence the way you behave.

## Economic factors affecting personal development

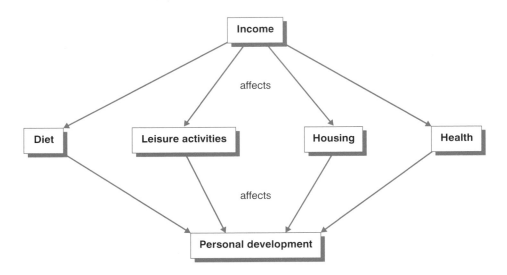

People receive income from a variety of sources, but mainly from:

- wages or a salary from an employer
- from the state in the form of Social Security or other benefits.

About one in five people live below the official poverty line. This is about £140 a week – about half the average weekly wage.

There are great differences between the lowest and highest paid jobs. The results of a survey of 8,000 jobs advertised in a Job Shop, before the minimum wage was introduced, showed that about 1,000 jobs paid £3.50 per hour and 3,000 paid £2.50 per hour.

On the other hand, the highest paid salaries can be very high indeed. A number of managers who manage large companies, such as electricity and water companies, can earn £600,000–£700,000 a year.

Many single and lone parents live in poor households. In the 1980s, nearly one in three elderly women living alone and single parents living without partners were living below the poverty line. Only 28 per cent of all other households lived below the poverty line. In the early 1980s, the average income of single-parent households was less than 40 per cent of the income of two-parent families.

## How can economic factors affect development?

### *Diet*
People with little or no money may not be able to pay for food or heating. Children and older people, in particular, need good, nourishing food for their physical development, such as bone formation.

### *Leisure*
People who have been unemployed for a long time, and who therefore have little money, are just able to buy the necessities for life: heating,

food and shelter. They have little opportunity for leisure activities because of the cost. Being unable to take part in leisure activities, buy luxuries or visit friends can lead to depression and possibly ill-health.

### Housing

Poorer people are more likely to live in cheap and poor housing and in crowded conditions. Cheaper accommodation is usually found in the middle of cities where the air may be polluted by car exhaust fumes and emissions from factories. Health can be affected by damp conditions and pollution. (See also the social effects of housing, on page 111.)

---

**Activity 18**

**a** Make a list of things that you think a family today would consider necessary in order to lead an ordinary life.

**b** Examine your own situation. Make a list of the important items in your home, such as the TV, cooker, fridge, furniture and heating. Highlight the items that you think are essential to life. Discuss your reasons for choosing each item with your group.

---

# 3.3 How relationships change over time and their effects on personal development

## Personal relationships

Personal relationships give some of the greatest pleasures in life. Unfortunately they also cause problems for some people. Good personal relationships are based on mutual understanding and trust. Misunderstandings can cause misery and stress.

## Childhood relationships

Children are not small adults. They are human beings who operate at a different intellectual, emotional and social level to that of adults. The development of relationships proceeds through a series of stages – a life-long process. The first two years of life are of vital importance in developing a person's personality, identity and ability to form social and personal relationships.

## Socialisation

In the UK men and women are expected to behave differently, perform various roles, which have a great effect on behaviour and personal relationships. A baby is not born with the knowledge of how to behave in social situations. It is acquired by the process of socialisation. As we have already seen, socialisation is the process by which we learn the patterns of behaviour which are expected of us. It is the process by which we learn language, the rules and regulations of society and what we believe in.

---

**Activity 19**

Write a definition of socialisation and give an example of how a person's experiences may have affected their ability to develop personal relationships.

---

Children learn by:

- repeating actions
- making associations between things
- observing and copying other people.

By watching others behave and observing the consequences of the behaviour for that person, the child identifies with and learns from the other person's behaviour.

*Children learn by observing and copying other people*

Learning is an active process and is done by the child. You cannot make a child learn; you can only provide the best situation possible for them to learn. For example, if a child's behaviour results in a kiss or hug or other form of pleasant behaviour then the child has good reason to carry on doing whatever it was doing. On the other hand, if good behaviour does not result in a reward, the child may have no reason to improve its behaviour.

Children do not simply copy some actions. The relationship of the person to the child is also important. The child is more likely to copy someone who is important or nice to them, such as parents, teachers or playgroup staff.

As all families are not identical and behave in different ways towards children, some will be strict and others not so. So each child's personality and its ability to develop personal relationships will inevitably be quite different.

## Language and the development of relationships

Humans are the only species that have the ability to use language. Language is an organised system of symbols that humans use to communicate and establish relationships with one another.

Before children produce recognisable words, they produce sounds that become steadily more varied and deliberate. Before speaking recognisable words, many children pass through a stage of jargon. This is the stage where an adult may feel sure that a child has said words, but cannot make out what the words are. The mother's influence on a child's acquisition of language is important. Mothers hold power and influence in the family. They are often the first socialisers of their children.

### Activity 20

Talk to a parent with a very young child. Ask what sounds the child produces and find out from the parent how they know what the child is trying to communicate.

Certain groups of children lag behind others in their ability to develop speech and relationships. Middle-class children tend to talk more than children from working-class backgrounds. Why do you think this is so?

Children who have a good early experience of being loved, find it easier in later life to make loving relationships. To develop good relationships in later life, therefore, children need to experience affection, approval and tender physical closeness from their parents. If these things are not experienced, it may be difficult to build up loving relationships later.

Loosening of ties between partners in a family, as a result of separation or divorce, can deeply influence relationships between children and their parents. However, in some cases it has been argued that single-parent families may be more child-centred than traditional families.

## Adolescence

### *The importance of the peer group*

Most teenagers become less and less reliant on their parents and involve themselves in a widening range of relationships. Many adolescents belong to peer groups that provide support while they establish new relationships. Teenagers breaking away from their parents feel safer if they belong to a group or are part of a crowd.

Belonging to a group gives teenagers a sense of identity, a feeling of being 'one of a gang'. Membership of a group also gives a feeling of **self-esteem**. When you have self-esteem, you value yourself and feel confident, you know yourself and trust your judgement. Groups give a feeling of security and stability within which social skills can be developed. Social skills such as making friends, both male and female, can be practised.

### *Relationships with parents*

Adolescence is a time of experimentation and rebellion. Although teenagers have disagreements with their parents, they still tend to agree with their parents on important issues such as the need for honesty and integrity. Many value their parents' opinions. However, parents and teenagers do disagree about such things as clothes, music and hairstyle. Many teenagers find that parents are difficult to get on with, but relationships improve as teenagers get older.

/ **Activity 21** /

Look back on your early teenage years. What can you remember of the relationship you had with your parents? Write your memories down and discuss your examples with your class colleagues.

## Adults

We have seen that childhood experiences will determine how easy or difficult it is for a person to make relationships in later life. Making relationships in adult life is not something that comes as second nature. It is something that we have learned to do during our childhood. If children have had a loving, stable relationship with their parents they will usually find it easier to develop good adult relationships.

**Case study**

Mary did not see much of her parents and when she did they kept her at a distance. Her parents were professional people with jobs that kept them away from home for long periods during the day. When they did come home they brought work with them. They only had time to put Mary to bed.

Both parents had difficulty showing affection to Mary and she never learned how to give affection or trust in return. She never got close to her parents, and had difficulty sharing her problems and concerns with them. She felt that she could not trust them with any intimate or important experiences.

When Mary grew up and began to form adult relationships, she had great difficulty in keeping friends or partners. She always wanted a lot of love and affection from them, but because of difficulty in giving love, the relationships never lasted very long.

ⓠ *Read the case study about Mary.*

ⓠ *What kind of early relationships with her parents would have enabled her to establish positive personal relationships with people of her own age?*

ⓠ *Discuss your ideas with your class colleagues.*

## Relationships between clients and carers

In the past, health and social care workers controlled services and made decisions about the kind of help to offer to clients. The power was in the hands of the carers. This does not help to build a relationship with a client that is based on trust. The client needs to have some control, or power, too.

### Establishing good relationships with clients

When working with clients we should help them to plan their own care by:

- not thinking that we know what they want or need better than they do
- involving them in all discussions about their future
- helping and supporting them to control their own situation
- helping them to recognise their abilities and life experience
- giving them accurate and honest information
- making sure that they have a choice.

To achieve this, we need to do the following:

- find out what the client's wants and needs are – this must only be done with the client's consent
- ensure that the client understands what is happening and agrees to any help offered
- involve all relevant carers and/or family in the process of finding out the client's needs or wants
- ensure that any care offered is based on agreement with all concerned – family, carer and client
- allow the client the greatest possible degree of choice in the services offered.

Health and social care services should be able to respond flexibly and sensitively to the needs of the client. This allows the client to feel independent and prevents their condition from getting worse.

Positive personal relationships can also be formed by focusing on the individual client and helping them within a charter of rights and a clear complaints procedure. That is, if the client sees that you are not judging them and that you are being objective about their situation, they are more likely to trust you and form a positive relationship with you. Helping is a contract between the carer and the client, made on the basis of trust and within a positive relationship.

You can use Activity 22 to provide evidence for Key Skills Communication C1.1 and C1.3.

### Activity 22

In this activity you are asked to make a report on the relationships of one client. You will need to identify what contributes to forming effective relationships, the needs of the client and how these needs are met by carers. You will also be expected to identify barriers to forming effective relationships. Write a report using the following headings:

**a** things that help to form effective relationships
**b** things that hinder or are barriers to forming good relationships
**c** how social and economic needs are met by carers.

## Confidentiality and its effect upon relationships

When, as a carer, you are involved in assessing a client, you will collect a lot of information. Because you have built up a relationship with your client, and because your client trusts you, he or she will feel able to tell you things that perhaps they have never told anyone else. They may say, for example, 'I've never told anyone else this, but…' or 'You won't tell my son, will you?'. You can never be certain what your client might tell you.

Your client will trust you not to tell anyone about anything that has been said in confidence. All clients have a right to expect this, and all carers should respect their right to **confidentiality**.

However, you will need to record information for assessment and you should make sure that your client understands this. Reassure them that only people directly involved in the assessment will have access to the records. They should be kept in a locked filing cabinet when not in use. It might be tempting to chat about a client on the bus, in the staff lounge, with other clients, with your family or your client's family. However, you should make every effort not to do so. You will be abusing your client's trust in you.

*Confidentiality establishes trust between carer and client*

### *Why have confidentiality?*
- It establishes a relationship of trust between carer and client.
- It enables the client to share information of a sensitive nature.
- The client will always know what happens to information given to a carer.
- It allows both the carer and client to respect each other.
- It prevents the client being exploited by others.

**121**

### Confidentiality: client rights

Clients and patients have many rights in respect of confidential information. Some of these rights are set out in laws outlining the procedures for dealing with confidential information:

- the Mental Health Act
- the Medical Records Act
- the Access to Personal Files Act.

The Patient's Charter is not a legal document, but it does guarantee:

- confidentiality of health records
- access for patients to their health records
- that relatives and friends may only be given information about the patient if the patient agrees.

Things that help to form effective relationships:

- seeing the client as an individual, not as a problem, such as a 'handicap' or an 'old person'
- respecting people, their wishes and opinions
- allowing and encouraging people to make choices for themselves
- keeping confidential any information a client may give to you.

Things that hinder or act as barriers to forming effective relationships:

- not respecting a client
- being angry or aggressive towards a client
- breaking confidentiality
- not paying enough attention to a client, not having enough time to talk to them or help them.

## Barriers to good relationships

### Stereotyping

Unless you treat each person as an individual you are likely to make assumptions about them – that is, make a judgement about them based on something you have seen or read. The judgement may be wrong but it affects your interaction with that person and acts as a barrier to good relationships. The assumption grows to a stereotype – we make the person fit the image we have of them rather than accepting them for what they are. The stereotypes act as barriers to good communication. Good carers try to be aware of the stereotypes they may make, particularly when the person they are trying to help may be from a different social class background, a different ethnic background or the opposite gender. Here are some examples of how we can easily misjudge people and get the wrong message.

## Judging on appearance

'The guy looked so punk I thought he was very threatening but he was really gentle when he worked with the toddlers.' *Day nursery assistant*

## Judging age

'Old people don't care about their appearance so I don't bother if the hem of her underskirt falls below her dress or Pop walks around with his fly undone.' *Care assistant in elderly persons' home*

## Judging disabled people – see the wheelchair and assume total immobility

'I was really surprised when I pushed the wheelchair to the toilet block and she got up and walked to the toilet on her own.'

## Judging academic ability to be the same as emotional and social

'Some of them are so slow you wouldn't think they'd be interested in anything romantic.' *Student working alongside some other students with learning difficulties*

By responding to people as individuals you are respecting who they are and what they want. You are giving them some scope to make a choice and exercise control.

An old people's home, offering respite care or temporary care for elderly people while relatives have a break, admitted a man of Jewish background. The staff could have assumed that he wouldn't mind just eating like everyone else for his fortnight's stay. They could have assumed that he was no longer practising his religion. They did, however, check his dietary requirements and took trouble to obtain the right kosher food. This made a huge difference to his stay.

## Key terms

After reading this unit you should be able to understand the following
words and phrases. If you do not, go back through the unit and find out,
or look them up in the Glossary.

*Pre-school child*                 *Life expectancy*
*Directed thinking*                *Intelligent*
*Identity*                         *Monogamy*
*Adolescence*                      *Polyandry*
*Puberty*                          *Polygamy*
*Oestrogen*                        *Socialisation*
*Testosterone*                     *Stereotyping*
*Psycho-social*                    *Language*
*Personality*                      *Self-esteem*
*Menopause*                        *Confidentiality*

## Test yourself

1  When does the process of personal development begin?
2  What is the average weight of a new-born baby?
3  What is a pre-school child?
4  When does puberty usually begin?
5  When do women experience the menopause?
6  What does socialisation mean?
7  What problems can living in high-rise flats cause for people?
8  What is a peer group?
9  What are basic physical needs?
10  Why have confidentiality with clients?

# Assignment for Unit Three

### Case Study: John Wexford

You are working in a residential home for elderly people and the
head of the home has asked you to produce a case study of the
personal development of John and his relationships.

Mr John Wexford was born in 1925 in a small village in Yorkshire;
he is now 75 years old.

John was one of eight children. His mother did not work and his
father worked as a labourer on a local farm. John, unlike his
siblings, carried on at school after 14 years of age and won a

scholarship to the local grammar school in a nearby city. Two of John's sisters died before they were one year old; John himself suffered from TB when he was 18. John was sent away to a local TB hospital where he spent two years before he was cured. At the hospital John met a nurse and after some years they were married. John's wife Mary had persuaded John to train as a teacher. John worked as a teacher until his retirement at 65. Mary had to stop work when she married John.

John was married for 40 years; when his wife died he was 65 years old. John has always lived in the city since he was 20 years of age and enjoyed the social life. He managed to buy his house when he worked as a teacher. When John retired he had only his teacher's pension and the old-age pension to live on. John had no savings, as he and his wife always liked to live life to the full. He also helped his four children when they each bought their own houses.

John has recently had a hip replacement, which was not a great success. The after-effect of the operation has restricted his mobility and he finds it difficult to sit still for long periods or play bowls. As a result, his social life has been severely restricted.

John decided some months ago that he would like to enter residential care, as he was feeling lonely. He was also finding it more and more difficult to look after himself after a recent fall, as a result of which he has lost his self-confidence. He has been in the Whiterock Home for one year and has not got on with any of the staff, as he feels that they interfere in his life and restrict his movements.

### Tasks

1. Identify typical basic features of John's life stages.

2. Identify and describe at least one basic physical, social and economic factor (this can be done in the form of a table).

3. Identify and describe three different relationships in the case study.

4. Show how social and economic circumstances affected John's personal development. Be sure to give information on where you got your information.

5. Identify positive and negative effects of relationships in the case study.

6. How would a different set of physical, social and economic factors have affected John's development? Give examples to predict the effect that different relationships would have had on the development of John's self-concept.

## Get the grade

To achieve a **PASS** you must complete tasks 1–3.

To achieve a **MERIT** you must complete tasks 1–5.

To achieve a **DISTINCTION** you must complete tasks 1–6.

## Key Skills

| | Opportunity |
|---|---|
| | **You can use this opportunity to provide evidence for the following key skills** |
| Application of Number N1.1 | Identify features of growth and development (if you use a table/chart). |
| Communication C1.3 | Identify and describe different relationships. |

# Investigating common hazards and health emergencies

## What is covered in this unit

*4.1* *Health and safety rules that apply in work settings*
*4.2* *Some common hazards that occur in care settings*
*4.3* *How to identify ways of reducing risk due to hazards*
*4.4* *How to recognise and deal with health emergencies*

At the end of this unit you will be asked to produce a demonstration of your understanding of common hazards and health emergencies, which includes a workplace safety survey explaining what may happen if you fail to follow correct health and safety procedures. You will also need to demonstrate some first aid procedures. If you would like to see further details of the tasks you are likely to need to carry out for assessment, please refer to the end of the unit where an assignment has been set (see pages 171–172). This unit will guide you through what you need to know in order to successfully put together your evidence. You will be assessed on this work and awarded a grade. This grade will contribute to the overall grade you will get for Unit Four.

## Materials you will need to complete this unit

- Manual of First Aid – Red Cross or St John Ambulance Association
- Copies of health and safety policies from the workplace (school, college, work placement etc.)
- Health and Safety Codes of Practice from the workplace
- Leaflets – publications of the Health and Safety Executive (HSE), Royal Society for the Prevention of Accidents (RoSPA), Health Education Council and local health promotion services.

# 4.1 Health and safety rules that apply in work settings

## Key health and safety factors in work settings

Going to work for the first time, or going to your first real work experience, can be exciting and a bit strange. It can also be dangerous. Every year over 500 people in the UK die at work and several hundred thousand have to stay off work because of injury.

Some hazards cannot be seen, such as:

- stress
- radiation
- inadequate information as to the handling and lifting of clients.

Some health hazards may affect workers slowly over many years, such as the effects of working down coal-mines or working with asbestos.

## What can you do about hazards in care settings?

Large organisations (such as factories, colleges and hospitals) will usually have:

- a health and safety officer who will have the overall responsibility for health and safety policy
- a system for reporting defects in equipment
- an accident book for recording accidents.

If you suspect that any equipment is faulty do not use it. Report your suspicions as soon as possible.

### Activity 1

You are working in a day centre looking after elderly people. You overhear a cleaner complaining to a care assistant about the lack of electrical power points in the TV room. She cannot find a free point in the TV room for her vacuum cleaner. The care assistant tells the cleaner to use a socket in the corridor. This will mean that there will be a long, trailing wire extension across the corridor and TV room.

**a** What accidents do you think could occur?
**b** What action should you take?

**DANGER**
High voltage

**DANGER**
Fragile roof

**DANGER**
Fork lift trucks

**DANGER**
Polluted water

*Some examples of hazard warning signs*

In this section we shall be looking at the following health and safety rules that apply in the work setting:

- Control of Substances Hazardous to Health Regulations 1988 (COSHH)
- Fire Precautions Act 1971
- Health and Safety (First Aid) Regulations 1981 (1982 in Northern Ireland)
- European Community Manual Handling Regulations 1993.

In section 4.2 we shall look at the Health and Safety at Work Act 1994, which controls health and safety in the workplace.

## Control of Substances Hazardous to Health Regulations 1988 (COSHH)

*quick fire*

*What do the initials COSHH stand for?*

These regulations lay down the essential requirements and a sensible step-by-step approach for the control of hazardous substances, such as poisons, gas or chemicals and for protecting people who are exposed to them.

### *What is a substance hazardous to health?*

Some substance used by carers are obviously dangerous. Others are not obviously hazardous until they are misused or used in the wrong place. For example, a bottle of bleach is not in itself harmful, but if it is left in a place where confused people or children could drink it, it would then become a hazard. Many substances can therefore be a hazard in one situation and not in another.

There is a wide range of substances capable of damaging health. Many are used for cleaning or decorating. The health of carers can be put at risk from these substances if the right precautions are not taken.

Many of these substances are labelled so that people know what they are dealing with. For example, labels indicate whether a substance is:

- very toxic
- toxic
- harmful
- irritant
- corrosive
- composed of any material, mixture or compound that can harm people's health.

Radiation controlled area

CAUTION Laser beam

CAUTION Chemical store

*Some examples of hazard labels*

The possible **toxic effects** of chemicals are:

- occupational dermatitis (skin disorder)
- headaches
- irritability
- nausea and vomiting (sickness)
- dizziness
- nose and throat irritation
- tiredness
- sleeplessness
- chest trouble
- worsening of asthma (a lung condition)
- reproductive hazards (may affect ability to have children)
- heart, lung, liver disease
- kidney damage
- cancer.

## Activity 2

In your own home, examine cleaning substances. Record how they are labelled and the instructions for use. What care needs to be taken when storing these substances?

### Safe use of chemicals

Poor working practices when handling chemicals, cleaners and powders may have a serious effect upon your health. Before you use chemicals (for example in cleaning equipment, toilets, floors etc.), assess the risks.

## Assessing the risks

- Read the label and the information supplied by the manufacturer.
- Find out how the substance affects the body if it is breathed in or absorbed through the skin.
- Find out what the signs and symptoms of over-exposure are.

Help yourself by:

- not keeping food near places where chemicals or cleaning materials are stored
- not putting pens, pencils or fingers in your mouth when handling these materials
- not storing substances in familiar containers such as milk bottles or jam jars
- never using anything that does not have a label on it
- always using rubber gloves or other protective clothing that should be supplied by your employer
- keeping cleaning materials, medicines and chemicals locked away
- knowing what first aid to do if an accident occurs with the substance.

You can use Activity 3 to provide evidence for Key Skills Communication C1.3

## Activity 3

Find out how many of the items on the list below are in your home and write down where they are kept:

**a** Caustic soda
**b** Bleach
**c** Methylated spirit
**d** Paint stripper
**e** Paraffin
**f** Lavatory cleaner
**g** Weedkiller
**h** Slug pellets

What might be the effect if a child ate or drank any one of these items?

### *What is the employer's responsibility towards people who do not smoke?*

Non-smokers sharing the same work space as smokers cannot help but inhale some of the tobacco smoke. This is called **passive smoking**.

Smoking is one of the most important causes of disease and premature death. Tobacco smoke contains a substance known to cause cancer. Passive smoking can also cause cancer in non-smokers and irritate the eyes, throat and lungs.

Employers have a duty to protect their employees from these hazards. To do this they should ensure that:

- non-smoking is regarded as the normal thing to do in the workplace
- smokers are segregated from non-smokers.

The European Union has issued instructions that smoking is **prohibited** (forbidden) in public buildings, such as schools, hospitals and colleges, except in places that are designated as smoking areas. However, the employer does not have to provide a place for smokers to smoke in.

## Activity 4

Find out what provisions have been made for people who want to smoke in your school, college or workplace.

## Fire hazards

The Fire Precautions Act 1971 is the main law controlling fire safety. It requires certain types of establishments, such as homes for the elderly, hospitals, schools, colleges and hotels, to apply for a fire certificate from the fire service. This certificate must be obtained before the establishment can operate.

Maryland Home for Elderly People

**FIRE RULES**

If you discover a fire:

**Raise the alarm** by operating the nearest fire alarm and proceed to the assembly point at the nearest exit (outside the Day Room Exit).

**Please go along the corridor through the Day Room and out through the double-opening patio doors.**

**Close the door of your room** as you leave and any others you may use.

**Do not:**

- use lifts as a means of escape
- shout or run.

**Study this notice** carefully so that you will know what to do in an emergency.

**Do not re-enter the building until told to do so by an appropriate person.**

*A fire action notice*

It is the management's responsibility to provide:

- adequate routes for escape
- a way of giving fire **warning**
- fire-fighting equipment
- written instructions for clients, workers and visitors displayed in prominent positions
- instructions and training for staff
- fire procedures and drills.

## Fire fighting

- Are portable fire extinguishers and/or hose reels provided in clearly visible and readily accessible places throughout the premises?
- Are they maintained at regular intervals?
- Are staff familiar with their use?

*quick fire*

*Why do establishments need a fire certificate?*

*The different types of fire extinguisher*

**Key Skills**

You can use Activity 5 to provide evidence for Key Skills Communication C1.1 and C1.3.

### Activity 5

**a** Draw a plan of your college or school. Identify all the different fire extinguishers and water hoses in public places and mark them on the plan.

**b** Make notes of what types of fire the extinguishers are designed to deal with.

## What should you do if you discover a fire?

You should notify a senior member of staff who should:

- ensure that the fire service has been called
- go to the scene of the fire and supervise the fire fighting until the fire service arrives
- clear everyone, except those actually engaged in the fire fighting, from the immediate vicinity of the fire
- order the evacuation of the building as soon as it becomes apparent that fire or smoke is spreading. Do not wait until the fire is out of control
- take a roll call of all staff and residents or clients when the premises have been evacuated (a list of absentees from the building should be available)
- *do not use lifts.*

Instructions should be given to caretakers and maintenance staff, setting out the action they should take in the event of fire. This should include:

- bringing all lifts to ground level and stopping them
- shutting down all services not essential to the escape of occupants or likely to be required by the fire brigade.

Lighting should be left on.

### Activity 6

Find out what the fire evacuation procedure is in either your school, college or work placement. Explain this procedure clearly to your colleagues.

| IF YOU DISCOVER FIRE | CLOSE | WHEN YOU HEAR THE FIRE ALARM |
|---|---|---|
| Break glass at call point | Doors and windows | Follow the evacuation procedure |

**FIRE!**

**ONLY USE EXTINGUISHERS ON SMALL FIRES**

# First aid regulations in the workplace

Immediate and proper examination and treatment of a person who has suffered injuries may save a life. This is known as first aid. First aid is also essential to reduce pain and help the injured person make a quick recovery.

The Health and Safety (First Aid) Regulations 1981 (1982 in Northern Ireland) state that employers must:

- provide adequate first aid for employees who are injured or fall ill at work
- provide sufficient numbers of **first aiders**
- appoint people to take charge of incidents
- appoint occupational first aiders whenever there are special hazards in the workplace.

## *What is a first aider?*

A first aider is a trained person who has gained a first aid certificate. The certificate has to be renewed every three years.

## *What is an occupational first aider?*

An occupational first aider is a person holding an occupational first aid certificate issued within the past three years. The certificate must be from an organisation approved by the Health and Safety Executive, such as a college or other training organisation. Occupational first aiders are trained to deal with the effects the particular hazards of the workplace, such as working with chemicals or special machinery.

## *First aid boxes*

A first aid box should be made of material designed to protect the contents from damp and dust. It should be clearly identified as a first aid box.

*What is the difference between a first aider and an occupational first aider?*

## The following are the most common articles found in a first aid box:

- first aid guidance card
- individually wrapped, sterile, adhesive dressings – various sizes
- sterile, unmedicated dressings with bandage attached
- eye pads
- crêpe bandages
- triangular bandages
- safety pins
- individually wrapped, moist cleaning wipes
- antiseptic cream
- scissors
- plastic forceps
- latex gloves
- sterile water or saline in sealed containers.

---

**Activity 7**

Locate the first aid boxes in your college or school. Find out why each one is located in its particular position.

---

## Lifting heavy loads

Lifting and carrying can, if not done properly, lead to ruptures, strains and back injuries. Safe lifting is a skill. It is easier to lift a heavy weight from the ground if the strain is taken by the leg and thigh muscles rather than by your back and abdomen.

---

### Did you know that:

- at some time in their lives four out of five people will suffer from back pain
- 24 million working days are lost each year at a cost of over £1 billion per year
- approximately 5 per cent of people have to change the nature of their work completely because of back problems
- 80,000 nurses are off sick with back pain each year.

---

The European Community Manual Handling Regulations 1993 state that care staff are not obliged to lift anything or anybody that may damage their backs. Managers must examine every situation in which staff are expected to lift people or objects and ensure that staff are properly trained for any lifting that they do.

At present in health and social care over 50 per cent of all reported injuries are due to manual lifting of loads. Loads do not have to be heavy to be dangerous. In the field of health and social care, the 'load' is usually the client or patient. Many clients and patients are too heavy to be lifted bodily. Remember that people are more difficult to lift than boxes or sacks of corn, because people may make unexpected movements when you are trying to lift them. Most difficulties arise when lifting people because of this.

Employers have the responsibility to make sure that staff do not put themselves at risk and must take all reasonable steps to protect them. In hospital and residential establishments, equipment, such as mobile hoists, should be available to move and lift dependent people.

### *Working safely when moving and handling clients*

Your back allows you to do everything – from sleeping to mountain climbing. People who experience back problems suffer pain and often have to take time off work. This can result in loss of earnings, inconvenience and even permanent disability.

*Mechanical lifts used in care situations*

Back pain and problems can be caused by:

- sprains due to faulty lifting
- disc trouble
- poor posture
- lack of exercise
- being overweight
- injuries
- diseases.

You can help yourself avoid back problems by ensuring that you maintain a good posture and making sure that you rest your muscles when you stand, sit and sleep. Follow the simple rules below.

Stand correctly with:

- your head high
- your chin in
- your chest forward
- your abdomen flat.

Sit correctly with:

- your knees higher than your hips
- your lower back firm against the backrest.

Sleep correctly with:

- a firm mattress
- a bed board
- your knees bent and lying on your side.

Before lifting:

- see what it is you have to do first
- think about when to get help and advice
- think about any difficulties you might have and how to deal with them
- always follow the rules and methods your tutors have explained to you
- make sure that the equipment you use is up to date
- keep up to date with new and safe ways of lifting.

General rules when lifting objects:

- Think about what you are going to do.
- Examine the object to be lifted.
- Clear the immediate area.
- Know how and where to position the item to be lifted.
- Get help if necessary.
- Stand close, with a firm footing and feet apart (Step 1 below).
- Straddle the object, keeping a straight back and bend the knees (Step 2).
- Grasp the item firmly to prevent slipping (Step 3).
- Breathe in – inflated lungs support the spine. Slowly straighten your legs, bringing them back to a vertical position (Step 4).
- Hold the item firmly and close to the body (Step 5).
- Avoid sudden, jerky movements.
- Turn your feet, not your back.

*Safe steps to lifting an object*

*Lifting or moving a client*

When lifting or moving a client some important and specific rules apply:

- Always wear flat shoes.
- It is advisable to remove rings and watches. These may scratch the client or get caught in hair.
- Explain to the client what you are going to do.
- Clear the area.
- Where there is more than one lifter, co-operate to lift together.
- Do not rush the procedure.
- Do not drag the client.
- Apply all the general rules of lifting.

> **Remember**
>
> Always follow the rules.

## Infectious disease

Infection means the passing of disease from one source (person, animal or soil) to another. This may occur in a number of different ways:

- by droplets or dust in the air
- by skin and mucous membranes
- by wounds
- by food and drink
- by soil or animals
- by infected articles.

Infections are caused by **microbes** (small living organisms or micro-organisms). These are so small that we need a microscope to see them. The main groups of microbes involved in infections are:

- bacteria – for example, cause TB
- viruses – for example, cause measles
- fungi – for example, cause ringworm
- protozoa – for example, cause dysentery.

When a person becomes contaminated by one of these organisms, they are said to be infected.

/ **Activity 8** /

Make a list of diseases caused by the four main types of organisms. Where might you find these organisms in the workplace or recreational facility?

Did your list include any of the following:

- bacteria: cholera? (water)
- viruses: influenza? (offices – enclosed spaces)
- fungi: athlete's foot? (changing rooms – swimming pools)
- protozoa: amoebic dysentery (tummy illness)? (kitchens – food ).

Micro-organisms multiply very quickly under conditions of moisture, warmth and a food supply. In these conditions, they reproduce by splitting in half about every 20 minutes. One or two germs could, therefore, multiply into millions in a few days.

In the home, day centre, residential home, nursery or playgroup micro-organisms are to be found in warm, moist places with poor ventilation, such as bathrooms, kitchens and bedrooms. They can also occur on food, face flannels, towels, floor coverings and mops. Micro-organisms can enter the body through:

- inhalation – breathing in through the nose and throat
- inoculation – through a break, cut or wound on the skin
- ingestion – through the mouth by swallowing.

The body has certain defences to protect against infection as shown below.

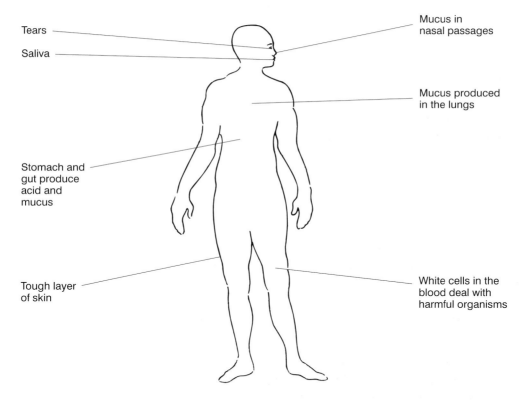

*The body's defences*

Carers should know how to prevent infection from spreading. If you use sensible hygiene practices, you should not be afraid of becoming infectious yourself. The following is a list of some of the ways in which the spread of infection can be prevented:

- adopting high standards of personal hygiene
- enforcing high standards of food hygiene
- providing good quality accommodation

- using disposable gloves, and washing hands before and after
- disinfecting or burning articles used by infected persons
- ensuring good ventilation
- making sure the establishment is clean throughout.

## Simple routines to prevent the spread of infection

### *Avoiding contact with blood and body fluids*
Always wear plastic gloves when in contact with blood or body fluids. If you are in contact with such matter, wash your hands thoroughly with soap and water.

### *Avoiding contact with cuts and abrasions*
Cover open wounds with waterproof dressings. Blue plasters should always be provided for food handlers.

### *Disinfecting*
- Wear plastic gloves and an apron when mopping up.
- Disinfect areas contaminated by blood and excreta with a bleach solution.
- Dispose of contaminated waste by using the appropriate bags and containers.

Carers must always be on the alert to the dangers of infection as these may make a person seriously ill. In particular, babies, young children and elderly people have less resistance to germs.

# 4.2 Some common hazards that occur in care settings

A basic function of all care organisations is to provide a safe and controlled environment for staff, clients and visitors. The wide-ranging nature of care organisations means that each organisation has its own particular requirements in terms of health and safety. For example, nurseries or playgroups have different requirements than a home for elderly people. Each will have their own particular hazards.

A hazard is something that has the potential to cause harm, including ill-health and injury. The hazard presented by a substance (poison, chemicals etc.) is its potential to cause harm. It may be able to make you cough, damage your liver or even kill you. Some substances can harm you in several different ways, e.g. if you breathe them in, swallow them or get them on your skin.

The risk from a substance or article is the likelihood that it will harm you when you use it in the workplace. Poor control can create a risk, even from a substance with low hazard (for example bleach or soap). However, with proper precautions, the risk of being harmed by even the most hazardous substance can be adequately controlled. How this can be done will be looked at in the next section.

### Common hazards in health care settings:

- Fire
- Use of work equipment
- Use of substances (i.e. bleach and other cleaning materials, medicines etc.)
- Manual handling
- Personal protective equipment, i.e. overalls etc.

### Activity 9

Look at the picture – write down the number of hazards that you can see. Discuss your list with your class colleagues.

Below is a list of hazards to look out for:

- Unguarded or unsupervised equipment
- Slippery or broken walkways
- Lose or broken wiring

- Poor lighting
- Leaks of water or gas
- Blocked doors and emergency fire exits
- Poor signing (fire exit etc.)
- Unhygienic toilets and slippery surfaces
- Broken tiles and mirrors
- Inadequate storage for cleaning materials
- Poorly maintained lifts and elevators.

### Activity 10

Draw up a checklist of potential health and **safety hazards** that you might find in a playgroup.

### Activity 11

Look at the picture – write down the number of hazards that you can see. Discuss your list with your class colleagues.

# 4.3 How to identify ways of reducing risk due to hazards

## Heath and Safety at Work Act 1974

This is the law that controls health and safety in the workplace. Both employers and employees (you) have responsibilities under this law to protect the health and safety of yourselves and other people.

### Responsibilities of the employer

An employer must provide a workplace that is safe from hazards and does not harm an employee's health. This includes:

- having a safety policy
- hygiene and welfare
- comfort
- cleanliness.

### *Safety policy*

Employers must tell their staff how they are going to ensure their health and safety. This is called a safety policy. It should tell you:

- who your key managers are, so that you can report any unsafe situation
- how they intend to protect you at work, including rules for safe procedures when carrying out particular tasks.

The safe procedure rules will cover, for example:

- the control of infection
- the wearing of protective clothing
- using correct lifting procedures
- training in the use of equipment.

The safety policy will, in many cases, be in the form of a booklet, or it may perhaps be a notice on a notice board. The document should also be published in a number of languages to make it accessible to all staff.

**What is a safety policy?**

A manager of a residential home for elderly people, for example, or of a day centre for children must ensure that all staff know their duties so that they pay appropriate attention to health and safety when they carry out their work.

The maintenance of a safe environment and the practice of safe procedures (see page 147) enables the client to feel secure and confident. That is one of the necessities of good social care. Make sure you know the safety rules and obey them.

## Important rules

- Learn how to work safely.
- Obey safety rules.
- Ask your supervisor or tutor if you don't understand any instruction or rule.
- Report to your supervisor, manager or tutor anything that seems dangerous, damaged or faulty.

### Activity 12

Find out what the safety policy is at your work placement. Obtain a copy, if possible, and compare it with others your class colleagues will have obtained from their work placements.

You can use Activity 12 to provide evidence for Key Skills Communication C1.2.

### *Hygiene and welfare*
This includes:

- separate marked toilets for each sex
- toilets kept clean and in working order and ventilated
- wash basin with hot and cold running water
- soap, dryers and nail-brushes where appropriate
- waste bins, regularly emptied
- facilities for taking food and drink
- safe methods for handling, storing and transporting materials. For example, drugs must be stored and used in such a way as to minimise risk to health. If a new cleaning product is introduced, an employer is obliged to tell employees of any possible harmful effects.

### *Comfort*
The employer should consider the comfort of employees, including:

- furniture placed so that sharp corners do not present a danger to staff or residents
- good ventilation in bathrooms, toilets and bedrooms
- thermometer in each work room so that staff can check temperature. This is important in areas where elderly people are cared for and also for babies and young children
- good lighting.

### *Cleanliness*
The employer should ensure that:

- workplace, furniture and fittings are kept clean
- all rubbish and waste food are regularly removed
- all spillages are cleaned up immediately
- dirty linen is stored appropriately
- dressings and medicines are disposed of according to instructions.

| PROHIBITION | MANDATORY | SAFE CONDITION | WARNING |
|---|---|---|---|
| Don't do | Must do | The safe way | Risk of danger |
| (red circle and red cross bar, for example 'No Smoking') | (blue circle, for example 'Wash your hands') | (green rectangle, for example 'First aid room') | (yellow triangle with black outline, for example 'Risk of electric shock') |

*Safety signs to take notice of in the workplace*

## Responsibilities of the employee

What are your responsibilities in the workplace as an employee? You have a duty to take reasonable care to avoid:

- injury to yourself – for example, a nurse or care assistant who injures their back by not using the correct lifting procedures, when they were aware of them, would probably not be successful in claiming any compensation for their injury
- injury to others – for example, if you injure a client by not using the correct lifting procedure (after you have been trained) or by not using lifting aids, you may be liable to prosecution (that is, you may be taken to court). You must report any hazards or accidents to your employers.

### It is your duty:

- to take care of yourself and anyone else – that means the clients, customers, their families and anyone who may be affected by your working activities
- to co-operate with your employer, helping in any way that you can to carry out the employer's duties under the Health and Safety at Work Act
- not to tamper with or misuse anything provided by the employer.

For example, it would be the duty of a care worker looking after people in their own homes to take care of themselves and anyone else, the clients, their families and friends. The care worker has a responsibility not to tamper with or use any equipment such as washing machines, irons, electric kettles or gas fires, that they may feel is faulty or may cause harm to anyone.

As a care worker you should be prepared:

- by being dressed appropriately for work. Wear any protective clothing you have been given by your employer, such as overalls or rubber gloves. Also remember to wear well-fitting, comfortable shoes

- always be on the look-out for **safety hazards**
- report any hazards or accidents to your supervisor immediately
- use only safe methods of working.

*If you have any questions or worries about safety, talk to your tutor or supervisor in the workplace.*

### What should you do if you are injured at work?

If you are injured at work:

- report the accident to your immediate supervisor or tutor
- record it in writing (it is usually recorded in an accident book)
- see a doctor – a medical examination should be carried after the accident and the result recorded.

> **Never:**
> - cut corners for the sake of speed
> - try to move or lift clients without appropriate help.

/ **Activity 13** /

A member of your class has fallen down the stairs. Find out how you should report accidents that happen on the college premises. What procedures are in operation? Your tutor or Student Union colleagues will help you with this.

### Safe procedures of work

Systems of work can affect your health and the client's health. For example, do you know what would happen to your work clothes if you were splashed by a chemical you were using to clean a floor? Could poor design of working areas like bathrooms lead to backache?

Are you aware of any potential safety hazard? Is there any risk of clients or patients transmitting disease? If you were working with old, unchecked electrical appliances in a client's home, would you know of the dangers or to whom to report your concerns? Are all students and staff aware of the procedures for staff who are vulnerable to physical violence?

### Safe systems – a checklist

- Do you know who your supervisor is?
- Whom do you report accidents and hazards to?
- Do you know the safe ways of doing the job?
- Are you are using equipment? Have you been instructed in its use and limitations?
- Has anyone assessed whether the equipment you are using is safe for the job?
- If things go wrong, do you know what to do?
- Are you aware of a system for checking that jobs are done safely, in the way intended?

> ### Case study
>
> One woman who had worked at a hospital for two years part-time had an unpleasant attack of irritant dermatitis (skin disease). Her duties included cleaning mop heads with a carbolic soap. The attack coincided with the introduction of a new brand. She experienced tingling and itchiness, and her hand blistered. She had only been given overalls – no gloves, glove liners or barrier cream.
>
> Her employer, the health authority, was taken to court and was found to have failed in its responsibilities under the Health and Safety at Work Act. This was because it didn't supply proper protection (rubber gloves) for staff to use when they were exposed to common toxic materials while cleaning hospital corridors.

**Key Skills**

You can use Activity 14 to provide evidence for Key Skills Communication C1.1.

### Activity 14

**a** List as many potential hazards that you can observe in:
- your work placement
- your classroom or laboratory.

**b** Make realistic recommendations as to how could you make them safer.

### *Safety audit (survey). How could you help prevent fire?*

The answers to all of the following questions should be 'yes'.

Are all parts of the premises clear of waste and rubbish, particularly:

- store rooms?
- attics and basements?
- boiler rooms and other equipment rooms?
- bottoms of lift shafts?
- staircases and under the stairs?

Smoking:

- Are enough ashtrays provided in all the areas where smoking is permitted?
- Are staff warned to use the ashtrays and not to throw cigarettes or matches into waste-paper bins, through gratings or out of windows?

Electricity:

- Do all parts of the electrical installation comply with the Institute of Electrical Engineers (IEE) regulations for electrical installations?
- Is the electrical installation inspected and tested at least every five years?
- Are staff trained to report frayed leads and faulty equipment?

If you do not have central heating:

- Are heating appliances fixed rather than portable?
- Are they provided with adequate and secure fireguards?
- Are the staff warned to keep combustible materials away from heaters?

### Activity 15

Locate the fire action notices in your college or school. List where they are displayed and copy down what they say.

### Activity 16

You have just been appointed the manager of a care setting: an old persons' home, a playgroup, a nursery, a day centre or a hostel. The owner of the establishment wants you to prepare a report (preferably word-processed) outlining:

- what the common hazards might be
- what equipment and safe systems might be necessary to prevent risks to staff and clients
- realistic suggestions for improvements
- what benefits the employer, staff and clients would get from a safe and healthy environment.

**a** Select which type of establishment you wish to make the report on. You may wish to base your assignment on your work placement. Whatever you decide to do you will need to visit your chosen organisation and talk to the manager, staff and clients:
   1. Select your establishment.
   2. Make arrangements to visit the establishment.
   3. Decide what questions you are going to ask the manager, staff and clients.

**b** Choose at least three common hazards from the following list:
   - fire
   - substances
   - unsafe equipment
   - unsafe working environment
   - infectious disease.
   1. Explain and list the health and safety regulations that apply to each of the three selected hazards.
   2. List your responsibilities as an employee in relation to the three selected hazards.
   3. Explain how you could reduce the risks to clients and staff presented by the three selected hazards in the workplace.

▶▶

**Key Skills**

You can use Activity 15 to provide evidence for Key Skills Communication C1.2.

**Key Skills**

You can use Activity 16 to provide evidence for Key Skills Communication C1.2 and Information Technology IT1.2.

> c Describe the safety equipment that the employer should provide to reduce the risks associated with the three selected hazards. For example, first aid equipment, alarms, emergency systems, fire doors, fire extinguishers etc.
> d List the safety precautions and safe working practices, such as lifting regulations, that apply to each of the three hazards you have selected.

# 4.4 How to recognise and deal with health emergencies

## Shock

Every injured person soon develops shock. Without proper treatment this can be fatal. However, with prompt and proper treatment the injured person nearly always recovers.

**Signs of shock** in an injured person:

**Remember the signs of shock:**

anxiety – pale – cold – sweating – restless – shallow breathing – rapid pulse – pain – much thirst

- Facial expression – the casualty may seem anxious and may stare in a vacant way.
- Skin colour is pale – white, ashen grey or slightly blue.
- Casualty is sometimes restless.
- Skin feels cold, yet it might be soaked in sweat.
- Breathing is rapid and shallow.
- The pulse is usually rapid and feeble.
- Casualty usually complains of pain and thirst.

## Treatment for shock

- Call an ambulance.
- Keep the casualty still.
- Cover wounds and stop external bleeding.
- Loosen clothing.
- Cover the casualty with a blanket or coat – do not over-heat.
- Comfort the casualty.
- Raise the casualty's legs to increase the blood flow to the brain.

*What are the signs of shock?*

## Concussion (head injuries)

Falls, blows and road accidents are the usual causes of head injuries. A blow to the head does not necessarily damage the brain, even if the skull is fractured. A crack in the skull will heal but a 'depressed' fracture (one which presses inwards on the brain) is serious and may produce symptoms of brain injury.

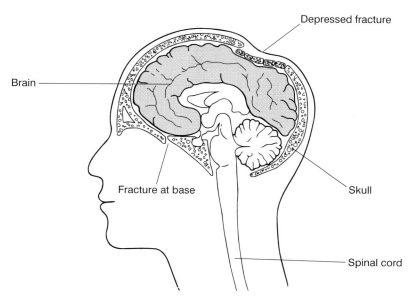

*Skull fractures*

## Symptoms of head injury

- Unconsciousness. There may be immediate loss of consciousness after the fall or blow, or unconsciousness may follow after the casualty experiences extreme drowsiness.
- Flushed face. This happens because the body temperature may rise.
- Slow pulse.
- Noisy breathing or shallow breathing.
- Convulsions.
- Twitching of the limbs.
- Abnormal pupils.
- Muscle weakness or paralysis.

*quick fire*

*What are the symptoms of head injury?*

## What do you do if you find a person with suspected head injuries?

With head injuries, the general condition of the person is important.

- Check the casualty's breathing – you or someone else may need to start artificial respiration (see page 164).
- Call for an ambulance.
- If the person is unconscious, place them in the recovery position.
- Once you have placed the casualty in the recovery position, check for any wounds. If there is bleeding from the head, do not try to stop it. Put a pad (see page 155) on it and keep it in place with a bandage.
- If the casualty regains consciousness, make them rest and watch them carefully for any signs of brain injury.

*The recovery position*

---

## Remember

Always make sure that you or anyone in your care sees a doctor if any of the following symptoms develop after a head injury:

- double vision
- continuous vomiting
- increasingly severe headache
- unconsciousness.

---

### Activity 17

**a** List the signs and symptoms of a head injury.
**b** What would you do if you came across someone suffering from a head injury?

---

## Burns and scalds

- A burn is tissue damage caused by dry heat.
- A scald is damage by wet heat.
- A chemical burn is tissue damage caused by chemicals.

The heat from a burn or scald damages not only the skin, but also the blood vessels that lie below the skin's surface. This causes a colourless fluid called **plasma** (which forms most of the volume of the blood) to leak. If a large part of the skin is damaged, the casualty may lose a lot of blood or plasma. This may cause them to go into shock.

*What is a burn?*

Children and old people react badly to severe burns. They are also particularly liable to extensive accidental burns.

---

### Activity 18

Mary, a care assistant, was preparing a bath for one of the elderly residents. She did not check the temperature of the water. When Joan, the resident, put her foot into the water, she was injured.

**a** Did Joan suffer a burn or scald?
**b** What is the difference between the two?
**c** How would you have treated either of the two?

---

## First aid treatment for burns and scalds

The aims of first aid treatment for burns and scalds are to:

- prevent shock
- avoid infection
- relieve pain.

### *Treatment*

- Cool all burns and scalds as quickly as possible, by drenching the burn with cold water. Continue this for at least 10 minutes. If the burn is a small one hold it under a running tap.
- Cooling relieves the pain and helps to stop plasma loss by closing up the damaged blood vessels.
- Remove any loose clothing near the burn.
- Do not remove clothing that has been burnt. Burnt clothing is sterile and will give some protection against infection.
- Do remove any clothing that is soaked in chemicals. Remember to protect your own hands when doing this.
- Remove rings, belts or anything tight from the burnt area. If the burnt part swells later, it may then be difficult to remove them.
- If the burn covers more than about the size of a 50 pence piece or if it is on the face, it needs medical treatment. Cover the area with a sterile dressing. In an emergency, you can use a clean cloth, such as a handkerchief or part of a sheet. The dressing will keep the plasma from coming into contact with the air and forming a route for infection.
- Remember that a badly burnt person may suffer from shock. If they do, lie them down and keep them warm.
- If blisters form, do not burst them.

### Activity 19

Make a list of the things you would do to help someone who has suffered a burn to their face.

## *Electric shock*

### What is an electric shock?

Electric shock is the body's reaction to the passage of an electric current. The electric current may cause sudden unconsciousness or just a slight tingling. An electric shock may cause the heart to stop beating and if the heart stops, breathing will also stop. The casualty may appear dead. However, a first aider must never presume that the casualty is dead.

The casualty may have severe burns at the point where the electric current entered and left the body.

### What do you do if you find someone who has suffered an electric shock?

- Switch off the current at the mains.
- Switch off at the plug or try to pull out the plug.
- Do not directly touch the casualty – you will also get a shock.
- If you cannot switch off the electric current, break the electric contact by pulling the casualty away from it. Do this by putting a rope around their legs or arms. Do this without touching the casualty.
- When you are pulling the casualty away, stand or kneel on a dry rug, mackintosh, rubber mat or pile of newspapers.
- It may be easier to push the contact (wire or equipment) away from the casualty. Do this with a broom handle after insulating your hand with rubber gloves, a dry cloth or newspapers.

*Use something non-metallic, such as a wooden broom handle, to push the appliance away from the casualty*

When you have removed the casualty from the electric current:

- Check for breathing and watch for signs that their heart may have stopped.
- If the heart has stopped, start chest massage (see page 165).
- If the heart is beating, but the casualty's breathing has stopped, start artificial respiration (see page 164).
- If the casualty is breathing, but unconscious, place them in the recovery position (see page 152).
- Report the accident to your manager or call an ambulance or a doctor.

## *Cuts*

Cuts are a common occurrence. Small cuts will need little treatment – the bleeding will stop as the blood clots. If the wound continues bleeding after four or five minutes, a doctor should be seen as the wound may need stitching.

### How do you control bleeding and dress wounds?

The body usually can stop bleeding itself but when there is serious injury the body is not able to cope. If the blood is flowing fast it does not get a chance to clot. Heavy blood loss can threaten life. For infants and children even the loss of half-a-pint of blood can be dangerous.

### How to stop the occurrence of bleeding

- Make the casualty lie down. This reduces the blood flow through the limb.
- Press hard on the wound, using a pad, folded handkerchief, bandage or dressing from a first aid kit.
- Maintain pressure for about 10 minutes by which time a clot should have formed.
- As soon as bleeding stops pick out any obvious foreign bodies from the wound, such as glass, pebbles etc. *Never remove foreign bodies embedded in a wound.*
- Apply a clean dressing. Bind it firmly with a bandage.
- If blood is oozing through the bandage, do not take it off but put another one on top of it.
- If the wound is serious, treat the casualty for shock (see page 150).
- Elevate the limb or wound if possible.
- Rest and support the injury.

*Different methods of bandaging*

*Activity 20*

Practise different types of bandaging on a fellow student.

## Points to remember

Minor cuts:

- clean with soap and water
- clean surrounding skin if dirty
- clean the wound
- apply clean or sterile dressing.

Major cuts and wounds:

- examine cut
- control the bleeding by applying direct pressure on the wound
- remove any foreign bodies on the surface of the wound
- apply dressing
- elevate the limb or wound.

Rest and support the injury.

### Remember

Always wear disposable plastic gloves when dealing with blood and wounds.

With a major wound, many people may go into a state of shock. Treat them for shock (see page 150). Young children may go into a state of shock even with a minor cut. Reassure the casualty whatever the age.

*Elevating a leg*

---

**Activity 21**

You are working in a playgroup and a child cuts their leg.

**a** What first aid would you give?
**b** What would you do to reassure the child?

---

## Broken bones

A break in a bone is called a fracture. There are three types of fracture:

- Open fracture – the broken bone penetrates the skin. This is very serious because of the danger of infection getting into the open wound.
- Closed fracture – no open wound.
- Greenstick fracture – a common fracture in children. The bones of a child are not as brittle as those of adults and are therefore more likely to bend rather than break. The bend causes a partial break.

*What is a simple fracture?*

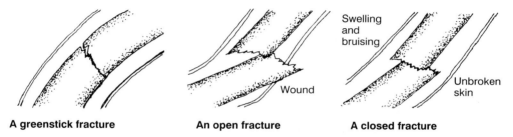

**A greenstick fracture**  **An open fracture**  **A closed fracture**

*The three types of fracture*

### General signs of a fracture

- Crack of bone breaking.
- Difficulty or loss of movement.
- Pain.
- Swelling and later signs of bruising.
- The limb may be deformed.
- The person may suffer from shock.

### What can you do in cases of fracture?

- Do not move the person. By moving the casualty or the broken limb, you may cause more damage and much pain.

- If help is not immediately available:

  1. Cover any open wound.
  2. Try to stop any severe bleeding by applying pressure alongside the broken bone. Alternatively, you can press the edges of the wound gently but firmly together.

3. Immobilise the injured part. Move the injured limb into the most comfortable position and bandage it to the casualty's body (see below).
4. Use lots of padding around the limb – blankets, folded clothes, pillows or towels.
5. Raise the injured part. This helps reduce pain and swelling.
6. Try to prevent shock. Loosen tight clothing, and cover the person with a blanket or coat.
7. Do not give anything to eat or drink.

## Activity 22

**a** List the three types of common fracture.
**b** Which of the three is mostly likely to occur in children and why?
**c** How would you deal with a person who has suffered a fracture?

*Ways of immobilising broken limbs*

## Heart attack

A heart attack is caused by a blood clot blocking a coronary artery. The blood clot prevents blood reaching the heart.

# What are the signs and symptoms of a heart attack?

Sudden chest pain

Breathlessness

Heart and breathing
may stop

Casualty may suffer
from shock

Casualty may become
unconsciousness

Weak, fast or
irregular pulse

Pale, cold and
clammy skin

*Signs of a heart attack*

# What can you do in a case of a heart attack?

- Telephone for a doctor or ambulance.
- Try not to move the casualty.
- If the casualty is conscious:
    1. Place them in the W position (see below).
    2. Loosen any tight clothing.
    3. Talk to the casualty and comfort them.

*The W position*

- If the person is unconscious:
  1. Place them in the recovery position (see page 152).
  2. Get medical help as soon as possible.
  3. Check the casualty's pulse and breathing every 10 minutes.
  4. If heart and breathing stops, start resuscitation (see pages 164–166).

---

### Activity 23

a  What can cause a heart attack?
b  Write down the signs and symptoms that might lead you to believe that a person has suffered a heart attack.
c  What first aid would you give?

---

## Poisoning

Poisoning may occur in a number of different ways, as shown in the diagram below.

Children are the most likely victims of accidental poisoning. They may drink substances left in pop bottles, cleaning substances left within their reach or they may eat things like poisonous mushrooms or berries. Also, people who are elderly and confused or absent-minded may take accidental overdoses of pills or other drugs.

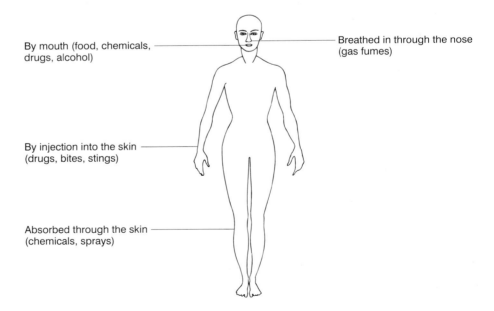

By mouth (food, chemicals, drugs, alcohol)

Breathed in through the nose (gas fumes)

By injection into the skin (drugs, bites, stings)

Absorbed through the skin (chemicals, sprays)

*How poison can enter the body*

---

### Activity 24

List the kinds of things commonly found in the home that could cause poisoning to a young child. What first aid procedures would you apply if you suspected poisoning?

---

## Signs and symptoms of poisoning

These will vary according to:

- the poison taken
- how it entered the body
- its effect on the person.

If a poison is swallowed, it may cause the person to be sick and vomit. This may mean that the body has rid itself of the poison. However, if the poison has been absorbed into the blood or inhaled, it can cause unconsciousness, stop breathing and eventually cause death.

## What can you do if someone has been poisoned?

- Call an ambulance.
- Find out what the poison is – ask the person or look around for the source.
- Never give salt or mustard and water to make them sick.
- If the person has swallowed a corrosive substance that has burnt or may burn their lips (such as petrol, household cleaners, paint stripper), *do not make them vomit*. This will only cause more damage.
- If the person has taken a corrosive substance and if they are conscious, try to dilute the poison by getting them to drink a pint of tepid milk or water.
- Keep any evidence, such as vomit, pills or container, to show the doctor or ambulance personnel what the poison was.
- If the casualty loses consciousness, put them in the recovery position (see page 152).
- If they stop breathing, start artificial respiration (see page 164).

---

/ **Activity 25** /

You are working in an old persons' home, You find an elderly, confused man unconscious in his room. He has been allowed to look after his own anti-depressant pills.

**a**  What signs would you look for?
**b**  What action would you take and why?

---

## *Common health emergencies and care procedures*

### First aid

As we have already seen, first aid is assistance or treatment given to a casualty before a doctor or ambulance arrives. The aim of first aid is:

- to save life
- to prevent the injured person's condition deteriorating
- to aid recovery.

In an emergency situation, the priorities of a first aider must be to:

- Stay calm.
- Quickly assess the situation:
  - first make sure that you are safe
  - make sure the person injured is safe from further injury
  - find out what is wrong with the injured person.
- Get help.
- Move the injured person only if there is risk of further injury to them.
- Give essential first aid treatment:
  - check the airway, breathing and circulation (A B C, see below)
  - check for severe bleeding
  - check for unconsciousness.
- Make arrangements to send the injured person to a hospital, to a doctor, back to work or home.
- Pass on information about the injury and the casualty's condition to the doctor, ambulance personnel etc.

## How to get help

Find the nearest telephone and dial 999. Give as much information as necessary:

- service required – ambulance, fire or police
- your telephone number
- where you are located
- what has happened
- the number and type of casualties.

## What is the A B C rule?

This is a very important rule for first aiders to remember. Thinking of the letters A B C will help you to remember the right order in which to do things in an emergency:

A = Airway – check that the airway is open. If not, open the airway (see page 163).

B = Breathing – check that the casualty is breathing. If not, resuscitation will be necessary (see page 164).

C = Circulation – check that the heart is beating by taking the pulse. If it is not, resuscitation and chest massage (CPR) will be necessary (see page 165).

If the airway, breathing and pulse are OK, you can then check for other injuries, such as fractures, cuts, wounds etc. (These are described on pages 151–157.) Every few minutes you should check (monitor) A B C signs.

If the person is semi-conscious or unconscious you should also try and measure their level of consciousness.

## Monitoring levels of consciousness

Unconsciousness can be caused by anything that interrupts the normal working of the brain. The most common causes are:

- suffocation
- shock
- heart attack
- head injuries
- poisoning
- epilepsy and diabetic emergencies.

Levels of consciousness are categorised as follows:

- Fully conscious – alert, responds to conversation in normal manner.
- Drowsiness – easily responds, may give muddled or slow answers to questions.
- Semi-conscious – aroused with difficulty, may only be able to carry out simple things like moving arm or leg or fingers, will be aware of pain.
- Unconscious – no response, no reaction to questions, pain.

### Keeping the airway open

Because a person's muscles are usually completely relaxed when they are unconscious they are at particular risk of choking. This is caused by the tongue falling backwards and blocking the air passage. This is one of the first things to look for in an unconscious person. So that air and oxygen can get to the brain, the first thing to do is to make sure that the airway is open.

### How do you keep the airway open?

- Tilt the person's forehead backwards by placing one hand underneath the neck and the other hand on their forehead. This will ensure that the chin moves upwards.
- Remove your hand from under the person's neck and lift the chin upwards and forwards. The mouth will open slightly and the nostrils of the nose will be pointing upwards. In this position the tongue will move from the back of the throat and unblock the air passage.

Once you have unblocked the airway and the person is breathing, you must place them in either of these positions:

- The prone position – 'prone' means face downwards and the elbows bent, so that the forearms and hands are under the forehead.

- The recovery position – The casualty is lying on their side, with the face turned towards the ground (see page 152). This position keeps the airway open and allows any fluid to drain from the mouth.

/ **Activity 26** /

Practise placing a person in the recovery position with a class colleague.

## Resuscitation

### *Mouth-to-mouth resuscitation*

The brain needs oxygen in order to function. The respiratory (breathing) system relies on our ribs, diaphragm, heart and lungs working together to transport oxygen from the air we breathe to the brain.

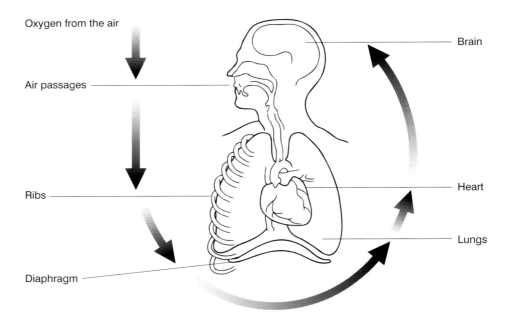

Oxygen from the air

Air passages

Ribs

Diaphragm

Brain

Heart

Lungs

*Factors in respiration*

A person who is not breathing, therefore, is being starved of oxygen. If the brain is starved of oxygen for more than four minutes it may be permanently damaged. One way to get air to someone's lungs is by breathing into their lungs. This is called artificial respiration or mouth-to-mouth resuscitation.

The air you breathe into the casualty's lungs will not be as rich in oxygen as the air they would normally breathe, but it will be enough to maintain life and avoid brain damage.

## How to do mouth-to-mouth resuscitation

Artificial respiration will do the unconscious person no harm, so don't waste time on fetching help or dealing with other injuries. The casualty will die if the brain does not get oxygen immediately.

Open the airway

Look for chest movement

Pinch nose closed

Take a deep breath and seal your lips around the casualty's mouth. Blow into mouth at rate of 10 breaths per minute

*Mouth-to-mouth resuscitation*

1. Lie the casualty flat on their back. Open the airway (see above).
2. Close the casualty's nose by pinching it, otherwise the air will escape through the nose.
3. Take a deep breath and put your mouth over the casualty's mouth.
4. Blow into the lungs and watch to observe if the lungs rise. The chest should rise as the air enters the lungs.
5. Carry on breathing into the lungs until they start to breathe again, or until professional help arrives. Don't blow too hard – just enough to make the chest rise.
6. As soon as the casualty starts to breathe again, put them in the recovery position.

With small children or babies, put your mouth over their nose and mouth and blow gently into the lungs until the chest rises.

## Cardio-pulmonary resuscitation

When a casualty has no pulse, it means that the heart has stopped beating. To restore the circulation, it is necessary to give chest massage (also known as chest compressions or heart massage).

Chest massage is best done combined with mouth-to-mouth resuscitation. This is called cardio-pulmonary resuscitation or CPR. It can be done either by one or two first aiders – one to give mouth-to-mouth ventilation and the other to do chest massage, but note that this procedure can be quite tiring.

How to do chest massage:

1. Lie the casualty flat on their back. Open the airway (see above).
2. Find the correct position for your hands (see 166).
3. Leaning over the casualty, with your arms straight, press down vertically on the breastbone to depress it about 4–5cm. Release the pressure without removing your hands.

*What does it mean when a person has no pulse?*

4. Continue giving compressions at a rate of about 80 per minute. Check the pulse after every 10 compressions.

**1** With two fingers, find the point where the ribs meet

**2** Slide the heel of your hand down to meet your fingers. This is the point where you will apply pressure

**3** Place the heel of first hand on top of other hand and interlock fingers

**4** Press down to depress breastbone about 4cm, then release pressure without removing hands. Repeat at a rate of 80 compressions per minute

*Position of the hands for chest massage*

For babies, place the tips of two fingers in a position just below the mid-point of an imaginary line between the nipples. Give chest compressions of about 1.5–2.5cm at a rate of 100 per minute.

With children under 5, put one hand in the same position as you would for an adult. Give compressions of about 2.5–3.5cm at a rate of 100 per minute. For children over five, use the same method as for adults.

### How to combine mouth-to-mouth resuscitation and chest massage

| Casualty | One first aider | Two first aiders |
|---|---|---|
| Adult | 1. Give 2 lung inflations<br>2. Give 15 compressions to every 2 lung inflations | 1. Give 2 lung inflations<br>2. Give 5 compressions to every lung inflation |
| Baby or child under 5 | Give 5 compressions to every lung inflation | |

### Activity 27

**a** Practise mouth-to-mouth resuscitation on a first aid dummy.
**b** Practise chest massage on a first aid dummy.
**c** Practise CPR on a first aid dummy, first on your own and then with a partner.

Your tutor will explain how you should do this.

**166**

**Activity 28**

You have been out rock climbing with your class. You come across a person who was climbing alone and has had an accident. You are the only member of the class who has had first aid training. The rest of the class think that the injured person has gone into shock.

**a** How could you tell if this is so? List the signs and symptoms of shock.

**b** What is the treatment for shock?

## Asthma

### What is asthma?

We usually do not think of how we breathe, as it is a passive and effortless procedure. To understand asthma, we must first understand how we breathe.

When we breathe in, the lung tissue is stretched. The natural elasticity of the lungs then forces the air out and we breathe out. When someone has forced, wheezy and difficult breathing it is called asthma. The breathing tubes (bronchioles) become narrowed so that it is difficult to breathe out naturally. Some people feel a great weight across their chest and have difficulty in breathing and they may make wheezing noises.

### What causes asthma?

Asthma is often an **allergic condition**. People may be allergic to:

*   pollens
*   smoke
*   animals
*   certain foods.

In Japan, for example, about half of the people who suffer from asthma are allergic to butterflies. Sometimes, if a person is worried their asthma may be made worse. Attacks usually occur suddenly and more commonly at night or the early hours of the morning.

### Who may suffer from asthma?

About 1 in 20 school children suffer from this disease. Many adults suffer. It is more common in men than women. Asthma also occurs later in life in individuals who suffer from chronic bronchitis (inflammation of the mucous membrane of the bronchial tubes).

How can you help someone who has an attack of asthma?

*   If the person is lying down, sit them up (in bed or in a chair) in a comfortable position. In many cases, the person themselves will

**167**

know which position is most comfortable. Sometimes the person suffering cannot bear to be touched and may want all their clothes loosened. Lean them slightly forward. In this position it is easier to use the chest muscles for breathing. Make sure that there is plenty of fresh air available.

- If this is a first attack, a doctor or ambulance should be called.
- If the casualty knows that they suffer from asthma, find out whether they have their inhaler with them. If so, help them to use it.
- Give plenty of reassurance until a doctor or ambulance arrives. The person will be very frightened, when they find difficulty in breathing. Young children may panic and will need lots of reassurance and emotional support.

---

**Activity 29**

You are travelling on a bus in town on a very foggy day. One of the passengers begins to have breathing problems. She manages to tell you that she suffers from asthma.

**a** What causes asthma?
**b** When is it most likely to occur?
**c** What is the first aid treatment for the condition?

---

## Epileptic fits

### What is epilepsy?

Epilepsy is a nervous disorder characterised by a sudden loss of consciousness. Convulsions also occur. These can be frightening when seen for the first time, but they are not in themselves a medical emergency. Epilepsy can affect people of all ages.

### Types of epilepsy

#### 'Grand mal' or major fit
This type of fit can be very frightening when seen for the first time. The person may make a strange cry and fall suddenly. Muscles stiffen and then relax. Jerking or convulsions occur, and they can be quite vigorous. Saliva may appear about the mouth. The person may also urinate (pass water). This type of fit may last several minutes. Then the person may recover consciousness, be dazed or confused. A 'grand mal' fit is not usually harmful unless it is followed by another fit.

#### 'Petit mal'
This type of fit may pass unnoticed by others. The person may appear to daydream or stare blankly. There may be frequent blinking of the eyes. This type of fit may cause problems for children at nursery or school as the child may not learn or pay attention during the periods of fitting.

## What causes epilepsy?

Epilepsy is not a disease or illness. It may be a symptom of some physical disorder, such as a disorder of brain activity. It may also occur after a head or brain injury. In children, in particular, there may be no precise medical explanation.

## Who may suffer from epilepsy?

Epilepsy can occur at any age. However, it is common in children. Over 100,000 children and young people have some form of epilepsy.

## How can you help someone who has suffered an epileptic fit?

- Most fits stop spontaneously. All that needs to be done is to protect the person from asphyxiation by preventing inhalation of vomit or swallowing of the tongue.
- Don't try to hold the person down or stop them jerking or thrashing about. Loosen tight clothing.
- As soon as they stop jerking, wipe the froth from their mouth and place them in the recovery position (see page 152). Make sure that any vomit is cleared from the mouth.
- When the person regains consciousness, make sure that they have a change of clothes if they have wet or soiled themselves.
- Do not put anything between the teeth. Do not give anything to drink.

/ **Activity 30** /

**a** How many types of epilepsy are there?
**b** What can you do to help someone who has just suffered a fit?

# *Choking*

Any foreign body (perhaps a fishbone or piece of food) that lodges or sticks in the throat or in the windpipe will cause choking. With children or elderly people the most common cause is food or drink 'going down the wrong way'. With small children, choking is a particular hazard, because of their habit of putting everything into their mouths.

## Symptoms of choking

- If the airway is not completely blocked, the casualty may be coughing.
- If the airway is completely blocked, the casualty will be struggling for breath and their face will turn blue as they try to get air into their lungs.

## Treatment for choking

1. Open the airway (see page 165).
2. Try to remove the obstruction with your finger.
3. If you cannot move the obstruction, give sharp blows with the heel of the hand between the shoulder-blades to try to dislodge it. Make sure that the casualty's head is lower than their chest.
4. If you cannot clear the obstruction, give abdominal thrusts.
5. If this all fails, get the person to hospital as soon as possible.

*Dealing with a choking adult*

*The abdominal thrust*

If a baby or child is choking, use the techniques shown below. Abdominal thrusts may be used on children over the age of 5.

*Dealing with a choking baby or child*

## Key terms

After reading this unit you should be able to understand the following words and phrases. If you do not, go back through the unit, and find out.

| | |
|---|---|
| *Prohibited* | *Toxic effects* |
| *Warning* | *Microbes* |
| *Safety hazards* | *Signs of shock* |
| *Passive smoking* | *Allergic condition* |
| *First aider* | *Plasma* |

## Test yourself

1  What is a healthy and safe working environment?
2  What does it mean when something is mandatory?
3  What is passive smoking?
4  Who is a first aider?
5  What can cause back pain?
6  What are the signs of shock?
7  What is the first aid treatment for asthma?
8  What is the first aid treatment for choking?
9  Name the three types of fracture.
10  What does A B C mean in first aid?

# Assignment for Unit Four

*The first part of this assignment is to carry out a school, college or workplace safety audit and explain what might happen if correct health and safety practice is not followed.*

*The second part is to demonstrate first aid procedures.*

### Tasks

1  Carry out a safety audit (survey) of your work placement, school or college. Correctly identify health and safety features (such as first aid equipment, alarms, emergency exits etc.) and basic hazards. Basic hazards could be wet floors, sharp edges, worn flooring, unprotected fires etc. These hazards and features could be shown on a drawing of the workplace.

2  Identify the possible immediate effects of failure to follow correct health and safety procedures, such as fire procedures or emergency first aid, or the consequences of not reporting or correcting an unsafe situation.

### Get the grade

To achieve a **PASS** you must complete tasks 1–2 and 7.

To achieve a **MERIT** you must complete tasks 1–4 and 7.

To achieve a **DISTINCTION** you must complete tasks 1–9.

**3** Identify and give a clear description of and the location of any hazards and health and safety features. This can be done in a written report or by using drawings.

**4** Clearly explain procedures for dealing with at least three emergencies (listed in the unit) over and above CPR.

**5** Explain why the health and safety features identified are in their specific location and state why they reduce risks. For example, why would a fire blanket be placed in a kitchen?

**6** Make realistic suggestions for improvements you have identified in your survey.

**7** Safely demonstrate CPR procedure.

**8** Demonstrate first aid procedures, relating correct symptoms and procedures.

**9** Competently demonstrate first aid procedures, relating correct symptoms and procedures, and explaining what you might do if the person had more than one symptom.

## Key Skills — *Opportunity*

| | **You can use this opportunity to provide evidence for the following key skills** |
|---|---|
| Application of Number N1.1 | Identify basic hazards and healthy and safety features. (For example, by using a drawing of the building and using measurements etc. to illustrate where safety equipment is located in relation to the hazard.) |
| Communication C1.1 | Demonstrate first aid procedures. Report to colleagues the results of your survey. |
| Communication C1.2 | Carry out the workplace survey. |
| Communication C1.3 | Present a written report of the results of your survey, including any drawings you may have used. |

# Planning diets

## What is covered in this unit

*5.1    What makes up a well-balanced diet*
*5.2    The different types of diet for different people*
*5.3    How to prepare meals hygienically*

At the end of this unit you will be asked to produce a plan for a **balanced diet** that would meet the nutritional needs for a person for one day. You will also need to prepare at least two courses from meal(s) identified in the plan and work within a given budget. If you would like to see further details of the tasks you are likely to need to carry out for assessment, please refer to the end of the unit where an assignment has been set (see pages 204–206). This unit will guide you through what you need to know in order to successfully put together this report. You will be assessed on this work and awarded a grade. This grade will contribute to the overall grade you will get for Unit Five.

## Materials you will need to complete this unit

- Appropriate access to cooking facilities and utensils
- Appendix 6 *Manual of Nutrition* (Department of Health and MAFF)
- Extract from the *Dietary and Nutritional Needs of British Adults Report* and the summary of *The National Diet and Nutrition Survey* available at http://www.doh.gov.uk/HPSS/INDEX.

## Introduction

What you eat plays an important part in your health. In this unit you will:

- look at your diet in terms of the amount you eat and the different food groups
- consider the importance of a well-balanced diet
- look at special diets and analyse them to see how they contain the balance of **nutrients**.

Having understood more about diets, you will then be able to plan and cost balanced diets to meet client needs and prepare food hygienically.

## 5.1 What makes up a well-balanced diet

### A balanced diet

The important aspect of your diet is balancing what your body needs for it to work as you want it to, with what you eat and drink. In doing this you supply all that is needed for the body to function without building up too much stored fat or causing any deficiency disorder.

| What is a balanced healthy diet? |
|---|
| A balanced healthy diet is one that provides you with enough of the various types of nutrient to meet your needs. It does not have excesses (too much) or deficiencies (too little) of anything. |

It would be easy to provide a balanced healthy diet if all the food you ate was made up of specific amounts of the required nutrients. This is the basis of many of the foods used by astronauts. However, no one food that you eat contains all the nutrients in the correct proportions.

If you are going to eat a balanced diet, you need to know:

- what your body needs – this depends upon your age, sex and activity level
- what nutrients are contained in the foods you eat.

### Nutrients

It is often very confusing to think about the food you eat in terms of what it contains. When you eat a sandwich, for example, you are not thinking about the protein and starch in the wheat that forms the flour to make the bread. You are presumably more interested in the fact that it tastes good and stops you feeling hungry.

'I don't eat a diet, I eat food.'

In this section, we are going to look in more detail at what food consists of and how your body uses it. We describe the content of food in terms of the nutrients it contains.

*Types of nutrients*

Macro means big and micro means small. All diets contain something of these major nutrient groups.

## Macronutrients

There are three main **macro** (large) **nutrients**:

- **protein**
- **fat**
- **carbohydrate.**

The table on page 176 summarises the main nutrient groups.

## Micronutrients

There are two important classes of **micro** (small) **nutrients**:

- **Vitamins** – chemicals produced by living organisms that are needed to help your body to function properly. The table on page 176 provides details of vitamins, their functions and sources.
- **Minerals** – chemicals that are not produced by living organisms (in most cases they could be extracted from rocks). They perform important roles in body chemistry. The table on page 177 gives details of minerals and common dietary sources. (Note: Although they can come from rocks and soil, we normally obtain minerals from plants and animals as part of our food.)

## *Water*

There is one important part of everyone's diet that does not fall into the category of micro or macronutrient. This is water. We all need it to replace water lost from the body in sweat, urine, breathing and faeces.

Its role is to allow biochemical reactions to go on inside the body cells. It also forms an important part of blood and is needed to transport things around your body. More people in the world are ill or die because of the lack of clean water than because of a lack of other nutrients.

*Name two macronutrients.*

*Name two micronutrients.*

*What is the role of water in the body?*

**175**

## The main nutrient groups

| Macronutrients | Importance in the diet | Major sources |
|---|---|---|
| Proteins | Needed for growth and repair of cells within the body. They form a large part of muscle tissue. | Meat, fish, eggs, cheese, beans and grains (rice, wheat, etc.) |
| Fats | Needed to provide energy (calories, kJ) for all body activity. Also needed to maintain cell structures (cell membranes are largely fat). | Meat, cheese, eggs, oils, butter, margarine |
| Carbohydrates | (a) Digestible sugars and starches provide energy (calories, kJ). (b) Indigestible **fibre** (roughage) helps food to pass through the digestive system. It has a protective effect against some diseases. | Sweets, drinks, potatoes, flour, rice Vegetables, wholemeal flour and bread, bran |
| **Micronutrients** | | |
| Vitamins | A group of substances given letters to describe them (vitamin A, vitamin C etc.). These are needed in small quantities to help take part in chemical reactions inside the body. | (See table on this page.) |
| Minerals | Chemicals that contribute to structures and reactions in the body, such as iron for carrying oxygen, calcium to build the skeleton and help muscles to work. | (See table on page 177.) |
| **Also** | | |
| Water | Many reactions take place inside the body in water. In fact your body consists of about 70 per cent water (figures for this vary depending upon how you measure it). Water is also important in helping get rid of poisons that we produce ourselves (such as getting rid of urea in urine). | |

## The major vitamins

| Vitamin | Deficiency disease | Functions | Major sources |
|---|---|---|---|
| *Fat-soluble vitamins* | | | |
| A (Retinol) | Night blindness. Xerophthalmia (drying of the cornea) | Essential for light detection by eye | Carotene in plants, such as carrots, spinach, lettuce. Also liver |
| D (Calciferol) | Rickets in children Weakened bones in adults Aids bone formation | Aids calcium and phosphorus absorption | Fish, liver, egg yolk Formed by action of UV light (sunlight) on skin |
| E (Tocopherol) | Degeneration of gonads, only demonstrated in animals | Poorly understood | Lettuce, peanuts, egg yolk |
| K (Phyloquinone) | Extended clotting times | Required for blood clotting | Leafy vegetables |
| *Water-soluble vitamins* | | | |
| B1 (Thiamine) | Beri-beri – muscle wastage and paralysis | Helps us use energy | Yeast, rice and most other plant and animal tissues |
| B2 (Riboflavine) | Dermatitis and skin sores | Required for aerobic respiration | Leafy vegetables, fish, and eggs |
| B5 (Pantothenic acid) | Poor muscle control Gastro-intestinal problems | Forms co-enzyme A which is important in fat metabolism | All animal and plant tissues |
| B6 (Pyridoxine) | Anaemia and vomiting | Helps make the best use of protein in the diet | All animal and plant tissues |
| B12 (Cobalamin) | Pernicious anaemia. Not treatable with iron | Required for correct red blood cell formation | Beef, kidney, liver |
| C (Ascorbic acid) | Scurvy – breakdown of membranes | Required to help hold cells together | Citrus fruits, green vegetables |

## A more detailed look at macronutrients

It is important to have a good understanding of macronutrients. Let us look at them in more detail.

### *Protein*

The word 'protein' describes a large group of chemicals that are made up of smaller building blocks called amino acids. There are about 20 different amino acids commonly found in proteins. A protein is made up of several hundred of the building blocks, each of which is one of the 20.

Our bodies can make some of the 20 amino acids. Those that we cannot make have to be obtained from food. It is important to understand that, while we eat protein-containing foods, what we really need is to get a good balance of amino acids.

### *What happens to the protein you eat?*

Protein is first digested to break it down into the individual building blocks (amino acids). These are then absorbed from the digestive system into your blood and transported around your body. They are used to make your own body proteins.

### The major minerals

| Mineral | Deficiency disease | Function | Major sources |
|---------|-------------------|----------|---------------|
| Calcium | Poor skeletal growth<br>Delayed blood clotting<br>Muscle spasms | Skeleton and teeth<br>Blood clotting factor<br>Muscle contraction | Milk, cheese, fish and hard water |
| Chlorine | Localised shortage linked to muscle cramp | Required for activity of nerve and muscle | Cooking salt, cheese |
| Cobalt | Pernicious anaemia | Part of vitamin B12 | Most foods |
| Fluorine | Weak tooth enamel | Helps to prevent dental caries | Drinking water, toothpaste (trace) |
| Iodine | Goitre (swollen thyroid) | Constituent of thyroxine (thyroid hormone) | Sea fish, shell fish (trace), iodised table salt |
| Iron | Anaemia | Constituent of haem-oxygen, binding part of haemoglobin | Liver, eggs, cocoa powder<br>Not easily absorbed from plants, such as spinach |
| Magnesium | Rare/not known | Constituent part of skeleton<br>Co-factor in energy transfer | Most foods |
| Phosphorus | Rare/not known | Skeletal formation<br>Energy transfer<br>Membrane structure | Most foods |
| Potassium | Rare/not known | Required for activity of nerve and muscle | Leafy vegetables, liver |
| Sodium | Localised deficiency causes muscle cramp | Required for activity of nerve and muscle | Cooking salt, bacon, most foods |
| Zinc | Rare/not known | Enzyme co-factor<br>Constituent of insulin<br>(see page 200) | Most foods (trace) |

Proteins in your body are used for:

- structural things like tendons ligaments and cartilage
- movement – they are a key part of muscles
- chemical reactions – the chemistry of your body is controlled by a large group of proteins called enzymes.

**quick fire**

What is protein used for in the body?

Protein in your diet is used to build and repair cells and tissues. As such, it can be described as being used for growth and repair. If you eat more than you need, it cannot be stored and so is broken down to form urea (a waste product in urine), with the rest being a source of energy.

### Sources of protein

In your diet you need to eat a balance of protein to provide all the amino acids (particularly the essential ones) that you need to make your own proteins. There are two sources of protein:

- Sources of first-class protein – These are foods that are rich in proteins that contain the essential amino acids. Meat contains the right proportions of amino acids to make muscle. Other animal sources that are very good are fish, milk (and products like cheese) and eggs. Milk and eggs naturally provide the nutrients required for the growing animal.
- Sources of second-class protein – These are foods that contain protein but not all of the essential amino acids. Second-class protein is found in vegetables (particularly beans, lentils, rice and grains, such as wheat). It is, therefore, important to eat different types of these foods to obtain all the essential amino acids. This is particularly important for people who eat no animal protein (meat, milk or eggs).

*Sources of first-class protein*

*Sources of second-class protein*

## Essential amino acids

Your body is able to convert many of the amino acids from one to another amino acid. There are about seven that you cannot make in this way. These seven are called essential amino acids and you must eat a balance of proteins to supply these.

## Fats

Like protein, the term 'fat' describes a broad group of chemicals. These are particularly important in two areas:

- providing energy within the body
- as part of membranes within and around cells.

Fats in the diet can largely be described as:

- saturated
- monounsaturated
- polyunsaturated.

The names refer to the chemical structure and the form of some chemical bonds.

There are some essential fatty acids (smaller molecules that form part of a fat molecule) that are a necessary part of your diet. These are required in small amounts and are important in membrane structure. It is unlikely that these fatty acids will be missing from your diet.

All fats can be used as an energy source. This means that they are broken down inside your body to provide the energy needed to keep you warm, alive and moving. However, any excess fat in your diet can be stored to provide for future energy needs. This stored fat is largely found in a layer of fat underneath your skin, called subcutaneous fat. This fat layer also acts as an insulating layer to help to keep you warm.

### *Sources of fat*

Sources of fat in the diet can be from two sources:

- animals – most animal fats are solid at room temperature and contain a high proportion of saturated fats

What two important things does fat do in the body?

*Sources of fat*

**179**

**What are the two sources of fat?**

- plants – fats from plant sources are often liquid at room temperature and are usually called oils. These are normally found in seeds and fruits, such as corn, olives and avocados, and often contain a high proportion of unsaturated fats.

## Carbohydrates

This is a group of chemicals made up from simple sugars. These are sweet-tasting chemicals such as glucose and sucrose. The most familiar sugar is the one sold as white or brown sugar made from sugar beet or sugar cane. This sugar is called sucrose.

Sugar molecules can be joined together to produce different carbohydrate molecules. As the number of sugar molecules joined together increases, the molecule becomes less sweet and eventually takes on one of two basic forms:

- Digestible starch – Starch molecules are complex carbohydrate molecules that can be digested and absorbed as simple sugars. They are found in potatoes and grains (like wheat and rice) in particular. The bulk of flour is starch. Starches and sugars are used by the body as an energy source. Any excess is converted to fat and stored under the skin.
- Indigestible cellulose – This is one of the components of dietary fibre.

*Sources of carbohydrate*

Digestible sugars and starches

Indigestible fibre

## Dietary fibre

**Fibre** is indigestible material, mainly from plants. It consists of carbohydrates like cellulose and other, more complex chemicals that help support plants.

The most noticeable effects of eating fibre are:

- speeding the passage of food through the digestive system
- increasing the bulk of faeces
- making faeces softer (stopping constipation)
- reducing hunger between meals
- slowing the absorption of nutrients.

The benefits of these effects are:

- toxic materials are not retained in the digestive system, particularly the bowel where they are associated with cancer
- going to the toilet (defecation) involves less physical strain and so there is less damage to the lining of the lower gut
- digested nutrients are absorbed over a longer period of time and this reduces the work of internal control mechanisms (see Diabetes, page 200).

There is some evidence that soluble fibre found in things like oats may affect blood cholesterol levels and reduce the risk of heart attacks. We do not fully understand the link and how it may work.

## Nutrients are important for:

- body building and repair – protein in particular
- energy and warmth – carbohydrate, fat and some protein. Some vitamins and minerals are also important
- healthy development and body maintenance – vitamins and minerals in particular.

### Activity 1

Food tables are not the easiest things to understand and so it is worth while taking a little time to look at them. Obtain a copy of up-to-date food tables (see page 182).

**a** Write down a diary of what you eat for a day.

**b** Carry out an analysis of the macronutrients you ate on that day. Use food tables to divide the foods into three groups:
- those that contain more protein than fat or carbohydrate
- those that contain more fat than protein or carbohydrate
- those that contain more carbohydrate than protein or fat.

**c** Look at the lists in each group and check the food tables again. This time note down which nutrient (fat, protein or carbohydrate) is the second largest amount for each food.

You will now have an indication of which foods are important in your diet, in terms of the main nutrient. You will also know which other main nutrient they contain. This will be very useful if you want to identify ways of changing your diet.

Note: Keep your food list because you will use it for a later analysis.

**Key Skills**

You can use Activity 1 to provide evidence for Key Skills Application of Number N1.1.

## Reference nutrient intakes

The table on page 182 shows some daily requirements for different groups of people – the **reference nutrient intakes**. You will see that carbohydrate is not included (other than fibre). This is because it is part of the energy intake (see page 184), and the amount required varies according to the amount of fat and excess protein in the diet. Throughout this unit we will not expect you to calculate carbohydrate intake unless you choose to find information for a diabetic diet.

## Food tables

To know what nutrients different foods contain, you can use food tables that give the composition of foods per 100g. You may also be able to use one of the many computer programs that help you to analyse your diet. However, the tables do not always give details of all possible foods.

### Reference nutrient intakes of selected nutrients, per day

| Age range | Vitamin B6 (mg) | Folic acid (mg) | Protein (g) | Vitamin C (mg) | Calcium (mg) | Iron (mg) | Zinc (mg) | Vitamin A (mg) | Thiamin (mg) |
|---|---|---|---|---|---|---|---|---|---|
| 0–3 months (formula fed) | 0.2 | 50 | 12.5 | 25 | 525 | 1.7 | 4.0 | 350 | 0.2 |
| 4–6 months | 0.2 | 50 | 12.7 | 25 | 525 | 4.3 | 4.0 | 350 | 0.2 |
| 7–9 months | 0.3 | 50 | 13.7 | 25 | 525 | 7.8 | 5.0 | 350 | 0.2 |
| 10–12 months | 0.4 | 50 | 14.9 | 25 | 525 | 7.8 | 5.0 | 350 | 0.3 |
| 1–3 years | 0.7 | 70 | 14.5 | 30 | 350 | 6.9 | 5.0 | 400 | 0.5 |
| 4–6 years | 0.9 | 100 | 19.7 | 30 | 450 | 6.1 | 6.5 | 500 | 0.7 |
| 7–10 years | 1.0 | 150 | 28.3 | 30 | 550 | 8.7 | 7.0 | 500 | 0.7 |
| Males 11–14 years | 1.2 | 200 | 42.1 | 35 | 1000 | 11.3 | 9.0 | 600 | 0.9 |
| 15–18 years | 1.5 | 200 | 55.2 | 40 | 1000 | 11.3 | 9.5 | 700 | 1.1 |
| 19–50 years | 1.4 | 200 | 55.5 | 40 | 700 | 8.7 | 9.5 | 700 | 1.0 |
| 50+ years | 1.4 | 200 | 53.3 | 40 | 700 | 8.7 | 9.5 | 700 | 0.9 |
| Females 11–14 years | 1.0 | 200 | 41.2 | 35 | 800 | 14.8 | 9.0 | 600 | 0.7 |
| 15–18 years | 1.2 | 200 | 45.0 | 40 | 800 | 14.8 | 7.0 | 600 | 0.8 |
| 19–50 years | 1.2 | 200 | 45.0 | 40 | 700 | 14.8 | 7.0 | 600 | 0.8 |
| 50+ years | 1.2 | 200 | 46.5 | 40 | 700 | 8.7 | 7.0 | 600 | 0.8 |
| Pregnant* | – | +100 | +6.0 | +10 | – | – | – | +100 | +0.1 |
| Lactating* –4 months | +11.0 | +550 | – | +6.0 | +350 | +0.2 | – | +60 | +30 |
| over 4 months | +8.0 | +550 | – | +2.5 | +350 | +0.2 | | +60 | +30 |

*For pregnant and lactating women, the figures given are to be added to the amount for the woman's age range.

Source: Table 25 from MAFF, Manual of nutrition (HMSO, 1995)

## But I don't want to have to carry a book of nutrients around with me!

Fortunately there is no need to carry round a book of nutrients. For most people it is sufficient to sort foods into different classes and eat samples from each class. This is the basis of the *Balance of Good Health National Food Guide*. In the *Guide*, foods are divided into five groups:

Fruit and vegetables

Bread, other cereals and potatoes

Meat, fish and alternatives

Fatty and sugary foods

Milk and dairy foods

## *Benefits of a balanced diet*

- By matching your diet to your needs, you give your body the opportunity to function at its best efficiency. In such a situation you are also more likely to be physically fit. This does not mean that you are athletic. It means that your heart, lungs and the rest of your body are in balance and little stress is being caused to any part.
- Monitoring and maintaining a balanced diet means that your weight should be correct for your height (see page 79). This again means that your muscles and skeleton are in balance and are not being damaged by too much weight.
- A balanced diet can help prevent disease. Clearly you will not suffer any deficiency diseases or diseases of excess. General health and resistance to infection is also improved. This is because a balanced diet assists all the body systems to be in balance. This includes those involved in preventing and fighting disease.

## The effects of an unbalanced diet

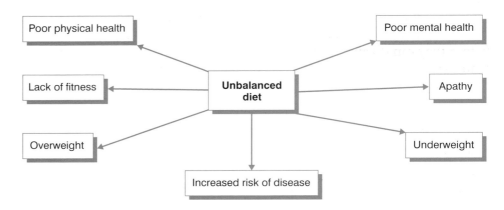

*Detrimental effects of an unbalanced diet*

Looking at the tables of minerals and vitamins you will see that the deficiency diseases are listed. These are the diseases that are caused by not having enough of the vitamin or mineral in the diet. If you have not heard of most of them it is not surprising. Deficiency diseases are very rare in the UK.

There are three major areas in which your diet may be unbalanced:

- your energy (calorie/kJ) intake
- too little fibre
- a specific lack of a mineral (most commonly this is iron).

### Unbalanced energy intake

The way to detect whether your energy intake is regularly too great or too little is to look at your weight in relation to your height. You can plot your height and weight on the graph on page 79 to find out if you are taking in too much (overweight) or too little (underweight).

As you have already read, excess quantities of the macronutrients are stored in the form of body fat. In fact, every 38kJ (9 calories) that is taken in and not used is enough to add about a gram of body fat.

This system of storing energy evolved as a way of preparing for times when food is scarce. However, in the UK it is unlikely that you will go through periods of starvation (unless they are self-imposed). The overall effect is that many people are storing too much energy and as a result their bodies are heavier than is ideal.

### Too little fibre

The fibre (or roughage) content of your diet seems to be an odd thing to consider. Why should something that passes through the digestive system be so important? To a large extent this is difficult to answer as we have only a limited understanding of how dietary fibre has the effects it does.

What we do know is that a lack of fibre in the diet is linked to cancer of the bowel. This is thought to be related to the amount of time food spends passing through the bowel. High-fibre diets mean that the food passes through quickly and so any cancer-producing chemicals pass out before they can do any harm. With a low-fibre diet, food may take more than twice as long to pass through the digestive system and so there is more opportunity for cancer-causing chemicals to have an effect.

## Vitamin and mineral deficiencies

Having said that deficiencies are unusual, there are some that do occur in the UK. In particular the intake of iron, calcium and vitamin D need to be monitored in some groups of people who are at risk.

- Iron (see the table on page 182). Particularly at risk from lack of iron are **vegetarian** women going through, and just after, puberty. Menstruation has started with its associated loss of blood. There is also a growth spurt. Both of these cause an increased demand for iron to replace and make haemoglobin. The limited uptake of iron from vegetables can mean that vegetarians do not absorb sufficient to cope with the extra demands. This lack of iron gives rise to anaemia, which means the blood's ability to carry oxygen is reduced. This shows up as increased tiredness, particularly with even mild exercise.
- Vitamin D and calcium (see the tables on pages 176 and 182). These two are linked, as vitamin D helps us to absorb calcium. There are two groups at risk: the first because of a lack of vitamin D (and hence calcium), the second because of changes in the way our bodies use calcium.
  — When a growing child has too little vitamin D (and/or calcium) in his or her diet, the bones fail to form properly. This deficiency disease is called rickets. The disease is associated with poverty in the UK and was, until recently, very rare. The increase in poverty in the UK has led to an increased number of cases of rickets in the poorest communities. This can be linked to the lack of vitamin D, but the effect of poverty cannot be ignored. The incidence of rickets in people of similar ethnic origins, but who do not live in poverty, is much lower.
  — Our reduced ability to absorb calcium in middle and old age means that some may be lost from the skeleton and not replaced. This makes the skeleton more liable to wear or break. It also means breaks take longer to heal. This condition is called osteoporosis. Women, during and after the menopause, are most at risk. During the menopause the ovaries stop producing hormones as well as stopping egg production. This change in the body's hormone balance means that calcium loss increases. To compensate, women often increase vitamin D and calcium in their diet. Many also use hormone replacement therapy to help control calcium losses.

*What is the effect upon the body of a lack of iron?*

**185**

### Activity 2

Select five of your favourite foods. For each these foods, do a micronutrient (see pages 175–177) analysis. To do this, calculate what percentage of your reference nutrient intake of vitamin C, vitamin D, iron and calcium is provided by 100g.

So far, we have identified that a lack of specific vitamins and minerals can lead to deficiency diseases. We have identified some factors relating to energy intake and also to dietary fibre. Let us now look at some of the less specific issues stemming from an unbalanced diet.

## The NACNE Report

In 1983 the National Advisory Committee on Nutrition Education (NACNE) produced some proposals for nutritional guidelines for health education.

The proposals concentrated on body weight and health. They also looked at issues relating to carbohydrate, fat and coronary heart disease. The relationship between salt and high blood pressure was investigated.

The Report concentrated on health education aspects of nutrition. It set targets for health education to meet in terms of changing people's attitudes and diets. In summary, it recommended a dietary energy intake of:

| | |
|---|---|
| Protein | 11% (no change) |
| Fat | 34% (a reduction)★ |
| Carbohydrate | 50% (an increase)★ |
| Alcohol | 5% (a reduction) |
| Total | 100% |

★ The types of fat and carbohydrate were recommended to be changed (see below). This would lead to a change in the types of food consumed and to an increase in minerals, vitamins and essential fatty acids.

The report concluded that even being mildly overweight increased health risks.

### Why did NACNE reach these conclusions?

#### Fats

There were two important parts to the recommendation:

- To reduce the total fat intake. As fat is high in energy, this would help reduce weight. Also, evidence from the medical profession stated that death rates from heart disease in the UK are among the highest in the world and that this is related to fat intake.

- To increase the ratio of polyunsaturated fatty acids to saturated fatty acids. This followed evidence that a diet with most of the fat as polyunsaturated fatty acids could reduce the incidence of heart disease. This is partly because the body makes cholesterol predominantly from saturated fats. Cholesterol has been linked to heart attacks.

Research has also identified certain types of polyunsaturated fatty acids as being particularly beneficial. For example, there is a very low incidence of heart disease in people who consume a large quantity of oily fish. The fats in oily fish have a lot of omega-3 fatty acids. This is linked to reduced blood cholesterol levels and fewer heart attacks.

### Carbohydrates

The recommendations were to:

- reduce sucrose (sugar) intake. This would help to reduce weight. Sugar is also a linked with dental caries (tooth decay). But the proposed reduction in sugar intake would have little effect on this
- increase the intake of complex carbohydrates as fibre. This would have the effect of slowing down absorption. This means that blood sugar levels do not change rapidly. Most complex carbohydrate is also associated with vitamins, minerals and indigestible fibre.

### Fibre

As we have already seen (pages 185 and186, low levels of dietary fibre are linked to large bowel disease, including irritable bowel syndrome, constipation, diverticulitis and colon cancer. The effect of an increase in dietary fibre is to increase the bulk of faeces and reduce the time material stays in the colon. We have also already mentioned the possible link with blood cholesterol levels.

### Salt

Very high intakes of sodium in the form of salt may lead to high blood pressure (hypertension). Some people tend to have high blood pressure and, for them, above average levels of salt can be dangerous. The recommendation to reduce salt intake is because of this. However, it is not easy to recognise people at risk.

### Alcohol

Alcohol and diet were not studied in detail. Alcohol supplies energy and so should be reduced as part of the move towards weight reduction. Alcohol causes liver damage and for this reason also it should be reduced. It should not necessarily be cut out altogether, as moderate alcohol consumption (a glass of wine per day) may reduce the risk of heart attacks.

### Protein

No recommendations were made about protein intake, although a suggestion was made that people should eat a little less protein as current intake was greater than required.

### So why is my diet so important?

The saying 'You are what you eat' is in many ways very true. The material that enters your body is used by you to make your body tissues. If your diet is wrong then your body becomes out of balance. An unbalanced diet can lead to:

- overweight – associated with heart disease and damage to joints
- underweight – giving rise to tiredness, reduced resistance to infection and, in extreme circumstances, starvation
- nutritional deficiencies, most commonly anaemia, and specific diseases, such as the consumption of too much refined sugar being linked to tooth decay.

## Key Skills

You can use Activity 3 to provide evidence for Key Skills Information Technology IT1.1 and IT1.2.

---

### Activity 3

In this activity you will be asked to produce a booklet about healthy eating.

The headteacher of the local junior/middle school is very worried that the children in their final year at the school are not eating a healthy diet. He plans to open a 'healthy tuck shop' and review the meal choices for school lunches. You have been asked to prepare an information booklet about nutrients to help the children to understand more about foods, nutrients and healthy eating.

The leaflet must have sections that:
- identify and give examples of macro and micronutrients
- identify and give examples of five good sources of the major groups of macro and micronutrients
- describe what the nutrient groups are used for in the body
- describe what constitutes a well-balanced diet
- describe the effects of an unbalanced diet
- give guidance about foods that should be selected from the 'healthy tuck shop' and also foods that should be available for lunches.

In order to do all of this you will need to plan each step carefully.
1. First you will need to gather together the information you need. Some will come from this book. Some may come from leaflets available from, for example, doctors' surgeries, health education units and supermarkets.
2. Think about foods that might be liked by junior/middle school children and that fit into the needs for promoting healthy eating. Any examples of foods that you use should be ones that the pupils are likely to want to eat. You might consider conducting a small survey of school children to do this.

3. Plan what information you want to put into the booklet. It should:
   * not be too long
   * be written so that the children can understand it
   * be interesting and eye-catching, using illustrations wherever possible to communicate information.

If you can, it is always useful to try out the booklet on people from your target audience.

4. You could produce the booklet using a word processor or desk-top publishing software if you wish.

## The problems of being overweight

One of the basic problems of being overweight is having to carry around the excess weight. This:

* puts a stress on the heart because it has to pump more blood per minute to provide for the extra energy needed
* means that the lungs have to work harder to provide the oxygen
* puts the joints under greater strain.

What tends to happen is that an overweight person does less, walks more slowly and reduces the amount of exercise taken. This reduces the energy being used and increases the risk of becoming even more overweight.

Lack of exercise contributes to a lack of physical fitness. This means that the individual is less ready to respond to any extra physical demands. Eventually the weight of an overweight person tends to stabilise at a point where the extra energy required to move the extra bulk balances the excess energy intake. At this point the person is effectively constantly working harder than necessary, without getting physically fitter. The resulting strain and wear and tear leads to heart disease and joint damage.

For many overweight people their lack of physical fitness makes many tasks harder. Feelings of apathy or not being bothered become common. There may be an intention to lose weight or increase exercise, but the effort of doing so becomes a barrier in itself.

### Poor self-image

Apathy also leads people to become unconcerned about the impression they make on others which, in turn, leads to a poor self-image as friendships fail to develop because of lack of effort.

Many overweight people have an image of themselves that they do not look or feel good. This can be reflected in their ability to make friends and can also lead to them being depressed. A cycle can develop of being unhappy and eating for comfort. This leads to greater overweight or guilt about eating. The extreme effects of this on mental health can be clinical depression.

**quick fire**

List two basic problems of being overweight.

An illness that appears to be linked to an image of overweight is anorexia nervosa. People suffering from this often have an image of themselves that they are overweight and the wrong shape. They effectively starve themselves (sometimes to death) while still feeling that they are overweight.

## *The problems of being underweight*

Many people do not recognise being underweight as a problem unless it is at the extreme of starvation or anorexia. Taking in too little energy means that the person cannot do everything because of a lack of energy. This leads to tiredness and, like overweight, a level of apathy and feelings of 'I can't be bothered'. The energy required to exercise is not available and physical fitness suffers.

Taking in too little energy to meet your daily needs causes the stored fat to be utilised. This is the basis of weight reduction diets. However, if the intake is not monitored, protein (in the form of the person's own muscles) is used, as well as fat. In the long term, this means that muscles become weaker. It is important to monitor the balance of foods even when going through a period of self-imposed starvation.

## *Ill-health and an unbalanced diet*

You have seen that lack of nutrients can lead to ill-health. Did you realise that eating an unbalanced diet can make you more prone to disease?

### Too much energy in the UK diet

Another problem of taking in too much energy is the type of food being eaten in excess. In the UK, sugar and saturated fat consumption is high. This means that most of the fat in the body is saturated and that most of the fat circulating in the blood is saturated. This has been linked by many people to an increased risk of heart disease.

The fat in circulation becomes attached to artery walls and has the effect of reducing blood flow and also putting a strain on the elastic structure of the walls. To overcome the reduced blood flow the heart has to work harder to push the blood around. Arteries can become blocked so that they starve the area they supply of oxygen. If the artery is one that supplies the heart with oxygen, then a heart attack occurs.

People who are significantly overweight or underweight tend to be ill more frequently. It is thought that the immune system that helps fight disease does not work well when the body is under stress. Overweight and underweight are both examples of physical stress and so they increase the risk of ill-health.

# 5.2 The different types of diet for different people

## *Balancing diets for different groups of people*

From what we have said so far, it is clear that a balanced diet is one that matches food intake with nutritional needs. However, it is not possible to specify a single diet that will provide for the needs of all people.

A quick look at the table of reference nutrient intakes on page 182 gives you an idea of some of the basic categories into which people are placed when considering a balanced diet. Let's look at some of these in more detail.

## Activity 4

**a** Using the table of reference nutrient intakes (on page 182), identify the amount of protein recommended (in grams) for:
- children aged 1–12 months
- children aged 8 years
- boys aged 12 years
- girls aged 12 years
- men aged 30
- women aged 30
- men aged 60 years
- women aged 60 years
- a pregnant woman
- a breast-feeding woman with a 2-month-old baby.

**b** Look back at what you need protein for and try to explain why the results of your calculations are not the same for each age range or sex.

**c** The table below gives the estimated average daily requirements for energy. Some people may need more, some less. Identify the average requirements for energy for the people listed in task **a**.

### Estimated average requirements for energy in the UK (per day)

| Age range | Males | | Females | |
|---|---|---|---|---|
| | MJ | kcal | MJ | kcal |
| 0–3 months (formula fed) | 2.28 | 545 | 2.16 | 515 |
| 4–6 months | 2.89 | 690 | 2.69 | 645 |
| 7–9 months | 3.44 | 825 | 3.20 | 765 |
| 10–12 months | 3.85 | 920 | 3.61 | 865 |
| 1–3 years | 5.15 | 1230 | 4.86 | 1165 |
| 4–6 years | 7.16 | 1715 | 6.46 | 1545 |
| 7–10 years | 8.24 | 1970 | 7.28 | 1740 |
| 11–14 years | 9.27 | 2220 | 7.92 | 1845 |
| 15–18 years | 11.51 | 2755 | 8.83 | 2110 |
| 19–50 years | 10.60 | 2550 | 8.10 | 1940 |
| 51–59 years | 10.60 | 2550 | 8.00 | 1900 |
| 60–64 years | 9.93 | 2380 | 7.99 | 1900 |
| 65–74 years | 9.71 | 2330 | 7.96 | 1900 |
| 75+ years | 8.77 | 2100 | 7.61 | 810 |
| Pregnant | | | +0.80 | +200 |
| Lactating: | | | | |
| 1 month | | | +1.90 | +450 |
| 2 months | | | +2.20 | +530 |
| 3 months | | | +2.40 | +570 |
| 4–6 months | | | +2.00 | +480 |
| >6 months | | | +1.00 | +240 |

*Source: Table 24 from MAFF, Manual of nutrition (HMSO, 1995)*

> **d** How would energy requirements change for very active and very inactive (sedentary) people? Why do you think this is?

## Children

Children have a range of dietary requirements, as you will have discovered from the activity above. If we ignore infants who obtain their balanced diet from breast milk or formula baby milks, it is still clear that requirements change between the ages of one year and 8 years.

### Protein requirements

Children grow rapidly in the first three years of life and then slow down. This is reflected in protein intake. Energy requirements in part reflect this growth, but also changes in physical activity.

A one-year-old child may be just starting to walk, while an 8 year old is likely to be moving about a lot more. The 8 year old needs more energy in the diet to support this increased activity. Balancing this, a one-year-old child loses heat faster than an 8 year old. This is because of the younger child's size. In the small child, there is a large area of skin in relation to body weight. Heat does not have to travel far before it reaches the skin and is lost to the air. So, relatively more energy from food is needed to keep a one year old warm compared to an 8 year old.

### Vitamin requirements

These are fairly constant throughout childhood or reflect growth rates. The exception is the recommended intake of vitamin D for under-5s which is significantly higher than for older children. This, in part, is because of the rate of bone growth, but is also to prevent rickets.

## Adolescence

### Protein requirements

The period of puberty is a time of rapid growth and great physical activity. These are reflected in increased requirements for protein and energy.

### Mineral requirements

Menarche, the first menstrual flow, is the start of a cycle of regular loss of blood. Iron is a key component of blood and so there is an increased requirement for iron in the diet compared with men, until menstruation ceases during the menopause.

## Adulthood

Throughout adulthood, differences in dietary requirements are largely related to physical activity and differences in size. If you carry out the calculations for different nutrient requirements per kilogram of body weight you will find that there is very little difference between men and women. The differences in the daily requirements are related to the fact that the average adult woman is smaller than the average adult man.

To a lesser extent, there are sex differences with regard to requirements for specific nutrients. The male hormone testosterone affects protein requirements and so men require slightly more than women for equivalent physically active lifestyles. As we have already mentioned, women have a greater requirement for iron.

### Pregnant women

It is often said that a pregnant woman needs to eat for two. This may be true, but in the early stages of pregnancy the growing foetus is so small that its requirements are very small. What is important is for the woman to eat a balanced diet, avoiding some of dangers associated with alcohol, drugs and smoking (see Unit Two).

As the foetus grows, there are increased requirements for nutrients – for both the mother's needs and those of the growing baby. Protein is required for growth of the foetus. Energy is required by the foetus as well as the mother, who is using more energy than normal because of the extra weight being carried. Towards the end of pregnancy the woman is carrying extra weight equivalent to several bags of sugar.

Vitamin and mineral requirements increase to provide for the growing foetus:

- calcium levels in the diet need to increase to provide for the developing skeleton and also for the growth of the mother's skeleton to cope with the increased weight
- iron requirements increase as the foetal blood forms with its need for iron. Pregnancy is a time when a woman becomes slightly anaemic (reduced iron levels in the blood). This is natural and allows the foetus to obtain oxygen more easily. It is important not to try to correct this mild anaemia with too much iron as this can damage the foetus.

### Elders

As people get older they tend to become less physically active. This is reflected in a reduced energy requirement. Growth ceases and repair processes become slower and less efficient with age. The protein requirement in the diet reflects this.

There is good evidence that levels of calcium and vitamin D need to be increased to prevent or delay the process of calcium loss from the bones. This particularly affects women after the menopause, but it also affects men.

_quick fire_

Why does a pregnant woman need calcium?

---

### Activity 5

In this activity you will be asked to research the dietary needs of individuals in a residential establishment.

You have been offered work assisting with the running of a week-long residential break for foster parents and their foster children at a seaside town. The person running the residential ▶▶

**Key Skills**

You can use Activity 5 to provide evidence for Key Skills Information Technology IT1.1, IT1.2 and Application of Number N1.1, N1.2 and N1.3

establishment is concerned that many of the people involved will have different dietary needs. You have been told that there will be at least one person on a weight-reducing diet, one with diabetes, several vegetarians and a vegan in the group of 30 people. The ages range from 1 to 60 years old.

The residential leader has asked you to research the different dietary needs of individuals.

1  Research and describe the nutritional needs for one of the adults and one of the children in the holiday group. You may decide the age and sex of the person that you are going to describe. Produce a table that shows the amount of nutrient each person will require in a day. The table should indicate the age and sex of the person you have identified.

2  The holiday leader is uncertain about how much activity any individual will undertake.

   a  Add to your table details of the nutrient requirements if the individuals:
   • are to be very active
   • spend most of their time reading in the holiday home.

   b  Add a paragraph at the end of the table to explain why nutrient needs vary for different people and the factors (age, sex, activity etc.) that need to be considered. Describe the effects of each of the factors on the amounts of nutrients needed. (This should be a general description and not just relate to your two chosen people.)

## *Factors influencing dietary patterns*

We all have different likes and dislikes in terms of food. We also all have different lifestyles. What you eat and when you eat is determined by a variety of things. These include:

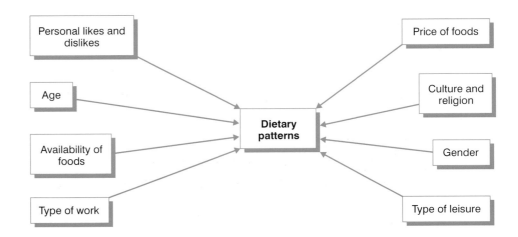

## Eating patterns

The pattern of meals for very young babies involves small intakes of food about every four hours. This pattern has evolved to provide the required nutrients without putting a great strain on the digestive system. It is thought that early people had a feeding pattern of frequent small meals with occasional large ones. This reflected the hunter–gatherer lifestyle.

Our current eating patterns are often governed by the requirements of work, school or college. Traditionally in the UK, there is a pattern of three meals a day: breakfast, lunch and dinner/tea. This means that a person's diet is based around these three meals, with associated between-meal snacks. These snacks form a very important aspect of the diet.

If we take the three-meals-a-day model, it is possible to identify common variations:

This pattern is fairly common but it puts a strain on the digestive system. Breakfast is, as its name indicates, a time for breaking a fast. Most people will not have eaten much for up to 12 hours before breakfast. Breakfast is an important meal enabling people to start the day with an energy intake.

Snacking mirrors early eating patterns and may be an ideal. The risks are that the snacks do not form a balanced diet. Too many snacks are high in fat and carbohydrate with few of the micronutrients. People who 'snack feed' tend to be those in a hurry who grab food when they can. Being in a hurry is a stressful behaviour and there are also risks associated with this.

Many people do need to ensure they eat enough to meet the needs of their work. Those involved in physically strenuous work will need to ensure that they have a high energy diet. There are a lot of people who are expected, or are tempted, to eat as part of their work. Included in this category are those involved in food preparation and those who have 'working lunches'. It is often difficult for these people to accurately control their food intake.

These people have developed a reflex to eat in certain situations. Often the foods are snacks and it is difficult to monitor the food intake.

## Eating patterns and elders

Many elders adopt an eating pattern that mimics the habits of young babies. They eat small amounts throughout the day. This reduces the strain on the digestive system and supplies the nutrients in a more consistent manner.

Elders follow this pattern for many other activities. For example, many elders punctuate their day with naps and continue this pattern through the night. It is important to identify such activities when planning meals for these people. It is also important to ensure that the small meals provide a balanced diet and do not over-emphasise high-energy foods.

**quick fire**

*Why do babies eat little and often throughout the day?*

## What influences diet choice?

Three factors have a major effect on diet choice, other than likes and dislikes. They are:

- availability of the food
- price of the food
- religious and cultural factors.

### Availability of food

In the past the availability of food was controlled by the seasons. For example, strawberries were only available for a short season during the summer. Now it is possible to obtain most foods at any time of the year. However, the fact that the foods are in the shops does not mean that everyone can have them. Even though they are available, strawberries are very expensive at Christmas!

South African Granny Smith 49p

Chilean Grapes 88p

Tomatoes Spain 45p

70p

Spring Onions Mexico Class 1 48p

King Edward Potatoes 22p

Parsnips 20p

Carrots Class I UK Loose Per lb

32p

Strawberries Spain Class 78p

*Good transport systems mean that foods are much less seasonal than they were. Transport costs, however, increase the prices*

When planning a diet it is better to use the foods in season for two reasons:

- if they are in season, they cost less than out of season
- they may have a greater nutritional content because they are fresher. Nutrients such as vitamins may be lost as a result of storage while foods are transported across the world.

The latter can be an important factor in considering different foods. For example, potatoes are a source of vitamin C. Freshly dug potatoes have a higher vitamin C content than those that have been stored. As freshly dug potatoes are not available through the winter they cannot be seen as an important source of vitamin C.

Similar comments can be made about many fresh vegetables compared with those that have been tinned. It is important to note the word 'fresh' is open to interpretation and to remember that many 'fresh' foods lose important nutrients if they are stored incorrectly for even a short period.

## Cost of food

As we have already indicated, the cost of food can have seasonal variations. More important here is a person's ability to buy the right food to produce a balanced diet. People living on low incomes or benefits may struggle to provide a balanced diet from the available income.

There are regular articles in the press from people suggesting that it is possible to provide a balanced diet on a low income. This may be true, but the choice of foods becomes limited and the diet, while nutritious, could become boring and monotonous.

## Religious and cultural factors

It is only possible here to touch briefly upon some issues relating to diet in religion and culture. It is important that you recognise this and use it only as a guideline if you are planning a diet for someone from a cultural or religious group other than your own. (If you are planning to do this, then it is important to ask about foods that should not be eaten.)

Some people will refuse to eat specific foods because of their religious beliefs. They may also require that the food that they eat is prepared in a special way. Neither orthodox Muslims nor Jews will eat pork. Both groups also require that their meat comes from animals that have been slaughtered or butchered in particular ways. These restrictions present few problems in providing a balanced diet, as the nutrients required can be provided from other sources.

Orthodox Jews also have dietary restrictions on combinations of food served in a meal. For example, it is not acceptable to serve beef in a meal that also contains milk products. Therefore, roast beef and Yorkshire pudding are clearly unacceptable, as would be a meal containing beef and a final course of cheese and biscuits or coffee with milk. Again, awareness of this enables well-balanced diets to be devised.

**Activity 6**

In this activity your task is to plan and cost a balanced diet for a week for an elderly person in a wheelchair.

- You must give the age, sex and any special dietary requirements at the start of your plan.
- The plan should be written so that it can be given to the cook to show what meals will be eaten.
- You should also have a shopping list for the cook with the price of the different foods on the list.

You will need to explain how the plan meets the client's dietary needs.

## Special diets

We began to see above that not all people have access to the same foods. In this section we will consider how people following special diets may have to plan their diet carefully.

### Weight-reduction diets

You may be surprised that in the whole of this unit, this is the first time we have described diets in the way that many people think of them – we think of 'being on a diet' as meaning trying to lose weight.

The simplest way to lose weight is to ensure that your energy intake is less than the amount of energy you use. As soon as you do this you will start to use up the fat stored under your skin and so start to lose weight. It would be so easy but for two things:

- the first is the will-power needed
- the second is that you do not eat energy, you eat food.

#### Planning a weight-reduction diet

- First of all, it is important to have an idea of how much energy you need. An estimate of this figure can be obtained from the table of reference nutrient intakes on page 176.
- It is also important to identify a target weight from the graph of ideal weights and heights on page 79.
- The next step is to identify how to cut down the energy intake while maintaining a balanced diet.

It is easy to cut out the energy from sugar as there are no other significant nutrients. Cutting down on margarine or butter reduces the vitamin D content of the diet. Clearly a weight-reducing diet needs to be planned to include all the nutrient requirements of a balanced diet with the exception of the energy intake. In the UK, many people eat more protein in the form of meat and dairy products than is necessary and so it may be possible to reduce the intake of these, while increasing the amounts of vegetables that provide fibre, reduce the hunger pangs and are good sources of many vitamins and minerals.

One further factor relating to diet that needs to be considered was mentioned earlier in the unit. Starvation (weight-reducing diets are a controlled form of this) can lead to apathy. What is actually happening is that the body reduces its energy requirements and slows down. In doing so the anticipated weight reduction does not work. To counter the apathy effect, it is important to increase exercise levels at the same time as dieting.

## Diets for people with diabetes

Diabetes is a disorder of the body's internal control of blood glucose levels. Insulin is produced by the pancreas and the mechanism is controlled by the level of blood glucose. Diabetics either produce:

- no insulin or
- too little insulin.

### Diabetics who produce no insulin

People with this form of diabetes usually have to inject a mixture of slow and fast action insulin designed to match their sugar intake and needs. The aim in controlling diabetes is to keep blood sugar levels within acceptable norms and as steady as possible.

The skill in planning a diet for a diabetic is to provide the carbohydrate in forms that allow sugar to pass into the bloodstream in a way that mirrors the available insulin. The diabetic person has to space out meals and eat carbohydrate between meals to match the energy requirements. This means that a diabetic planning to undertake vigorous exercise may prepare by eating a sweet biscuit to balance the sugar required for the exercise.

A high-fibre diet is useful for insulin-injecting diabetics, as it helps reduce the swings in blood sugar levels and balances the fast and slow acting insulin that is injected.

### Diabetics who produce some insulin

These people need to try to balance their carbohydrate (starches and sugars) intake with the amount of insulin produced. One important way of doing this is to have a diet that is high in fibre. This has the effect of slowing the digestion of the starches and so releasing sugars at a reasonably steady rate. These are absorbed from the intestines into the bloodstream at a similar steady rate. The limited amount of insulin produced is sufficient to cope with this steady intake of sugar. Without the fibre the digested sugars would be absorbed rapidly and overwhelm the limited supply of insulin.

Key things to monitor in diets for diabetics are:

- sugar content (glucose and sucrose)
- complex carbohydrates (starches and fibre).

## Vegetarian diets

Vegetarians are people who do not eat meat. There are a wide variety of preferences within this, but we will use the term vegetarian to indicate those people who eat no meat or fish, but who do eat eggs, milk and milk products. Those people who eat no animal products are called vegans (see below).

There are few problems in vegetarian diets, as all nutrients are available. Milk and eggs are first-class protein sources (see page 178). However, their protein contents need to be monitored as these foods also contain a lot of saturated fat. Beans and grains provide second-class protein sources. It is important, therefore, for the diet to contain a mixture of beans and grains to provide all the essential amino acids.

The vitamin and mineral content of the diet is normally reasonable as cheese, milk and eggs are good sources of the B and D vitamins that are commonly provided by meat in non-vegetarian diets.

## Vegan diets

This much stricter form of vegetarianism requires a closer attention to balancing the diet. Because protein has to come from plant sources, it means that at least two different sources are required to provide the correct balance of amino acids.

There are two micronutrients that are difficult to provide in a vegan diet:

- Calcium is available in small amounts from green vegetables and flour that is fortified with calcium carbonate. It is a legal requirement for some flours to contain added calcium.
- Vitamin B12 is more difficult to provide. It almost always comes from animal sources and these are unacceptable for vegans. One natural source is yeast extract which contains less than 0.4 per cent of the amount from the best animal source. Most people on a vegan diet therefore take supplements of vitamin B12 extracted from bacterial sources.

### Activity 7

This activity requires you to plan and cost a meal. You need to research the information yourself. What we can do is give you some guidelines on how to undertake your initial research.

*Identify your client's dietary needs*
You will need to identify a client for whom you are going to plan the meal. If this client is a real person, it would be useful to find out what foods he or she likes and how much money would normally be spent on food for a week. If you are not working with a real person, make up the details of your client. Base the money available on things like state benefits.

▶▶

**Key Skills**

You can use Activity 7 to provide evidence for Key Skills Information Technology IT1.1, IT1.2 and Application of Number N1.1, N1.2 and N1.3.

Obtain a copy of the most up-to-date reference nutrient intakes that you can and also a copy of food tables. These may be available in the form of a computer program that will help you to analyse the diet.

Use the table of reference nutrient intakes to identify your client's needs.

*Research the cost of foods*
This can be carried out with the help of your colleagues. Make a list of all of the foods you are likely to want to provide. This list should cover all of your ideas and those of your colleagues. Divide the list up, with each of you taking one part, and find the prices from your local shops. (Hint: Many supermarkets include on their price labels a price per unit, such as the price for 100g.)

Get together and produce a computer database or spreadsheet that lists the foods and their prices.

*Present the menu to your client*
When you are satisfied that your meal meets the dietary requirements and that the costs are acceptable, you should prepare a written menu for your client. This should include:

- details of each course
- the cost of each course and the total cost
- a description of how the meal meets the needs of your client
- an outline of the roles of each of the nutrients you have analysed in the diet.

# 5.3 How to prepare meals hygienically

When preparing food you must keep hygiene in mind. You must ensure that all work surfaces and equipment are clean before and after use. Good hygienic practices will make for a more pleasing workplace and will reduce the risk of infections spreading. In your work placement, you should read the basic guidelines relating to hygiene and safety rules that must be enforced.

## Hygiene

- The most important thing is to wash your hands in warm water with soap before touching food.
- Wash after touching raw foods and before touching ready-to-eat foods.
- Wipe your hands on a separate kitchen towel.
- Bleach, disinfect kitchen cloths often.
- Always wear protective clothing when working in the kitchen.
- Make sure that jewellery and hair are not likely to get into food.

- Cover cuts and grazes.
- Clean up spilt food straight away.
- Avoid cross-contamination of raw and cooked foods by preparing them on separate surfaces and washing hands and equipment after use.

## Cross-contamination

This will involve mopping up spills and wiping work surfaces, tables and chairs as required. Proprietary cleaners in the correct dilution should be used. Hand basins should be cleaned at least once every 24 hours using a proprietary cleaner, hot water and clean or disposable cloths. You will find that different establishments use a variety of cleaning agents, including bleach solutions. Check the health and safety regulations in the workplace before you use these cleaning materials.

## Food poisoning

- Always dispose of waste matter carefully, using appropriate containers.
- Always make sure you have instructions from your supervisor.
- Never leave cleaning materials where people, especially small children, can reach them.
- Protect yourself by always reading instructions on labels of cleaning agents that you use and avoid coming into contact with them by using gloves and overalls or aprons.

## Food storage

To avoid food poisoning, areas where food is prepared, whether in a caring establishment or a client's home, need to be kept scrupulously clean. All work surfaces must be wiped frequently. Bleach solutions are appropriate for this.

- Always keep chilled food in the fridge or freezer.
- Always keep the coolest part of the fridge at between 0°C and 5°C. Make sure that the freezer is below –18°C.
- In the fridge keep raw meat and fish apart so that they cannot drip on to or touch other food. Make sure that they are thoroughly wrapped and kept separate from other foods.
- Always read the labels on food. This information will tell you the sell-by date, name of the food, ingredients, weight or volume, usage and storage instructions.

*Why keep raw meat separate from other foods?*

When you cook:

- use a separate board and knife for raw meat
- make sure that meat and poultry are well cooked
- cool cooked foods as quickly as possible and then put them in the fridge or freezer

*Why should ill people not eat raw eggs?*

- make sure that people do not eat raw eggs or uncooked food made from them (raw eggs contain bacteria that can lead to food poisoning)
- when cooking for babies or elderly or ill people make sure that eggs are cooked until white and yolk are solid
- do not reheat cooked meat.

## Key terms

After reading this unit you should be able to understand the following words and phrases. If you do not, go back through the unit and find out, or look them up in the Glossary.

| | |
|---|---|
| *Balanced diet* | *Micronutrients* |
| *Nutrients* | *Minerals* |
| *Macronutrients* | *Fibre* |
| *Protein* | *Reference nutrient intake* |
| *Fat* | *Vitamins* |
| *Carbohydrate* | *Vegetarian* |

## Test yourself

1  What are the seven types of nutrient?
2  Which of the seven types are:
   (a)  macronutrients?
   (b)  micronutrients?
3  What is the function of protein in the diet?
4  What is the main vitamin found in oranges?
5  How does the nutritional requirement for a young child differ from an adolescent person?
6  Using the *Balance of Good Health* guidelines, which foods should you eat lots of?
7  What types of food does a vegan not eat?
8  Name two religious groups who do not eat pork.
9  What are the detrimental effects of being overweight?

# Assignment for Unit Five

*In this assignment you are asked to prepare a plan for a balanced diet that would meet the nutritional needs of one person for one day. You must prepare two courses from meal(s) you have identified in your plan.*

Remember this menu is for your client and so it should be produced so that he or she can understand it. If it is for a very young child, it should be written so that the parent or carer can understand it. If the menu is for a real person, ask for his or her views on the menu you have planned.

Suggestions for clients (remember you can adapt these for vegetarians):

A 6-year-old child who takes a packed lunch to school.

Your teacher who never has time to cook a big meal other than at weekends.

An elderly relative who likes to have breakfast, lunch, tea and supper.

A new friend who has just moved to your town, who is a Sikh, Muslim or Jew.

An 8-year-old child who is violently ill if he has milk or milk products (including yoghurt, cream, butter and cheese).

*Tasks*

1　You will need to find out what are the commonly available foods from the five food groups when planning the diet.

2　When planning the meal you need to take into account your chosen person's preferences and requirements. You will also need to work out what a standard serving is for each of the foods:

(a)　Food tables normally give nutritional details per 100g of each item of food. For as many items as possible, weigh or estimate the weight of a standard serving. Use this figure to calculate the nutrient content of the serving. Many packaged foods give details of the nutrient content. If they are not listed in the standard tables try to get a copy of the information on the label.

(b)　Write out your proposed menu for the day. Then produce your own food table with the following headings for each item of food in the meal:
  * energy per serving
  * protein per serving
  * fat per serving
  * fibre per serving
  * iron per serving
  * calcium per serving
  * vitamin C per serving
  * vitamin D per serving
  * cost of the food.
  At the bottom of each column add up all the values to get the total figure for that meal.

　　▶▶

To achieve a **PASS** you must complete tasks 1–4.

To achieve a **MERIT** you must complete tasks 1–7.

To achieve a **DISTINCTION** you must complete tasks 1–9.

(c) When you have done this try to put together the meals that provide the daily requirement for energy, adjusted to suit your client's needs. *You may need to change the foods to get the costs to meet your target.*

(d) Once you are satisfied that you have the energy requirements and costs right, you can then work out the daily intake of protein and fat.

(e) Calculate how much of each of the micronutrients (vitamins and minerals) the meal contains. For each micronutrient divide the number by seven to calculate the average daily intake.

3  Prepare the food hygienically and safely (make sure that you meet any specific requirements of the food preparation area in which you are working).

4  Present the meals to the person you have chosen hygienically and as planned.

5  Show different ways of meeting your chosen person's dietary needs.

6  Prepare and cook the two courses within a realistic time frame and meet deadlines.

7  Combine food appropriately in both courses and present the dishes in an attractive way.

8  Evaluate your diet plan, taking into account the nutritional content, time, resources and available budget. Also explain how the plan meets the needs of your chosen person.

9  Independently present the two courses in a way that appeals to and suits your chosen person.

## *Key Skills*  *Opportunity*

| | You can use this opportunity to provide evidence for the following key skills |
|---|---|
| Communication C1.1 | Plan the diet by discussion with the chosen person. |
| Communication C1.2 | Plan the diet by reading and getting information. |
| Communication C1.3 | Plan the diet by writing two different types of menus. |
| Application of Number N1.1 | Produce a plan for a balanced diet (when using nutritional tables for example). |
| Application of Number N1.2 | Prepare two courses from the plan for the day. Work within a given budget. |

# Exploring health and recreational activities

## What is covered in this unit

6.1 **The benefits of recreational activity**
6.2 **Learning about the recreational facilities available in your community**
6.3 **How local facilities can be used by clients to enhance their well-being**
6.4 **Barriers that might make it difficult for people to use health and recreational facilities**
6.5 **Health and safety factors associated with health and recreational facilities**

At the end of this unit you will be asked to produce a report about locally available recreational activities. If you would like to see further details of the tasks you are likely to need to carry out for assessment, please refer to the end of the unit where an assignment has been set (see pages 235–236). This unit will guide you through what you need to know in order to successfully put together this report. You will be assessed on this work and awarded a grade. This grade will contribute to the overall grade you will get for Unit Six.

### Materials you will need to complete this unit

- Information from local facilities, i.e. craft centres, day centres, leisure centres, nurseries, sports centres and youth clubs
- Local directory of local services, usually published by the Local Council for Voluntary Services
- Local telephone and trade directories
- Map of the local area.

### Introduction

Recreation covers a broad range of activities. In this unit you will look at the role of recreation in supporting:

* physical development
* intellectual development
* social development.

You will not only be considering your own recreation, but also looking at appropriate recreation for a wide range of people.

## 6.1 The benefits of recreational activity

Recreational activities are important for health and well-being. You will already be familiar with the ideas of keeping fit to maintain health, but recreation helps to maintain more than just physical health. The role of recreational activities in maintaining intellectual and social well-being is also important. It is useful to consider the three areas of **intellectual, social** and **physical recreational activities**.

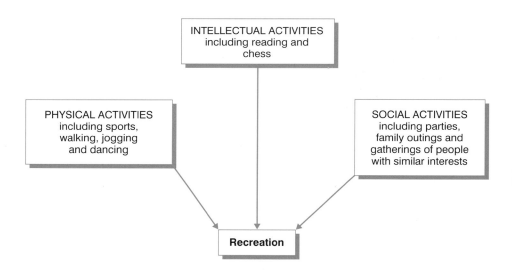

Recreation can be taken to mean anything that is done as a leisure pursuit. Hobbies are recreational. For some people their paid work may also be an enjoyable recreation. However, for this unit, we will limit recreation to leisure activities. In some cases these may also form part of a therapy. That is, they may be part of a programme to maintain health and well-being – many occupational therapy activities are recreational.

*Recreation can take many forms. Different activities appeal to different groups of people*

**Key Skills**

You can use Activity 1 to provide evidence for Key Skills Communication C1.3.

**Activity 1**

**a** For each of the following activities write down the type of person most suited to it. Give reasons for your choices:

- Disco dancing
- Ballroom dancing
- Riding a tricycle
- Playing with dressing-up clothes
- Football
- Cricket
- Swimming
- Crown green bowling
- Ten-pin bowling
- Alpine skiing
- Playing chess
- Reading
- Hill walking
- Playing pool
- Listening to jazz music
- Drawing and painting
- Model making
- Knitting

**b** What might stop someone from undertaking any of the activities?

In Activity 1 you will have identified some recreational activities that are associated with different client groups. For example, disco dancing is seen as an activity for young people. Crown green bowling may be seen as a pastime for older men. The stereotypes are not accurate, but they do help us to consider some issues about different recreational activities.

## The benefits of recreation

---

### Activity 2

a Write down what recreational activities you do.
b Why do you do these activities?
c Analyse the activities in terms of the three types of recreation (physical, social and intellectual). Write down a few sentences about your findings.

---

The answers to the questions in Activity 2 most probably have a very strong theme of liking what you do. Recreation normally has the emotional benefit that you enjoy doing it. This is a very positive benefit as it fits in with the idea of recreation bringing a balance back to your life. Where work, school or college may be stressful, recreation provides activities that, while being demanding, are also relaxing.

## Physical benefits

Physical activity contributes to fitness in several ways:

- *strength* – the ability of muscles to work over short periods of time. It is required for lifting or in the act of jumping
- *stamina* – the ability for muscles to continue working without fatigue (becoming tired)
- *suppleness* – the flexibility of the joints. Exercise to develop suppleness is part of warming up and avoids strains to muscles and joints
- *speed of reaction* – the ability to respond rapidly to changes. This is linked to things like hand–eye co-ordination. Linked to these are improved balance and agility
- *heart and lung efficiency* – regular physical recreation makes the heart, lungs and circulation work. Exercise improves these organs' ability to provide oxygen to the body. This has the benefit of reducing risks of heart disease
- *determination* – regular physical activity has a knock-on effect in providing the determination to follow tasks through to a finish. Different physical activities develop different aspects of fitness. Jogging and dancing develop stamina. Gymnastics improves suppleness. Badminton improves strength, suppleness and stamina.

**Why was the NHS formed?**

Clearly activities need to be balanced with ability and age. Well-thought-out physical recreation provides benefits to physical health. It is also important to recognise that there are many activities that are not considered to be sports, but that also contribute to physical health, such as recreational dancing and walking for pleasure.

*Problem-solving provides mental stimulation for people of all ages*

## Intellectual benefits

You may think that all your mental activity should be confined to school or college. Recreation should be relaxing. Intellectual activity can, however, provide a stimulating, satisfying and, at the same time, relaxing recreation. The types of activity often involve problem-solving in some way, such as in games like chess.

Reading also provides an intellectual stimulus. Reading for relaxation can involve stories that stimulate your imagination. Using your imagination stimulates mental activity and satisfaction in the enjoyment of the story. Many books also involve problem-solving as part of the enjoyment. Mysteries and detective stories often give sufficient information to enable you to solve the problem before the main characters.

Problem-solving activities and using your imagination both lead to a more active mind. You can use your experiences from reading to help make connections and solve problems for yourself in your life. Strategy games or books that involve thinking about choices help to make you analyse questions, such as 'What would happen if . . .?'. This can carry over into your daily activities where you start to think further about the consequences of your actions.

Many hobbies like collecting, learning new skills (such as playing musical instruments) or making objects (models or pottery) involve intellectual skills. Meeting with others with similar interests in clubs and societies provides some of the social benefits of recreation.

## Social benefits

People are naturally social animals. One of the worst possible tortures is to deprive a person of contact with other people. To be social animals we need to know how to interact with other people.

Young children often appear to be very selfish. They do not know how to share. They always want things for themselves and their needs are most important. Many recreational activities for young children help them to learn about playing with other children and sharing. A major importance of pre-school activities is in learning these social skills. A second important aspect is to see many different children acting in different ways. These different role models help the child to learn how to interact with other people.

The need for social contact is recognised in most caring systems. For older people, there is a risk of isolation. Where a husband or wife dies, the surviving partner may be left to live in a house with little contact with other people. This isolation can be worsened by difficulties in moving out of the house. Many social services departments recognise this and organise day centres to support people by coming together for social interaction. Other recreational activities are often provided to support this. Dances, bingo and special swimming sessions for pensioners, for example, can all be provided to help maintain social interaction.

Any social interaction helps people to understand each other. For adolescents, the social interaction may be in situations where individuals can start to explore relationships. Many youth clubs, discos and youth organisations are offered to provide an opportunity for individuals to meet and learn about each other. In some cases, these relationships may develop further into friendship or, in some cases, marriage.

Shared recreational activities imply shared interests. This is the first step towards friendship. The benefits of recreational activities are normally a mixture of physical, intellectual and social. The mixture contributes to a balanced personality and a balanced lifestyle.

**You can use Activity 3 to provide evidence for Key Skills Communication C1.2.**

### Activity 3

Read the comments below. Describe the benefits each young person is gaining from his or her activities.

**a** 'I really enjoy playing tennis. Even though sometimes I feel a bit slow, I know when I start to warm up that I'll feel better. I seem to have more energy when I play than when I don't bother going down to the sessions.'

**b** 'When I've been working in the evening, I look forward to going to the youth club. It gives me a chance to catch up on the gossip, to relax and unwind with my friends.'

**c** 'I like the challenge of climbing, of pushing myself to the limit of taking a risk. Although I'm scared, it's still a inspiring experience.'

**d** 'I need to get out of the house a bit at weekends. That's why I like to meet up with my friends and go to town. I need to talk to people of my own age. I think I need to have my own space – some independence.'

**e** 'I like going away on training weekends with the football club. It's interesting thinking about meeting new people and even more interesting when you might arrange to see someone again afterwards.'

**f** 'I'm not much good at art really, but I love painting, using colour. I feel really free when I settle down to paint, focused but free – strange really.'

**g** 'We have some really good discussions down at the youth group. The sessions really make me think about big issues like politics, religion and relationships.'

**i** 'When I'm at school, I feel I'm one of a huge number, but when I'm helping at the old persons' home, I feel important, wanted and useful.'

How did you get on? Could you describe how the activities were of value to the young people? Did you think about how they might need physical challenges, company of people their own age, time to relax, chances to take risks, time to be away from parents, opportunities to meet people, chances to make friends with the opposite gender, time to be alone, space to concentrate, a forum to sort out what they really think, a way of raising self-esteem and self-identity?

# 6.2 Learning about the recreational facilities available in your community

## Surveying local recreational activities

A major task for this unit is for you to identify what recreational facilities are available locally and look at their use. This can best be done as a series of tasks in Activity 4 below. You will need to work in co-operation with your colleagues.

**Key Skills**

You can use Activity 4 to provide evidence for Key Skills and Communication C1.2 and C1.3 and Information Technology IT1.1.

### Activity 4

Choose a local facility, such as a local sports centre or day centre for elderly or physically disabled people. Visit your chosen facility and find out the following:　▶▶

a What are the recreational activities available?
b What are the opening hours and costs of activities? Are there any days when it is not open, such as Sundays or Christmas?
c Name the main groups of clients who use the facility.
d What is the nature of the client groups – age, physical condition (for example, are they expected to be fit), any special needs they may have (for example, a social recreation club for physically disabled and able-bodied people)?
e How often is the facility used and when is it used?
f How long do people spend on the chosen activity (for example, some people may play squash for 40 minutes or a chess club may involve people for 3 hours or more)?
g What are the physical, social and intellectual benefits. Which benefit might the people involved in the activity identify?
h What are the barriers to access, if any – physical barriers, attitudes, costs, specialist equipment, clothing, location or transport? Is there easy public transport? Do people attend from all over the district or are they very local? Are there times when the facility is not available because it is booked on a regular basis by one group of people? Where there are barriers, try to suggest ways in which they can be overcome.

## 6.3 How local facilities can be used by clients to enhance their well-being

### The suitability of an activity

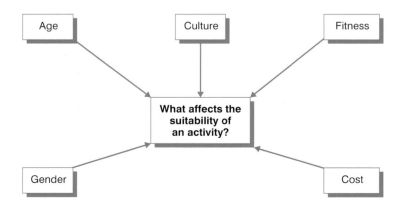

## Age

The age of a person can be very important in identifying recreational activities. This can be because the activity is one that can be dated as to when it became popular.

Many recreational activities become popular for a short time and then another takes its place. This may be related to something new being made available or it may be that someone has popularised the activity. For example, ice skating became very popular after Torvill and Dean won several competitions. Chess increased in popularity with television coverage of the world championships.

The age of a person may also give clues as to the books he or she reads. The books of J.R.R. Tolkein, for example, were very popular in the 1960s and 1970s. Popular books in the early 1990s have been adventure stories that allow the reader to make decisions and solve problems.

Age has an effect on physical recreation. Some activities require skills and strength to be developed and are most appropriate for people when they are at their fittest as adolescents and young adults. Such activities may be inappropriate for elders, where speed of reaction is reduced. The risks of injury in such situations may be of importance in choosing types of physical recreation.

Here are some activities that may be inappropriate recreation for different groups because of their age:

- *Young children* would find games with complex rules or requiring good hand–eye co-ordination difficult. Team games involving the use of a ball fit into this category. Young children have difficulty understanding the idea of rules and are not sufficiently physically developed to cope with the moving ball.
- *Elders* could well find physical recreation requiring rapid reactions difficult. Bones and joints become weaker with age and so physical activities that put these under strain need careful checking. As with children, but for different reasons, many games like hockey, netball and tennis become less accessible.

It is important to recognise that these are generalisations and individuals do not always fit into the stereotype for their age.

## Fitness

Fitness is often linked to age. This is a combination of strength, suppleness and efficiency of the heart, lungs and circulation. It is unwise for anyone to undertake physical activity without considering personal fitness. Most of us would not expect to be able to run a marathon. However, many people of all ages do develop fitness over time to enable them to do so.

## Gender

Many recreational activities are considered to be suitable for just males or just females – we call these gender stereotypes.

---

### Activity 5

**a** For each of the activities listed below, note down the sex of people most often associated with it. In some cases the answer may be 'both'. Take football, for example. We know that women and girls do play football, but it is generally associated with being a male sport.
  - Squash
  - Badminton
  - Netball
  - Aerobics
  - Hockey
  - Swimming
  - Disco dancing
  - Ballet
  - Chess
  - Reading
  - Snooker and pool.

**b** How would you react if you were asked to be involved in an activity that was considered not for your gender?

**c** How would other people react to you?

---

The issue of gender is not just that only men or only women are able to do certain things. Difficulties may also arise because of:

  - stereotypes. In many cases it is less easy for one sex to get access to an activity
  - a person's socialisation. For example, some women may feel uncomfortable in mixed sex swimming.

There are gender differences in many team activities. Where physical strength is involved it is unusual to find mixed sex teams of people beyond their early teens. This does not mean that the activities are not enjoyed by both sexes and it is often the case that the club involved has separate teams for men and women.

*The designers of this club didn't think women would be using it!*

## Culture

When considering suitable activities, a person's culture may affect the choice. Culture refers to beliefs, values and religion. For example, there are religions that have dress codes that make some physical activities less accessible. Muslim women would not be expected to show their legs in mixed company. Swimming would therefore have to be in single sex swimming sessions.

## Cost

One of the biggest factors concerning the suitability of activities is related to the amount of money available. Even a free activity may have hidden costs related to the equipment required. Often organised activities involve costs that put them outside the reach of many people. Even where costs are low, they may be too great for some people. Access to a playgroup may be a benefit to both parent and child. The cost, including travel, may make it an infrequent luxury.

*There are often hidden costs that reduce access to some recreational activities*

Cost also needs to be considered for the different groups:

- *Children and adolescents* may pay for activities from their limited amount of pocket money. Immediately, they have to balance the value of the recreation to them with the value of other demands on their money. Many activities are available to children at a reduced cost to reflect this.
- Similar considerations need to be made for *elders*. Many elders have a low income and the cost of activities needs to be balanced against their need for other things. Again, this is recognised in price reductions for pensioners.
- For *families*, the cost of any activity needs to be balanced against the already high costs of running the family. If the family undertakes recreational activities together, the cost may be several times the cost for an individual. There are, of course, many activities where the purchase of family tickets reduces the cost.

With all of these groups the cost of any specialist equipment is not reduced because of age or family size.

When considering suitability of any activity, the amount of money available becomes an important consideration. Factors include not only the daily costs of undertaking the activity, but also the costs of any materials, equipment and travel.

## Activities beneficial for different client groups

After completing Activity 5, you will have the tools to help you to consider aspects of recreational activities that affect choice. Broadly speaking, the different groups of people to consider are:

- children
- adolescents
- elders
- families.

For activities to be beneficial they need to match the needs and abilities of the individuals. There should also be a balance in terms of physical, social and intellectual pursuits.

### Children

Most of us would consider playing or play to be the major recreational activity for children. Play provides physical, intellectual and social benefits. The type of play will depend upon the stage of development that the child is at (see Unit Three). Some physical activities, such as swimming, are appropriate for children of all ages. Other activities such as team games (football, hockey, netball etc.) require physical, intellectual and social development before they are appropriate. Young children may not have:

- the physical co-ordination to catch or hit a ball
- the intellectual development to understand rules
- the social development to play co-operatively in a team.

#### *What recreational activities are suitable for young children?*
For young children, much of their recreation occurs in and around the home. Often it involves supervision and co-operation from an adult. Typical activities and the areas that they address might include:

- drawing, painting and colouring – physical and intellectual
- looking at books – intellectual
- playing with dolls – social and intellectual
- dressing up – intellectual and social
- pretend cooking – intellectual, social and physical.

This list could, of course, be extended. Most toys for young children support their need for physical, social and intellectual activities.

For most children, recreation involving social interaction with other children takes place with friends in the home or in organised groups. Organised groups include playgroups, crèches and nurseries. These groups also provide recreational activities that clearly support physical and intellectual needs.

Some organised physical recreational activities are available for young children. Most swimming pools have specific times for parents and young children. Gymnastic activities are also available in association with national gymnastic associations. Both of these clearly provide for physical recreation.

Many local authorities provide playgrounds for children with climbing frames, swings and slides. These offer opportunities for recreation, particularly physical, but also involve social interaction. Fantasy play, for example by turning the climbing frame into a fortress, is a form of intellectual recreation.

---

### Activity 6

This activity can take place anywhere that children play. It is important that any adults present know what you are doing. It would be a suitable activity for a work placement.

**a** Observe a young child playing. List the different activities being undertaken in a period of 15 minutes.
**b** Next to each activity write down the areas it benefits (physical, intellectual or social).

---

*Examples of young children undertaking social and intellectual recreation*

### *What recreational activities are suitable for older children?*

As children get older the availability of organised recreational activities increases. The child's development makes organised team games possible. Parental involvement may reduce and the child may undertake some recreation away from home and parental supervision. Growing independence can make playgrounds and parks more available.

There are many organisations that provide supported recreation for children They include national provision through organisations like the Scouts, Guides and Woodcraft Folk. Each of these supports recreational activities across a wide age range.

Physical recreation through team sports, swimming and gymnastics are frequently organised by schools, sports or leisure centres. Discos are often organised for children, providing both social and physical recreation.

Normally, as children get older they learn to read. Reading becomes available as a form of recreation. It also makes games with written rules available for recreational activities.

Childhood is also a time when hobbies develop. These can involve:

- model-making in some form
- collecting
- developing skills in dance or playing a musical instrument.

All of these provide an intellectual side to recreation. They also offer opportunities of meeting people with similar interests, so bringing in the social aspects.

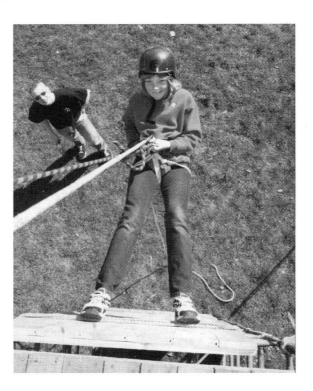

*The Guide Association provides opportunities for social, intellectual and physical recreation (such as rock climbing) that might not otherwise be available*

## Adolescents

This follows on from the developments in childhood. Again, as people get older, their independence increases. Recreation outside the home may be more easy to access. The range of activities includes social gatherings in youth clubs and other organised functions.

For many people adolescence is a time of peak physical fitness. It is also a time when recreation patterns become established and are maintained throughout the rest of life. Access to and availability of recreation facilities can be very important at this stage of life.

The social aspect of recreational activities now becomes very important. It is a time where relationships are being explored and many recreational activities involve social groupings.

Adolescence is a time when gangs may form. The term 'gang' describes a group of people who may behave in ways that are unacceptable to other people. Sometimes a gang may form partly because there are no other facilities available for recreational activities.

*Social and physical recreation are important aspects of being at a disco*

## Elders

A common stereotype of elders implies that physical recreation has to be limited. This view is incorrect. What must be taken into account is the need to ensure the physical recreation is appropriate. Care needs to be taken to ensure that the activities help maintain the body, rather than damage it. Activities can be physically demanding without causing damage.

Elders are not at a peak of physical fitness because:

- reaction speeds reduce with age
- bones become more fragile and injuries take longer to heal
- heart, lungs and circulation are less efficient than when they were much younger.

All of these will affect the choice of activity. Often recreation that is physical and also has a social focus is appropriate. The stereotypical game for older people is often considered to be bowls. It meets the needs on many counts. It involves some physical activity. There is a very strong social element of meeting with other people and having time to talk. The skill of controlling the ball and playing to win involves an intellectual challenge.

## Families

Potentially a family includes all the groups of people already mentioned (children, adolescents and elders) together with adults. Suitable activities ideally meet the needs of all members. This is difficult, but not impossible. Certainly it is possible for all members of a family to benefit from swimming, for example.

There are difficulties, and shared activities have to involve co-operation from all members of the family. An adult can transfer an enthusiasm for reading by reading to younger children. The enthusiasm can also be transmitted by being together while reading separate books.

Some recreational activities have been designed with families in mind. Theme parks often attempt to provide recreation for all members of the family. In these situations a variety of activities are available for people of different ages.

*Reading is a shared recreation that provides intellectual stimulation. Parents can communicate an enthusiasm for reading to their children*

## Recreational activities for people with specific needs

So far we have considered recreational activities in general. There are many people who, for a variety of reasons, may have specific recreational needs. For example:

- people living alone need to be able to take part in social activities
- people with disabilities may need support to take part in some forms of recreation

- elderly people may have a variety of specific needs for recreation that reflect age, mobility or living alone
- other people may have needs because of their concerns about their own obesity (overweight).

In all of these cases, the choice of recreation has to be made to provide for the need. To suggest that a person living alone undertakes solitary recreation, such as jogging, does not meet the need for social recreation. To encourage an obese person to take up physical activities involving strenuous exercise would be dangerous to his or her health. You would also need to consider the feelings of an obese person who may be embarrassed to exercise where others may laugh at their obesity.

Many of the issues associated with specific needs can be addressed by increasing awareness of the issues. In the case study of Jane (page 231) we will see how awareness enabled a person with disabilities to participate in recreational activities. Let us now consider specific groups in more detail.

### Activity 7

Read the comments below. Decide what needs are being satisfied by each activity:

a 'When I practise yoga, I feel so completely relaxed that I sleep better and seem to be less harassed during the day.' *Mother of three young children*

b 'I was delighted when Phil was asked to swim for the school. He had been a bit low after that bullying incident.' *Father of a 10-year-old boy*

c 'Sometimes I think I won't go to the day centre when I feel in one of those "can't be bothered" moods. But then I urge myself to get going, have a wash and shave, change my shirt and make an effort. I always feel better for having made the effort. I need that motivation for a bit of self-discipline.' *Seventy-six-year-old man*

d 'I'm so glad I've mastered the Eureka computer. It gives me a chance to write my poems.' *Adolescent girl with very little sight*

e 'I look forward to playing a bit of snooker on Friday nights at the club. I can meet my friends and I'm improving – we have a laugh.' *Teenage boy*

f 'One thing about gardening, it's a good excuse to get out in the fresh air. It's an interest. I look forward to the spring, and in the winter I'm busy with seeds. All that bending and stretching, I don't need to go to keep fit. It's a pity I'm not so enthusiastic about housework!' *Older woman*

g 'I've always danced – I think I danced before I walked! I love to move and I feel I can interpret the music when I dance. The classes help me to improve.' *Seventeen-year-old boy*

## People with physical disabilities

This covers a wide range of disabilities and may include people who:

- are visually impaired
- are hearing impaired
- are wheelchair users
- have a limited range of movements (such as severe arthritis)
- have poor muscle control (such as cerebral palsy, Parkinson's disease, multiple sclerosis).

All of these people have one thing in common – they suffer from the attitudes of others. Many well-meaning people try to take control of their lives and tell them what they ought to do in terms of recreation.

While some people with disabilities may feel unable to participate in some recreational activities, most will be able to identify activities they would like to undertake. In many cases, the recreational activity can be developed to support the specific need.

People with disabilities have the same needs for recreation as everyone else:

- physical recreation
- social recreation
- intellectual recreation.

Physical activities may have an important health-related role in improving mobility, but that is also true for everyone else.

One aspect of physical disability that creates issues for able-bodied people is social recreation. There is a tendency for activities to be organised for people with similar disabilities. These can be very useful as self-help groups, but they do tend to limit contact with others. The reactions of able-bodied people to those with disabilities provides a barrier to many activities in general. This can cause feelings of isolation from society, with social links only developing among other people with similar disabilities.

Recreational activities for people with disabilities should cover all of those available in general. Allowances may need to be made for disability. After all, if marathon races were segregated then few of the runners would have any contact with the competitors in wheelchairs.

It may be necessary to allocate facilities and times specifically for people with disabilities. This goes against much that has just been said, but in competitive activities where the disability is significant then it would be reasonable. Other situations should encourage participation of all. As we will see in the case study of Jane (on page 231), adaptations to the environment are more important than providing separate activities.

*Many recreational facilities are made available to people who find access difficult*

## People with specific health-related problems

This category would include obese people and those with heart and circulation problems. There are two issues involved in selecting recreational activities. These are related to:

- self-esteem
- health and safety.

### *Self-esteem*

Any recreational activity that exposes a person to embarrassment will lower his or her self-esteem. An obese person may feel unable to participate in an activity because of the possible comments of others. This is an instance where self-help groups can be important.

In health terms, an obese person needs to lose weight. Recreation may be directed to this goal, with physical activity and diet contributing. If the physical activity is carried out with others who are obese, the

**225**

embarrassment factor can be reduced. There is also an element of understanding and pressure from colleagues that helps a person to continue in the activity. This social aspect of the recreation is important.

*Providers of facilities are concerned about health and safety. Notices and lifeguards remind people of hazards*

*List two issues to be considered when selecting recreational activities.*

Swimming is a very appropriate activity for both obese people and those with heart and circulatory disorders. The buoyancy provided by the water reduces the stresses on joints and the exercise can be tailored to meet specific needs. Swimming provides exercise that improves muscle tone and joint flexibility. It improves breathing and increases the heart rate. Both benefit the respiratory and circulatory systems.

## Recreation for elders

Many elders maintain a healthy, independent lifestyle. They organise their lives to meet their recreational needs. It is not this group that we will consider in this section.

For some elders, specific recreational support is needed. Those living alone may need support in maintaining social activities. Others may have very little mobility and need assistance in physical activity. There are also needs to provide intellectual stimulation.

Facilities available that provide recreation specifically for elders include day centres and residential homes. Some leisure centres also run specific sessions to support the recreation needs of elders.

Day centres and residential homes provide a variety of activities. For example, they provide a place where people meet socially, offering

*A day centre provides a place for social and intellectual recreation for elderly people*

opportunities for conversation and other forms of social recreation. They also provide intellectual recreation in a variety of ways:

- It may be associated with playing games. These may be group games, such as bingo, or individual challenges, such as chess and draughts.
- With some people the intellectual stimulation has to be organised on a one-to-one basis by the care workers. Conversation with care workers, involving talking about things that have happened in the past, is important. Using photographs and things from the past to stimulate memories also enables people to think about the present.
- Intellectual recreation can also include activities related to occupational therapy. Intellectual activity may come from concentrating on painting, sewing or knitting. It may come from practising a skill like cooking. All of these also have benefits in physical activity. They do not provide exercise like swimming, but they support fine movements, and help maintain hand and finger mobility.

# 6.4 Barriers that might make it difficult for people to use health and recreational facilities

## Factors influencing activities

So far we have only been able to touch on some of the factors relating to recreation for people with specific needs. Some (cost, accessibility, the time, requirements of health and safety and physical access) affect everyone, not just those with specific needs.

The major difference is that specific needs may require support. It may be to:

- *help a person gain independent access to recreation*. An example of this would be the provision of grab rails around a swimming pool to allow people with mobility difficulties to use the pool safely. Your survey of local facilities from Activity 4 should have identified some similar examples
- *provide the support of another person*. For example, a visually disabled runner may need a companion to run alongside. At a riding school for disabled people, each rider is accompanied by a helper. Without the support of the helper the individual would not be able to undertake and enjoy the activity.

## Availability

One common complaint is that there are not enough facilities available to meet the needs of everyone. For example, the availability of golf courses does not meet demand and so there is often a long waiting list for membership of golf clubs. The same complaint can be levelled at the provision of almost any recreational activity, but it would be impractical to provide facilities for everyone who wanted them. There will always be some level of rationing.

The facility may be available locally, but bookings may mean that it is not available at convenient times. Many local authority-owned swimming pools, for example, have limited access for the general public because they are booked for clubs or school swimming lessons. There are also times when the pool is booked for specific groups, such as elders or parents and toddlers.

Availability affects activities like reading, just as much as physical activities. Often you may wish to borrow the latest bestseller from the library and it is already on loan. The only answers are either to buy the book (too expensive) or to reserve it and wait until it is returned!

Social recreation is often controlled by the availability of the activity. Rooms may only be available for dancing at certain times. Organisations such as the Scouts or youth clubs normally have regular meeting times during the week. There may also be irregular meetings at other times. Many leisure centres and libraries offer rooms for hire, but these are often booked well in advance, so to organise a leisure activity may require planning.

---

### Activity 8

**a** Go to a recreational facility close to your home and find what activities are available. Obtain a timetable of the activities, if this is appropriate.

**b** Find out whether you would need to book a room, a court or a pitch, and how you would do so. Also, find how far in advance you would need to book to get the facility you would like.

**c** Check whether any organisations have regular bookings that reduce your freedom of choice in the time that you could use the facility.

**d** Find out any costs involved.

**Key Skills**

You can use Activity 8 to provide evidence for Key Skills Communication C1.2 and C1.2.

## Improving availability

The availability of recreational resources is a difficult problem to address. It is possible to campaign for a new sports and leisure centre to be built in your locality. However, it is unlikely, though not impossible, to be successful. Even if successful, it would not solve the problem of availability for several months or years ahead.

What is more useful is to press for improved availability of existing facilities. For example, opening times may be extended. Schools and colleges may be prepared to make facilities available outside normal opening hours if there is sufficient demand. Improving availability often involves groups of people getting together to demonstrate a need.

## Physical access

Access to a recreational activity can be affected by the following factors:

- *The ability of different people to get to the necessary facilities.* Easy-to-identify problems, such as lack of wheelchair access, can stop some people from being able to participate in the recreation.
- *Availability of the activity in a specific locality.* It would be difficult for a rock climber to spend an evening after work climbing if he or she lived in an area like the Fens of Lincolnshire, for example. The area is flat and there are no natural rock faces. Someone living in the Peak District of Derbyshire would be much more able to have an evening climb.
- *Travelling times.* Even in areas where the facilities are available, travelling times can create problems. For example, a long journey to spend 40 minutes playing badminton may become unacceptable to a player. A difficult bus journey for someone with arthritis may stop attendance at a bingo session.

*Some thought and simple changes can remove barriers to physical access*

## Improving physical access

Problems of physical access to any facility should be easy to identify. Barriers produced by closed minds are more difficult. Many people stereotype disabled people and assume that some recreational activities should not be available to them. They may also limit access just to specific times when support can be given. For such situations, improved access to facilities can often be negotiated with support coming from volunteers.

### Case study: Jane

Swimming is an excellent physical recreation that provides exercise for almost all groups of people. Many swimming pools have barriers to some potential swimmers. For example, Jane has multiple sclerosis. She is able to walk, but very unsteadily. She was beginning to find it increasingly difficult to go swimming. Getting to the changing rooms was no problem. However, the pool had large baskets for clothes which had to be taken to an attendant for safe keeping. Jane could not safely carry the basket.

Going from the changing room to the pool involved walking through a footbath. Jane was very concerned that she would slip over. The same was true for her journey to the side of the pool. Once in the pool, Jane was able to swim and enjoy the ability to move around. The water supported her and made it possible to move much more freely than on land. However, getting out of the pool was a problem. All of the ladders were vertical and climbing out proved almost impossible.

The local authority, which owned the pool, were sympathetic to Jane's problems. Together they worked out what could be done. Hand rails were fixed in the changing rooms, the footbath and to the side of the pool. Steps were fitted that had a slope more like stairs. Immediately Jane was able to move about much more safely.

While they were discussing the adaptations, Jane also pointed out that adding Braille to signs would make access easier for people with impaired sight. The side of the pool could also have water depths in Braille.

The effects of the changes were monitored by the local authority. One of the things they noticed was that the number of parents with young babies attending swimming sessions dramatically increased. They started to ask why and realised that people carrying babies also have concerns about balance and slipping over. The rails and steps provided increased safety and more parents were happy to bring their babies swimming.

One thing that Jane said about her discussions with the local authority was that changing attitudes is the hardest part. If people talk to those with disabilities then change does not have to be expensive. The changes introduced do not have to make the people with disabilities feel singled out by having their disabilities emphasised.

## Cost

Cost can also be a barrier to access. It includes the cost of:

- specific equipment or clothing
- membership of a facility
- entry to a facility.

We have discussed some of these matters earlier, but it is worth repeating.

Where an activity is scarce the cost may be high. Membership fees for golf clubs can seem exorbitant. Private sports facilities often have membership fees that provide a barrier. Local authority-run facilities often have reduced rates for different groups of people, but these are often only available at specific times – another barrier to access.

Costs may not be obvious. Walking as a recreational activity often means that different routes are used for variety. The cost of transport to the start and finish of a walk may be a barrier. To be limited in the number of routes available can lead to boredom and becoming less enthusiastic about the activity.

Many social activities have implied costs. Most youth clubs, cinemas or theatres have food and drinks available. Expectations of friends may mean that an individual spends money on food and drink. This adds to the cost of the activity and may make it too expensive for some people with low incomes.

## Overcoming problems of cost

This can be approached in two main ways. The first is *by looking for recreation that involves little or no cost.* Many physical activities do not need specialist equipment or facilities. Walking and jogging only require the roads and paths that are readily available. Reading does not mean that expensive books have to be bought. Public libraries are able to obtain copies of almost any book you wish to ask for. There may be a small charge, but it is less than the cost of the book. The second way is *by trying to reduce costs.* This can be done in a number of ways, such as:

- Sharing transport costs often makes it possible to get to places that would otherwise be too expensive. This has the knock-on effect of increasing the social nature of the recreation.
- Many recreational facilities have special rates for groups. They may also have discounts for groups of people on low incomes. It is not unusual to find discounts for students, unwaged people and elders. It is also possible to find discounts offered for times when fewer people want to use a facility. For example, visiting the cinema in the early afternoon is often cheaper than the evening.
- Expensive equipment does not always need to be purchased. Many organisations offer to hire the equipment necessary to participate in an activity. This can extend to the hire of specific

uniform items. A local Scout or Guide group may loan equipment to help members participate fully.

## Attitudes

As we saw in the case study of Jane, attitude can be a barrier to access. This may be the prejudice of adults with regard to children. Statements like these need to be challenged: 'Children wouldn't want to . . .'; 'Children only mess around so we are not prepared to . . .'; 'It wouldn't be safe for blind people/people with cerebral palsy/disabled people to . . .'.

Where there appears to be no demand for something, then consider what the real barrier to access might be.

# 6.5 Health and safety factors associated with health and recreational facilities

It is important that, when taking part in recreational activity, both the carer and the client must be aware of any potential hazards in taking part in the activity. The following information is intended only to give some examples; each activity will present hazards, which are individual to the particular activity, for example rock climbing or mountaineering.

## Hazards – children's play

Are the grounds safe, i.e. soft, clear of broken glass etc.?

- Is the play equipment made of suitable materials – rubber, plastic or wood?
- Play equipment should be designed so that a child can't fall too far.
- Children using and playing with cycles should always wear a protective helmet and at night they should also wear bright coloured clothing and something reflective so that motorists can easily see them.

## Equipment

### Inspection

All equipment should be inspected to make sure it is safe and it should also be regularly maintained.

### Cleaning

This will prevent breakdowns and accidents.

### Regular testing

This will make sure that the equipment is running properly.

### Replacement

Equipment should be replaced when it begins to wear out or after a certain period of time (sometimes the makers will say when it should be replaced).

## Codes of practice

People taking part in recreational activities should always abide by the rules of the activity or the code of practice published by the sport's governing body. The United Kingdom Activity Centre Advisory Committee (ACAC) drew up a code of practice after an accident in which four teenagers lost their lives in a canoeing tragedy in 1993.

Remember also that the Health and Safety at Work Act applies to many recreational facilities such as sports halls and swimming pools.

| Some hazards at sports and leisure centres | |
| --- | --- |
| Slippery floors | Unhygienic toilets |
| Damaged sports equipment | Water too hot |
| Poor lighting | Blocked emergency exits |
| Use of untrained staff | Poor exit signs |

### Activity 9

You have been asked to organise a party of twenty under 5s in a local church hall.

Identify potential health and safety issues (in relation to the activities that will be carried out by the children and also the state of the hall and its equipment). How would you put right any health and safety issues that you identify?

### Key terms

After reading this unit you should be able to understand the following words and phrases. If you do not, go back through the unit and find out, or look them up in the Glossary.

*Intellectual recreational activities*          *Physical recreational activities*
*Social recreational activities*

## Test yourself

1 What are the three broad classes into which recreation can be divided?
2 Playing chess and reading are examples of what type of recreational activity?
3 Swimming with a group of friends falls into which recreational categories?
4 Give two examples of social recreational activities.
5 What factors might affect a person's choice of recreational activity?
6 What factors might be a barrier to a child playing golf?
7 What might put an obese person off physical recreation?
8 What benefits are gained by recreational activities?
9 Suggest a suitable physical activity for an active elderly person.
10 What safety issues might you need to consider for an elderly person undertaking strenuous physical activity?

# Assignment for Unit Six

### Report: Produce a booklet for your local leisure centre

You have been placed for work experience with the Local Leisure Centre. The first job they have asked you to do is to produce a booklet for local people.

You will need:

- a map of the area you are considering
- a Phone Book, Yellow Pages and a Thomson Directory of the area.

Use the directories and your own knowledge to find out what is available and where it is available. You may also find that your public library has a list of recreational organisations and clubs. As a guide, look for:

- sports centres
- swimming pools
- leisure centres
- outdoor pursuits centres
- cinemas
- theatres
- sports clubs, such as squash, bowls, athletics and archery
- societies and clubs, such as rambling associations, chess clubs and groups for collectors of items
- public libraries
- crèches, pre-school playgroups and nurseries.

### Get the grade

To achieve a **PASS** you must complete tasks 1 to 4.

To achieve a **MERIT** you must complete tasks 1 to 7.

To achieve a **DISTINCTION** you must complete tasks 1 to 9.

*Tasks*

1  Identify the main local recreational facilities and also identify at least six of these services on a map. Photographs could also be used.

2  Describe at a basic level how one client group could benefit from these facilities. Identify the client group that you wish to study. Use your previous activities to see whether there is any local provision for the group. It may be that you are working with (or have worked with) the group while on work experience. Arrange to talk to someone involved with the provision of the recreational activities for your client group. Write out a series of questions that you would like the person to answer. These might include questions about:

   * the activities that are appropriate and available
   * the needs, in terms of physical, social and intellectual activities
   * factors such as cost, time, health and safety, access and physical ability that affect the types of activity
   * any risks involved with the activity.

4  Identify basic health and safety issues related to the activities and the client group.

5  Identify and describe the barriers that people might have to overcome to make the best use of the facilities.

5  Demonstrate a sound understanding of the physical, social and emotional benefits of different recreational activity.

6  Identify how potential barriers to access might be overcome for specific recreational activities. It would be helpful if you visited at least two facilities in order to gain information.

7  Describe clearly how health and safety issues can be addressed.

8  Analyse the specific benefits (physical, social and intellectual) to clients of using recreational facilities.

9  Justify your selection of one particular facility for use by a client group, explaining why you rejected other facilities.

## Key Skills

| | You can use this opportunity to provide evidence for the following key skills |
|---|---|
| Application of Number N1.2 | Compare different facilities and use charts or diagrams. |
| Communication C1.1 | Orally present your findings. |
| Communication C1.2 | Identify local recreational facilities. |
| Communication C1.3 | Write a report on locally available facilities. |

# Exploring physical care

## What is covered in this unit

**7.1** **The reasons why and the ways in which people need help with daily living activities**

**7.2** **Where care is given to people and who gives physical care**

**7.3** **The types of equipment available to help people**

**7.4** **The importance of support and encouragement, the maintenance of independence and respect**

**7.5** **Health and safety issues**

At the end of this unit you will be asked to produce an investigation into the physical care of a person in a caring situation, including the physical needs and support required. You will also be required to demonstrate practical caring skills while observing safe practice. If you would like to see further details of the tasks you are likely to need to carry out for assessment, please refer to the end of the unit where an assignment has been set (see page 267–268). This unit will guide you through what you need to know in order to successfully carry out this investigation and demonstration. You will be assessed on this work and awarded a grade. This grade will contribute to the overall grade you will get for Unit Seven.

## Materials you will need to complete this unit

- Nursing manuals from first aid organisations
- Information from statutory and voluntary organisations (leaflets etc.)
- Information from local suppliers of care equipment (leaflets, catalogues etc.)
- NVQ L 2 Care Units.

## Introduction

Many people need physical help with a number of activities that they do every day. Any assistance offered to dependent people must be provided in a manner that will not harm the client or the carer. This chapter sets out to show how physical assistance can be offered in a way that is safe and that maintains the client's independence and dignity.

You have chosen to do this Foundation course because you want to work in social care, you have a caring personality and you want to help people. Your most important assets are your personality and your attitude towards the people you are caring for. Your attitude is most important when working with people with disabilities. They may, for example, have no control over movement, they may be unable to speak, or may have impaired sight or hearing. While you are in college you are the focus and attention of the tutors and other staff, but when you are working with clients you become part of a caring team. The clients are then the focus of your attention.

## 7.1 The reasons why and the ways in which people need help with daily living activities

### Why do people need help with daily living activities?

The quality of life of a client will depend to some extent on their being able to move around freely without pain, discomfort or danger. We all take mobility (a person's ability to walk, wash, dress, feed themselves etc.) for granted from the time we first learn to walk.

If a person's mobility is reduced, the scope of their daily lives can become severely limited, as they may be unable to get out of bed, wash or feed themselves. A number of clients will need physical assistance with **daily living activities**, such as eating, walking, hearing or seeing. This support and assistance has to be provided safely and using equipment such as wheelchairs, walking frames and hearing aids where necessary.

Many factors contribute to loss of, or reduced, mobility in elderly people:

- arthritis
- strokes
- breathing problems
- heart conditions
- foot problems.

List as many daily living activities as you can.

Many of these problems can be alleviated by assistive aids to mobility. **Assistive equipment** includes wheelchairs, walking frames, hoists, specially designed knives, spoons, forks etc.

One important aspect of providing support to any client is to do so in a way that maintains the client's independence and dignity.

## Key Skills

You can use Activity 1 to provide evidence for Key Skills Communication C1.1.

---

### Activity 1

**a** In pairs, ask your partner to assist you to blow your nose (use clean, disposable tissues only). How does it feel to be dependent on another person?
**b** Discuss your feelings with the rest of your group.
**c** Discuss situations when an elderly client might find dependency upsetting.

---

To help people in a sensitive and caring manner, remember that you will need to pay constant attention to the way you talk to them. Be polite and respectful when talking to them and talk in a clear voice. Always talk to the person about what you are doing and why. This will help them to feel at ease and understand what you are doing.

Aim to:

- listen and respond to communications from clients
- use good eye contact and keep smiling
- be sincere, sympathetic and understanding
- be kind, gentle and tactful
- be willing to assist, but always allow the person to do as much as possible for themselves
- encourage them to be as independent as practical.

When working with people with disabilities it is important to be careful not to oppress them. You could do this by exercising power over their lives, by doing things for them or making decisions for them. The language used to describe dependent people can be oppressive. For example, labelling everyone over the age of 65 as elderly can be damaging to their self-esteem or self-confidence.

## Effects of advancing age

When discussing services for elderly people we are usually referring to people who are past retirement age. In men this is at 65 years and for women there is the option of retiring at 60, otherwise it is also 65 years.

### Percentage of elderly people in population, 1900–2001

| Year | Percentage |
|------|------------|
| 1900 | 4.7 |
| 1930 | 9.0 |
| 1950 | 10.8 |
| 1970 | 16.0 |
| 1981 | 17.4 |
| 2001 | 16.0 (estimated) |

Old age can be divided into two categories:

* early old age (from 65 up to 75 years old)
* late old age (over 75 years old).

### It's a fact

* People are living even longer now than ever before.

* In 1900, fewer than 1 in 20 people were over 65 years of age.

* By 1990 approximately 1 in 7 were over 65.

* Between 1995 and the year 2001, the number of elderly people over 85 years of age is expected to double and most of these will be women.

### Number of people over retirement age in Britain

| Year | Number of people over retirement age | Percentage of retired people over 85 years |
|------|--------------------------------------|--------------------------------------------|
| 1991 | 10 000 000 | 8 |
| 2021 | 12 000 000 | 10 (estimated) |
| 2051 | 12 000 000 | 15 (estimated) |

## Key Skills

### Case study: helping Mrs Jackson

Mrs Jackson is 90 years of age. She was a nurse all her working life and, by the time she retired 30 years ago, she was a matron of a large hospital.

Her family all live overseas and she sees them infrequently. She lives alone in a small house with one room, a kitchen and bathroom and toilet downstairs and one bedroom upstairs. She suffers from glaucoma and arthritis of the hands, wrists and hips. She has difficulty in using cooking appliances and getting upstairs. She cannot get into the bath. She also has difficulty in writing letters because of the pain in her fingers from the arthritis.

Mrs Jackson has very restricted mobility and will need much physical assistance to allow her to live as normal a life as possible in her own home.

◎ *The first step to helping Mrs Jackson is to talk to her about how she feels and what she wants. One other important consideration is Mrs Jackson's ethnic background which has not been mentioned. Would you give Mrs Jackson different consideration if she was of Asian background?*

◎ *After the social worker had talked to Mrs Jackson and obtained her permission, she asked a number of professionals to assess her needs. What services and physical aids do you think Mrs Jackson might need? Explain why you are recommending each one. Did your answers include any of those listed below?*

| Physical aids | Reason for aid |
|---|---|
| Stair lift | To allow Mrs Jackson to get up and down stairs |
| Bathroom hoist | This will assist the nurse or carer to help Mrs Jackson in and out of her bath |
| Bath aids | Rubber grip mats to stop Mrs Jackson slipping in the bath |
| Bed comfort | Aids such as adjustable back rests, triangular pillows and cushions to help her sleep and rest |
| Feeding aids | Specially designed knives, forks and plates to help with eating |
| Kitchen aids | Special taps to allow her to turn sink and bath taps on or off |
| Walking aids | Walking stick or zimmer frame for mobility |
| Sight aids | A magnifying glass to help her read |
| *Personal support:* | |
| Nursing service | To help her in and out of bed |
| Home help | Cleaning and cooking, shopping |
| Friend | Writing letters |

Triangular pillow

An adjustable backrest

Bed cradle

Cushions

Fleece pads

Easy grip cutlery

Long-handled taps

Large handles on plugs

Reacher to pick up objects

*Some aids that might be useful for Mrs Jackson*

## Old age and disease

Old age is not necessarily a time of problems. Many elderly people will not require assistance from carers. There is no standard model elderly person. Elderly people differ widely in needs, lifestyles and expectations. Also, they have the same emotional and human needs as young people.

While age cannot be equated automatically with dependency, many people, as they grow older, find themselves generally slowing down. Some of their faculties (eyesight, hearing, speech etc.) may start to decline or certain disabilities may develop.

The ageing body is increasingly subject to **degenerative diseases**. These are diseases that gradually worsen over time and can be any of the following:

- atheroma – a gradual build-up of fatty deposits on the walls of the arteries giving rise to coronary heart disease and strokes
- osteo-arthritis – where changes occur in the joints, giving rise to pain and loss of mobility
- brain degeneration – caused by either Alzheimer's disease, which is the excessive degeneration of the nerve cells, or atheroma of the arteries supplying the brain. Both these conditions can lead to gradual loss of intellectual power and ability
- cancer – there is an increase in the incidence of many cancers with advancing age.

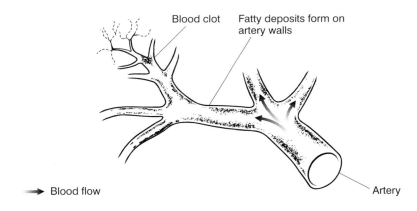

*Atheroma restricts the flow of blood through the arteries. Clots may form and block small blood vessels*

### quick fire

*Name two degenerative diseases.*

### Key Skills

You can use this opportunity to provide evidence for Key Skills Communication C1.1, C1.2 and C1.3.

### Case study: Mrs Delaney

"I worked in a factory since my 14th birthday. It was a wonderful feeling working. I can remember how proud I felt. I have already tried to keep active and work. I used to read a lot and go out three evenings a week to see my friends at the local club. I liked playing cards.

A few years ago, after my retirement, I got arthritis in my hands and pains in my legs. I began to have great difficulty in putting on my stockings and shoes and also doing up my buttons. I get very angry with myself. I feel that people should be able to do things for themselves. I do have a friend who helps me dress in the mornings and also cuts my food up, although I still have difficulty getting it off the plate because it slips about the table or tray. I feel embarrassed at having to get someone to adjust my clothes when I want to go to the bathroom. I feel like a baby."

ⓠ *Describe the difficulties you think that Mrs Delaney has with her mobility.*

ⓠ *List and describe the assistive equipment she could obtain to help her with her daily living activities. Be sure you describe assistive equipment that might help her with feeding and dressing. Make drawings of the aids.*

ⓠ *Describe how Mrs Delaney is feeling as a result of her loss of mobility. Why you think she is feeling so? Remember that she has always been a very independent person.*

ⓠ *What situations might be contributing to Mrs Delaney's loss of dignity, and why?*

ⓠ *What steps would you take to restore Mrs Delaney's dignity?*

The onset of one of these degenerative diseases can seriously affect an elderly person's ability to carry out daily living functions, such as walking, eating etc., without assistance.

### Activity 2

In this activity you will be expected to investigate two clients needing different pieces of equipment. You will need to:
- describe the main source of equipment
- describe the support networks available to each client
- discuss how the equipment helps the clients maintain independence.
- describe any potential risks to health and safety
- suggest how any health and safety risks could be addressed.

Mrs White: "I have been having difficulty with my hearing for the past few years. I have been using a hearing aid for some time now".

**a** Find out what types of hearing aids are at present available from the statutory and private sectors.

**b** What support groups are available to help Mrs White with her hearing difficulties? List the groups and the services they provide.

**Key Skills**

You can use Activity 2 to provide evidence for Key Skills Communication C1.2, C1.3 and Information Technology IT1.2.

▶▶

c Explain how the use of a hearing aid helps Mrs White retain her independence.

Mr Jones has been having difficulties with arthritis of the knee joints. He uses a zimmer frame to move about the house and a stocking gutter to put on his socks. Find out what types of aid to help with walking are available from the statutory and private sectors.

a What support groups are available to help Mr Jones?
b List the groups and the services they provide.
c Explain how the use of a walking aid helps Mr Jones retain his independence.

## 7.2 Where *is* given to people and who gives physical care

In Unit One the roles and responsibilities of many of the people involved in supporting and providing physical assistance to clients were discussed. We looked at the support that professional workers like the occupational therapist, the physiotherapist, the social worker, the GP and nurses could provide. The diagram below shows all the services that could be involved in delivering physical assistance or emotional support to an elderly person with a disability.

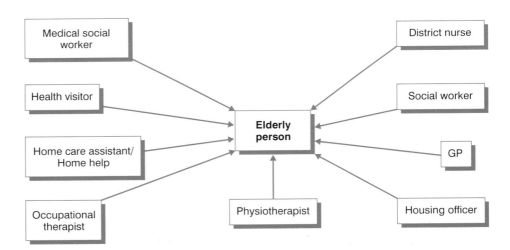

*Professional support workers*

As you can see, there are many people involved in providing services and assistance to an elderly person with a disability. All of these people must work together to provide the best service possible. It is also important that they co-operate very closely with relatives and friends of the client.

However, most important of all is that everyone, professional workers and carers, must take into account, and act upon, the wishes of the client. What the client wants is the most important thing, not what is available to offer them or what we as carers might think is the best thing for them. It is the elderly person who must have the final say in what services and support they want.

So that the client can make informed decisions, the carer should:

- explain what process they are involved in
- let the client put forward their own views
- agree with the client what services they would wish
- talk through with the client how the services can be delivered
- involve the client fully in reviewing the situation as appropriate.

The diagram below shows the different organisations that may be involved in offering support.

*How could you help people make informed decisions?*

**Organisations**

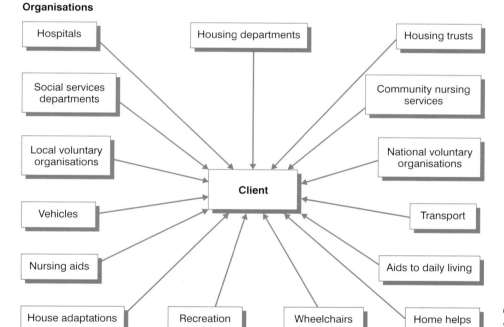

Hospitals

Housing departments

Housing trusts

Social services departments

Community nursing services

Local voluntary organisations

National voluntary organisations

Vehicles

**Client**

Transport

Nursing aids

Aids to daily living

House adaptations

Recreation

Wheelchairs

Home helps

**Services**

*Organisations offering support and physical assistance to elderly, dependent clients*

## Support groups to help elderly people with dependent needs

The voluntary organisations play an important role in the provision of care for elderly, dependent people. They can be very flexible in the services they provide and how they provide them. They are not bound by rules and regulations that may hinder statutory services. (See Unit One to remind yourself about statutory organisations.)

Voluntary organisations and self-help groups can be of great help to elderly people, particularly those who are housebound. They can:

- provide information about services available and help people get appropriate support
- provide information about assistive equipment
- visit and provide support. Age Concern, for example, provides a wide range of services for elderly people
- visiting service for elderly people offering companionship
- good neighbour scheme, provision of visiting, shopping, gardening and other household tasks
- holidays
- a telephone link – volunteers contact the housebound elderly person at pre-arranged time each day to check they are OK and also to offer support
- day centres
- coffee shops and luncheon clubs
- free transport.

## Who gives care?

Other groups, such as the Association of Stroke Clubs, provide self-help and information to members. Cross-roads is a voluntary scheme providing a support system for people in their own homes by offering temporary or regular care relief. This provides support and a rest for the carer by allowing the volunteer to attend to the personal needs of the client. Six million people are involved in providing voluntary services in the UK. The day-to-day work that the volunteers do is varied. They offer an informal system of caring that bridges the gap between the elderly client and the statutory services.

# What services may be provided by voluntary organisations?

## Case study: helping Mr Butterfield

Mr Butterfield worked as gardener for all his working life. He loved working outdoors but, four years after he retired at 65, he had a serious stroke. This left him with restricted mobility in one leg and arm. He finds difficulty in feeding himself as he cannot keep the plate from moving and slipping when he eats. He also finds that he cannot grasp the knives and forks as he cannot grip the utensils. He is also depressed at having to stay indoors all the time.

ⓠ *How would you help Mr Butterfield?*

ⓠ *What assistive equipment would you recommend to him?*

ⓠ *What other steps would you take to make him more mobile?*

Did your answer include any of the following?

| Physical aids | Reason for aid |
|---|---|
| Special non-slip plates | To allow him to feed himself |
| Knives/forks/spoons with thick handles to allow better grip | To allow him to grip feeding utensils and feed himself |
| Walking stick | To allow him to get about the house |

Did you also give some thought to the fact that, as Mr Butterfield was a very active man in his working life and liked the outdoors, he might improve his spirits if he could get out of the house? It could be arranged for a volunteer to take him out by car a few days a week or the Social Services Department could be asked to arrange for Mr Butterfield to go to a **day centre**.

## Activity 3

In this activity, you are asked to investigate and identify physical assistance for two elderly clients. You will need to indicate the physical assistance needed with daily living activities and safe lifting techniques, remembering that at all times you must maintain the client's independence and dignity.

**a** List the three ways of identifying whether someone needs physical assistance.

**b** Give three examples of each of the three methods.

# 7.3 The types of equipment available to help people

How can the use of assistive equipment can help a dependent person to live as independent a life as possible in their own home? Assistive equipment improves the client's ability to do certain tasks such as feeding, bathing or other personal tasks. It can also make life easier in residential establishments by helping with mobility and feeding and bathing for example.

How can assistive equipment help people?

The range of equipment available to the dependent person, either in their own home or in residential care, is vast. It ranges from knives and forks to large and very expensive pieces of equipment, such as hoists or stairlifts. However simple the aid, the purpose is to help the elderly or disabled person to move about or carry out daily living tasks as well as they can.

## The categories of assistive equipment

Assistive equipment falls into the following categories:

- personal care support
- hoists and lifting equipment
- eating and drinking aids
- help with dressing and undressing
- mobility aids
- reading and hearing aids.

## Personal care support

This includes such aids as rails in bathrooms, showers and toilets, also commodes, bedpans, urinals and waste disposal units.

Using a rubber mat in the bath can prevent the client from slipping. Hand rails allow the client to walk unaided in bathrooms or toilets. The rail also allows the elderly person to lower themselves on to the toilet. Sometimes a raised toilet seat also helps. A bath seat allows the person to swing themselves, on their own, into a bath or shower, thus not stripping them of their dignity or self-respect.

## Hoists and lifting equipment

Hoists and lifting equipment not only help maintain the independence of the client, but they are also an enormous help to the carers. They make lifting safer and easier. Some hoists are fixed, perhaps beside a person's bed or bath, but most are portable. This means that they can be used in a number of situations in the home with safety. They may be either manually or electrically operated.

(a)    (b)

Urinals (a) for men, (b) for women

Bed pan

A commode

Raised toilet seat

Rails in toilet, bath and shower

A bath seat

A mobile shower chair

*Examples of items for personal care*

## Case study: Mrs Patel

Mrs Patel is an 86-year-old Hindu woman who has only just been admitted to a residential home. She is the first person from an ethnic group to have been admitted. She became incontinent and the female care worker took her to the bathroom, removed her clothes and, using the bath hoist, safely lowered her into the bath. "I felt very embarrassed and hurt when the staff did not ask me if I needed a bath. No one talked to me about my culture or religious beliefs. Hindus prefer to wash with running water. I would have rather had a shower."

## Remember

Discuss with people what they want. Always ask about any religious, cultural or personal preferences.

*Examples of a bath hoist and a stair lift (see also page 255)*

A bath hoist

A stair lift

### Eating and drinking aids

To help people feed themselves, there are a number of aids available: cutlery, plates, trays, drinking aids. For example, clients with arthritis of the hand, which may cause poor grip, can have knives and forks with thick handles. Plates with rubber bases to stop the plate from slipping are useful for people with the use of only one hand.

### Help with dressing and undressing

Elders and people with disabilities sometimes have problems with dressing and undressing. They are simple tasks, but can be made difficult by even the simplest disability, such as a broken finger or a muscle strain. Arthritic joints make it difficult to do up buttons or lift arms above the head. Clients can use Velcro instead of zips or buttons. A number of aids to dressing can be used as illustrated.

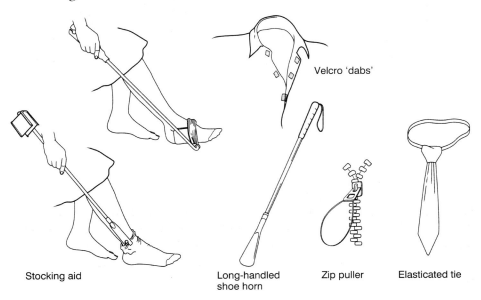

Velcro 'dabs'

Stocking aid

Long-handled shoe horn

Zip puller

Elasticated tie

*Examples of dressing aids*

## Mobility aids

Getting around the house or residential home can cause problems for many disabled or elderly people. Help can be available in the form of a simple walking stick or walking frame.

Wheelchairs can be either electrically or manually propelled.

Buildings can be adapted to help people. For example, kitchen worktops can be lowered to allow wheelchair users to access them. Ramps can be installed so that people can get in and out of buildings.

*A selection of sticks, crutches and a zimmer frame*

(a) hand propelled

(b) electric

*Examples of (a) a hand-propelled wheelchair and (b) an electrically propelled wheelchair*

## Reading and hearing aids

For those people with arthritis of the fingers or wrist, help is available in the form of page turners and writing aids. Those with sight problems can obtain reading glasses or computers with large letters that partially sighted people can read. Talking books and large print books are also available.

## What are the main sources of assistive equipment?

There are four main sources from which clients or their families or carers can obtain aids to daily living and adaptations to make it safer and easier in their own homes.

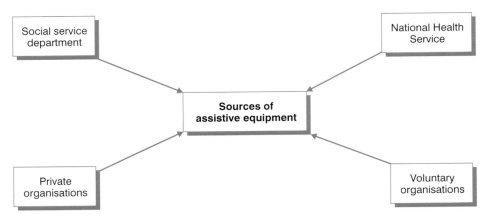

## Where can a client get information?

There are centres where people can go to see aids and adaptations and try them out. These centres are provided by:

- some Social Services Departments
- some of the larger chemist chains
- voluntary organisations, such as the Spastics Society, Red Cross or Help the Aged.

The DSS also provides a leaflet (reference no. HB 2) that gives information about centres and where people can get help.

---

**Activity 4**

Find out if your local Social Services Department or any other local organisation provides a service that allows people with disabilities to see aids and try them out. If such a service exists, make arrangements to visit it.

---

On a national level, the Disabled Living Foundation (380–384 Harrow Road, London W9 2HU) runs a free information service for clients, their families or carers. They will either give helpful information or refer you to someone who can advise. They also have a permanent exhibition of aids and other equipment that can be tried out.

### Social Services Departments

Since 1948 local authorities have had a responsibility to provide aids to daily living for people living in their own homes.

The increasing demand for support for those with a disability living in the community led to the Chronically Sick and Disabled Persons Act 1971. This stated that Local Authorities had a duty to find out the number of disabled people living in their area and their needs. The Act also stated that public buildings must have access for disabled people. Televisions and telephones could also be provided by Social Services Departments.

Social Services Departments now also have the responsibility for providing non-medical aids and equipment to help with everyday life. Aids are provided free by Social Services Departments, but in more and more cases there may be a charge. Wheelchairs may be loaned, as well as the more personal non-medical aids such as cutlery, eating aids, hoists, commodes and walking aids.

If you ask the local Social Services Department for help, they will usually ask someone, such as an occupational therapist, to visit and discuss the suitability of the various aids available.

The Social Services Departments can also alter a client's home or put in some specialist equipment to help make life easier for them. They can:

- install hand rails in bathrooms, hallways and stairs
- provide stair lifts
- provide ramps for wheelchair access
- widen doors
- build specially designed bathrooms or toilets.

Clients usually make a financial contribution towards the costs of alterations or large adaptations.

## National Health Service

Through the NHS the district nursing service can provide aids to help with home nursing, such as commodes, incontinence pads and bed aids. GPs can prescribe a number of medical aids, such as wheelchairs. Hospitals can also provide aids, such as support collars, callipers, wheelchairs, walking aids, hearing aids and low vision aids.

## Voluntary and private organisations

If some clients experience difficulty in getting appropriate aids, they can be obtained from either a voluntary organisation or bought from large chemists. Some voluntary organisations, such as the Red Cross, provide equipment and aids on short-term or long-term loan. They can supply such items as wheelchairs, commodes, bed rests, feeding cups etc.

## 7.4 The importance of support and encouragement, the maintenance of independence and respect

### Activity 5

"I was a very fit person until I fell down the stairs and broke my hip. I was in bed for some time and now have great difficulty in walking. At first, as I was not able to get about to the pub and football, I felt that life was not worth living. I could not enjoy my life or see my friends. I felt very silly having things done for me – personal things such as washing. I asked the social worker if she could do anything and she said that when I got a bit stronger she would ask the occupational therapist to see me. OT talked to me and asked me to do things, like trying to walk, dress myself and wash. We discussed what I wanted to do and I explained that I wanted to see my friends at the pub and go to football matches. She let me try lots of different walking aids. One type of walking stick helped me to steady myself and walk very slowly. I can now go to the pub and see my friends. I feel great and I am looking forward to going to football in a few months when I get stronger and more secure."

How did the social worker balance the best level of support of this person with their need for independence?

## It's a fact

Over a third of people over 65 live alone and about the same percentage live with their spouses (husbands or wives) who are also elderly.

As women live longer than men, it is women who are more likely to live alone. About 39 per cent of women live alone, compared to approximately 21 per cent of men. However, it is women who are more likely to suffer from chronic (long-term) illness.

Nearly one in ten elderly people are unable to leave their homes and walk down the road on their own.

About the same number cannot manage stairs or steps on their own.

For those over 85 years, the percentage increases dramatically. Half of people over 85 years of age are unable to walk down the road on their own and about 33 per cent cannot manage stairs or steps.

Many elderly people have difficulty with self-care, such as cutting toenails, bathing, showering or washing all over, feeding, brushing hair or shaving.

## How can you maintain the client's independence and dignity?

One of the ways in which we can support clients to maintain their dignity and independence is to give them choice and allow them to make decisions that affect their lives.

Giving this choice is central to the quality of care. It takes the power and control from the carer and places it where it belongs, with the client. Society, that is us, tends not to listen to people who have disabilities. However, by offering choice to people we **empower** them. This gives them a sense of dignity and worth.

*What does empowerment mean?*

We can empower people with disabilities by:

- being sensitive to their needs
- listening to what they are saying
- not 'talking down' to them
- not labelling those people with disabilities
- negotiating with the client, carer and any other professionals
- giving appropriate support as necessary.

### Case study: Jack Rudd

Jack Rudd was bereaved by the loss of his wife, upon whom he depended a great deal. A few weeks later he suffered a stroke which restricted his mobility and physical competence: "I felt helpless and lonely at home and I think I was getting depressed. I wanted to go into an old persons' home, but the social worker and home help kept telling me that I was better off in my own home. I got very angry, but was afraid to argue in case they wouldn't give me any help."

Q *Do you think that the social worker and the home help were empowering Jack? How could they have made him feel better and worth listening to? Discuss your ideas with your fellow students.*

Did your answer include any of the following?

- Ask Jack what he wanted.
- Explain to him what is available to help his mobility.
- Ask him if he would not mind being visited by an occupational therapist or physiotherapist.
- Discuss with him the results of any assessment.
- Let him make the final choice.

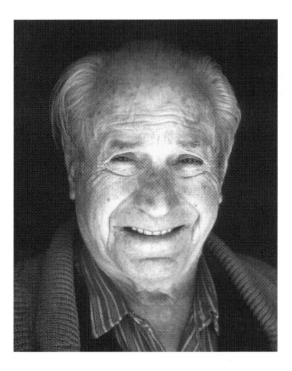

People such as Jack should be encouraged to make their own decisions and to be involved as much as possible in making decisions about their own lives. In this way we empower people and allow them to keep their dignity and self-respect.

## Non-verbal communication

A way to show respect for people is by trying to find out what they really want. We do this by observing them and listening to what they are saying. We don't just listen to what they are saying verbally, we also have to 'read' their **body language** (or non-verbal communication, such as how you sit, stand, hold your hands or fists etc.).

When talking to people with disabilities, we should choose the words we use very carefully and the body language we use should re-enforce what we are saying. When talking to people who are anxious, we should give them enough time to understand what we are saying and give them time to respond. We use body language to communicate with people. It is unavoidable. We send messages by the way we use our face, the way we stand, sit or gesture. Body language indicates a person's mood, feelings and attitudes. If you recognise some of these methods of communicating, you become more sensitive to other people and their needs.

What are these signs that we make to show how we feel? If you have done something well, we may communicate it by the thumbs-up sign, for example. This non-verbal communication indicates that we are happy.

List as many signs, or non-verbal communications, as you can that would indicate you were happy or unhappy. Did your list include:

*   Smiling?
*   Frowning?
*   Turning your back on the person?
*   Bored face?
*   Angry gestures?

## Facial expressions

Expressions are probably the most important aspect of non-verbal communication. Your face is very flexible and capable of showing your innermost feeling to others. Smiles are one of the most obvious signs we use to communicate. Smiles indicate warmth and openness. Smiles make other people react positively to you.

### Eye contact

Eye contact is an other important way that we communicate. When we communicate with clients, we normally have eye-to-eye contact. A strong gaze shows that you are paying attention. Breaking eye contact can indicate embarrassment. A lack of eye contact could indicate that you do not like the client and therefore do not wish to enter into meaningful conversation.

Do you feel at ease with those who keep eye contact with you? Do you remember when you told white lies to one of your parents? Did you look your parent straight in the eyes when telling an untruth? Have you heard the expression that someone has 'shifty eyes'?

Did your list in answer to the quick fire question include:

- rubbing their hands together?
- sitting or leaning forward?
- looking directly at you?
- nodding in agreement with you?

How you move your body, and the way you sit or stand reflects your attitudes and feelings towards other people. How you use your posture can affect the way a client reacts to you. When you sit with a client, you can make them feel important by leaning towards them or sitting with your arms unfolded. Sitting with your arms folded may indicate that you are not willing to listen to them.

### Height

If you sit in a higher position than your client, you can make them feel inferior. For example, when talking to someone in bed or in a wheelchair, it may be important to sit down so that you can maintain good eye contact with the client. People can feel that they are being told off when someone stands over them.

| Some of the ways that people could indicate friendliness by using non-verbal communication |
|---|
| Smiling |
| Non-threatening gestures, handshakes, pat on back |
| Using eye contact |
| Sitting or standing with unfolded arms |

## How can you recognise clients who might be feeling threatened?

How do you behave when you feel under threat? Do you fold your arms or cross your legs? Do you withdraw eye contact, become verbally aggressive or do you stand your ground? The important thing is to listen to them. Listening is more than hearing. It is paying attention to what people say, as well as to their non-verbal communication. You show that you are listening by keeping eye contact or perhaps nodding. There is very little point in trying to listen seriously to a client when you are clearing away the tables or writing a report.

We show respect to clients by listening to them and treating them as individuals. To do this you must find out what is important to the client, how they dress, what their interests are, their religion and ethnic customs. Do not judge other people's actions.

### Case study: Jack Rudd

After some effort, Jack Rudd managed to get himself admitted to the residential home of his choice. However, he became very unhappy after living there for some months. "I was really happy when I found that I was to be given a place at Hill Edge Home. It is only half a mile away from my old home and I could keep in touch with my old friends. The day I was admitted to the home, they said they were short-staffed and I was left waiting around in the TV room. I felt very embarrassed as I knew no one. I also found that I was not allowed to bring in any of my furniture or personal effects. I was given a room, but when I asked for a key the staff said, 'What would happen if you became sick in the night?' I did not understand what they meant. I do not like the way I am always accompanied to the bathroom by a member of staff when I am having a bath. I also have to be in bed at the same time as everyone else – that is 11 o'clock. Breakfast is at 8 in the morning, lunch is at noon and evening meal is at 5 o'clock. I am allowed to make a drink at 9 in the evening if I wish. I do not smoke and I do not like watching TV in the TV room because everyone smoked and it made my eyes and throat sore and my clothes smell."

ⓠ *How would you have organised things to show respect for Jack's individuality and to empower him in this situation?*

Did you list any of the following points?

- The staff should have explained what was happening during the admission process.

- Staff should have introduced Jack to other residents in the
  TV lounge.
- Jack should have been able to bring his personal possessions into
  the home. These would have made him feel more at ease.
- What Jack wanted at bath time should have been discussed with
  him.
- If staff had fears for his safety, they should have discussed this with
  him and a system worked out to the agreement of each person.
- Jack's dignity and self-respect were affected by not having any
  privacy in his own room.
- A non-smoking client should not have to share the same facilities
  as smokers. Jack does not smoke. He should not have to be
  subjected to the problems caused by passive smoking.

If we are to show respect for Jack, value his individual identity and
respect his choice, all of the above points should have been taken into
consideration. Jack lost his dignity and individuality when he was not
allowed to do things for himself. Clients, such as Jack, with such
personal care needs should to be treated with great respect so that they
can maintain their dignity. For example, they should be allowed as much
privacy as possible when performing personal tasks such as bathing.

## Confidentiality

People have a right to privacy. Confidentiality is of the greatest
importance. You have no right to intrude into client's lives. Through
your work as a carer you are likely to obtain information about clients.
Any information, of whatever nature, must remain confidential to you
and the appropriate staff. You may wish to use situations you have
experienced or observed in your work experience to put in your
portfolio. If you do this, you should have the permission of the client.
You must also maintain the confidentiality of the client and the staff of
the work placement.

Health and social care organisations need to keep records of patients and
clients. These records are kept in personal files or on computer. In most
care settings, only certain people will have access to personal
information. However, clients may tell you things about themselves or
relatives, and this information should remain confidential to you. This
will help the client maintain trust in you. You must respect the client's
right to confidentiality.

If you feel that a client has told you something that you should pass on
to another member of staff, talk to the client and see if you can get their
permission. If you cannot, then in most situations you should not pass
on the information. Remember to respect the client's wishes.

The key to the practice of confidentiality is respect for the client.
A breach of confidentiality is a breach of trust between the carer and
the client.

People now have a right to see their records whether they are held on computer or in manual records such as case files.

---

### Activity 6

What would you do if a client said to you: "If I tell you something, promise not to tell the manager"? Discuss your decision and your reasons for making it with your colleagues.

---

# 7.5 Health and safety issues

## Safety and care of assistive equipment

Equipment must be serviced regularly according to the manufacturer's recommendations. Any loose screws, damage or other worries you may have about a piece of equipment should be reported to your supervisor.

Lifts and hoists should only be used according to the instructions. These will indicate where the equipment should be used, in a bathroom or bedroom for example. The instructions will also explain the maximum weight that the equipment will bear. Very heavy weights will need special equipment to move them. Lifting a person who is too heavy could either break the equipment or unbalance it, possibly causing serious injury to both the carer and client.

## Moving and handling techniques

Sometimes as a care worker you will be asked to lift or move clients. You may have to move them from a bed to a chair, into a bath or on to the toilet. Lifting techniques in general are described on page 266. In this unit moving and handling techniques relating specifically to clients will be discussed.

### Lifting or moving a client

When lifting or moving a client some important and specific rules apply:

- Always wear flat, comfortable shoes.
- It is advisable to remove rings and watches. These may scratch the client or get caught in hair.
- Explain what you are going to do to the client.
- Clear the area.
- Where there is more than one lifter, co-operate to lift together.
- Do not rush the procedure.
- Do not drag the client.
- Apply all the general rules of lifting.

### Remember

Always follow the rules.

## Case study: Mr Jackson

"I live by myself and have done so for a number of years. My home is a usual two-storey, three-bedroom semi with living room, dining room and kitchen on the ground floor. The bathroom and toilet are on the first floor. I had a serious car accident some months ago. As a result of my injuries I must live in a wheelchair for the rest of my life. As soon as my home has been adapted to my new needs, I can leave hospital and go home."

Ⓠ *Read the case study about Mr Jackson.*

Ⓠ *List the statutory, voluntary and private agencies that might be involved in supporting Mr Jackson in his own home.*

Ⓠ *Describe the services each agency might offer.*

Ⓠ *List the adaptations to Mr Jackson's house that might be necessary to allow him to live an independent life.*

Ⓠ *Describe the assistive equipment that Mr Jackson will need to be able to perform daily personal tasks.*

Ⓠ *Describe the procedures you should carry out before lifting a load.*

Ⓠ *List the special difficulties that might arise when lifting people.*

Ⓠ *What equipment would you use to lift Mr Jackson?*

The European Handling Regulations came into effect on 1 January 1993. They place the responsibility for the safety of workers on the management of the organisation you are working for. All employers must ensure the safety of their workers in the following ways:

- All manual-handling tasks that might injure anyone should be avoided where possible. If it is not possible to avoid a hazardous manual-handling task, it must be assessed first to decide how it is to be done.
- Once the task has been assessed, action must be taken to reduce the risk of injury.
- The employer must ensure that they have a safe manual-handling policy and must give training before staff begin lifting.

As a care worker, you too should always be aware of the appropriate and safe way to carry out a manual-handling task. You should also call for assistance when you think it is necessary.

There are some special difficulties with lifting clients:

- many clients are too heavy to be lifted bodily
- clients are unwieldy and difficult to grasp
- many dependent or injured clients will make unexpected movements
- most injuries occur to care staff because of the physical behaviour of the client.

## Things to look for when assessing whether a lifting task is necessary

### *The lifting task*
- Does the client need to be lifted?
- Could the client move themselves?
- Could a lifting aid be used?
- How long will it take to lift the client?

### *The client*
What is wrong with the client? Remember that if a client has suffered a fall or other injury, you should not lift them until either you, a qualified first aider or a doctor is satisfied that it is safe to move them.

What is the weight, height and shape of the client? How much can the client assist you? How is the client going to behave? A confused client or one in great pain may make sudden movements.

### *Where is the lifting to be done?*
Are there any potentially dangerous objects about, such as furniture, equipment etc.? How much space have you in which to carry out the lift? Is the client in a confined space such as a toilet, bath or in their bed? Is the floor safe? Is there water, loose carpets, rugs, clothing or other hazards on it?

### *What lifting techniques will you use?*
Will you use a lifting aid or hoist? Will you be lifting manually? If so, how many staff are required to do the lift safely?

### *Who will lift the client?*
Is the person who will lift the client trained? How much experience have they of lifting this type of client? How skilled are they at communicating with clients?

There are many different ways of lifting a client. Your teachers will show you how safe lifting is carried out. You can only learn how to lift safely by practising under supervision. *Never practise without supervision.*

### Remember, when lifting from the floor:
- Keep your back straight.
- Bend your knees and hips.
- Use your stomach and thigh muscles.
- Keep your feet apart.
- Avoid twisting your back.
- Let the person you are moving help you as much as possible.
- Be careful.

### Remember, it is unsafe to:
- lift at arm's length
- lift at a distance from the body.

## Key terms

After reading this unit you should be able to understand the following words and phrases. If you do not, go back through the unit and find out, or look them up in the Glossary.

*Daily living activities*  *Empower*
*Degenerative disease*  *Body language*
*Day centre*  *Confidentiality*
*Moving and handling techniques*  *Assistive equipment*

## Test yourself

1 What do you understand by the term 'daily living activities'?
2 List four degenerative diseases and describe them.
3 List eight services that are available to elderly, dependent clients.
4 What rules apply when lifting a client?
5 List six ways that you can empower clients.
6 What do you understand by the term 'body language'?
7 What does the term 'confidentiality' mean?
8 Where can clients go to ask for assistive equipment?
9 What services may be provided by voluntary organisations?
10 What does the term 'body language' mean?

# Assignment for Unit Seven

**Produce an investigation into the physical care of one person in a caring situation.**

**Case study: Mrs Tavistock**

"I worked in a shop with my husband since my 20th birthday. It was a wonderful feeling working together. I can remember how proud I felt. I have already tried to keep active and work. I don't understand the young ones today who don't want to work and lie about all day. I think keeping active is important; it helps to keep your mind young. I used to read a lot and I liked playing cards at home with my family.

Ten years ago, I broke my arm and I got arthritis in my arm. I began to have great difficulty in dressing and bathing. I get very upset with myself as I feel that I should be able to do things for myself like my parents did when they were old.

### Get the grade

To achieve a **PASS** you must complete tasks 1 to 3.

To achieve a **MERIT** you must complete tasks 1 to 5.

To achieve a **DISTINCTION** you must complete tasks 1 to 7.

I do have a relative, who lives nearby, who helps me cook my breakfast in the mornings and also cuts my food up, although I still have difficulty getting it off the plate because it slips about the table or tray.

I have difficulty shopping, as I cannot carry heavy things. Since I have had arthritis I cannot drive, as I cannot afford to adapt a car."

## Tasks

1 Read the case study and list the physical care needs of Mrs Tavistock and the difficulties that she may be experiencing.

2 List and describe the appropriate physical support that is needed by Mrs Tavistock and how the aids to daily living operate.

3 Demonstrate the provision of practical support for an individual. Identify any basic health and safety issues such as hygiene and suitable temperatures for food.

4 Explain how physical care support can maintain the client's dignity and independence.

5 Describe clearly the potential risks to health and safety in relation to the support you have identified for Mrs Tavistock.

6 Make realistic suggestions as to how the health and safety risks could be addressed.

7 Show that you understand the need to balance support for Mrs Tavistock with her need for independence.

## Key Skills  Opportunity

| | You can use this opportunity to provide evidence for the following key skills |
|---|---|
| Communications C1.1 | Obtain information from the case study. |
| Communications C1.2 | Demonstrate care skills. |

# Preparing for employment in health and social care

## What is covered in this unit

**8.1 How to look for jobs and training**
**8.2 How to choose a job or training that suits you**
**8.3 How to write a job or training application**
**8.4 How to prepare yourself for interview**

At the end of this unit you will be asked to produce an employment folder. If you would like to see further details of the tasks you are likely to need to carry out for assessment, please refer to the end of the unit where an assignment has been set (see page 304). This unit will guide you through what you need to know in order to successfully put together this folder. You will be assessed on this work and awarded a grade. This grade will contribute to the overall grade you will get for Unit Eight.

### Materials you will need to complete this unit

- Job descriptions you have collected
- Local newspapers
- Information about the roles of health and social care workers (see Unit One)
- Information from careers advisers
- Your curriculum vitae
- National Record of Achievement.

## Introduction

After you have read this chapter and carried out the exercises you will have an understanding of:

- employment opportunities in health and social care
- the range of jobs in health and social care and their purpose
- the skills and qualifications needed to obtain those jobs.

# 8.1 How to look for jobs and training

## The main providers of health and care

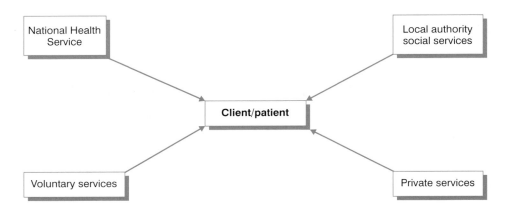

National Health Service → Client/patient ← Local authority social services

Voluntary services → Client/patient ← Private services

## The National Health Service

Health care has not always been free in the UK, but today we do have a system of free health care – the National Health Service (NHS). As we saw in Unit One, until 1948 people had to pay for medical and social care. Many found this difficult to do because they were poor. One way to pay for these services was by taking out insurance, for example, through friendly societies or trade unions. Then they knew the money would be there when they needed it.

In 1948 the government nationalised the health services and created the NHS. This brought various health and care services under the control of one person, the Minister of Health. The intention was to try to provide a fair and free service for everyone. However, there are still some people today who choose to pay for private health services.

The people who work in the NHS and who look after those who are sick do so in hospitals, health centres, nursing homes, GPs' centres or surgeries and also in the client's or patient's own home.

## Hospitals

Hospitals are the places where people go for treatment when they are too ill to be cared for at home. They are normally referred to a hospital by their general practitioner (GP). They may be seen first as an out-patient in a clinic and may later become an in-patient if they need special treatment or an operation.

### Activity 1

Find out how many hospitals there are in your locality and the main services they provide.

Discuss your findings with your class colleagues.

## Main jobs in health care

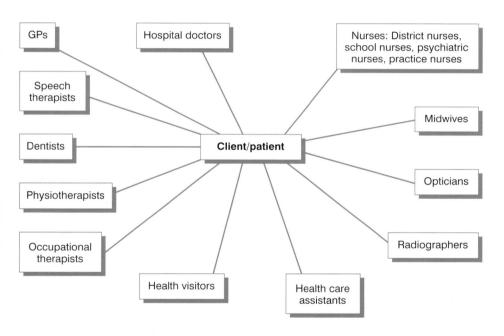

## Doctors

### Hospital doctors

In hospitals patients are looked after by teams of doctors, who specialise in particular areas, such as:

- paediatrics (children)
- obstetrics (childbirth)
- geriatrics (elderly people).

The senior doctors in the team may be referred to as specialists or consultants.

The role of the hospital doctors is to:

- *diagnose* – find out what is wrong with the patient
- *prescribe* – decide on the treatment to help the patient
- *monitor* – review the condition of the patient and change the treatment if necessary.

The doctors are supported by other health and social care workers such as:

- nurses
- physiotherapists
- occupational therapists
- radiographers
- hospital social workers.

You will find out more about these workers later.

**What does the term diagnose mean?**

### General practitioners (GPs)

GPs (or family doctors) are the main route for most people to good health care. GPs are paid by the government through the Local Health Authority. Their pay depends on the number and type of patients registered with them.

Most people select their own GP when they are over 16 years old from the list of GPs kept by the Local Health Authority. The role of the GP is to:

- diagnose and treat illness
- monitor patients with chronic (long-term) illness
- prevent disease through screening programmes
- refer patients to other services, such as hospitals and social services
- offer advice and support to patients, and also to their carers, relatives and family.

GPs work in the community. They are based in surgeries (or practices) covering particular areas. Sometimes a number of GPs work together in a group practice.

GPs employ receptionists and clerical staff to run their practices. They also often employ practice nurses. Social workers, health visitors and midwives are also often based at GPs practices. You will find out more about these workers later.

*Training*: Initially doctors undertake a five- or six-year degree course, before going on to specialise in a particular area of medicine or becoming a GP.

*Entry requirements*: A wide range of GCSEs, plus 4 A-levels in science subjects.

*What do the initials GP mean?*

## Nurses

Nurses work with sick people, both in hospitals and in people's own homes. They assess the patient's nursing needs and then carry out a plan of health care to help the person back to health. They also help people to make decisions about their own health and how to live a healthy life. Nurses may be:

- **registered general nurses (RGNs)** who mainly work in hospitals, carrying out practical tasks, such as giving injections, dressing wounds, administering drugs, washing and feeding patients
- registered mental nurses (RMN), or psychiatric nurses, who work with people who are mentally ill, either in hospitals, day centres, hostels and in the patients' own homes (where they are called community psychiatric nurses or CPNs). The RMN carries out the same tasks as an RGN, but also provides counselling (for both patients and carers), and other types of therapy. CPNs sometimes help patients to get jobs or encourage them to mix socially with other people in the community
- registered nurses for the mentally handicapped (RNMH) who work with those suffering from learning difficulties. They teach patients everyday social skills and life skills, such as how to dress and feed themselves.

*Training:* The RGN, RMN and RNMH qualifications have been replaced by a new training programme called **Project 2000**. This is a three-year training programme for nurses. Most nurse training takes place at universities. In the first half of the programme the student nurses study subjects common to all fields of nursing. When they have passed the first part, they can then decide to study a specialist area, either:

- adult nursing
- mental handicap nursing
- mental health nursing or
- children's nursing.

*What is the difference between a RGN and RNMH?*

*Entry requirements:*

- Age – over 17 years.
- At least 5 GCSE passes at grade C or above.
- Other equivalent qualifications – BTEC National Diplomas or appropriate GNVQs may also be considered.

In addition, you need to have:

- an interest in caring
- good communication skills
- the ability to work in a team
- the ability to remain calm under pressure.

*A nurse may decide to specialise in children's nursing*

### Practice nurses

Practice nurses are RGNs. They are usually employed directly by a local GP practice, where most of their work is carried out. They perform such tasks as:

- dressing patients' wounds
- blood and urine tests
- giving injections
- offering family planning advice.

There are approximately 4,000 practice nurses employed in the UK.

### District nurses

District nurses are RGNs. They are employed by local Health Authorities. They provide the link between hospitals and the primary health care team (GPs, nurses, social care staff and others) by **monitoring the person's ability** to cope in his or her own home.

They provide physical, social and emotional support and nursing care for acute (short-term) and chronic (long-term) patients and their families in their own homes. They carry out a range of tasks, including:

- assessing patients' needs
- giving injections
- changing dressings
- taking blood tests
- washing and feeding patients
- giving advice and teaching people about practical care.

There are approximately 20,000 district nurses employed in the UK.

Where does a practice nurse work?

### Health visitors

Health visitors are RGNs who have had further training, leading to the Health Visitor's Certificate. By law health visitors have to visit (or see) regularly all children under the age of 5 to ensure that their progress is physically, emotionally and socially normal. They also offer parents support and advice about feeding, safety and child development.

Other roles of health visitors include:

- health education – advising people how to keep healthy and prevent illness
- running antenatal classes for expectant mothers
- running child health clinics
- supporting patients, particularly elderly people, in their own homes and helping ill people to live with their disabilities.

There are about 13,000 health visitors working in England, Wales and Scotland.

### Midwives

Midwives are independent, professional nurses in their own right. They are usually RGNs who have completed an 18-month midwife course.

They are responsible for:

- supervising the antenatal care of pregnant women – monitoring the health of the mother and the unborn baby, and offering advice on diet, exercise, parenthood and care of the baby

- postnatal care once a woman has had her baby, either in hospital or at home – they look after the mother and baby for 10 days after birth, after which time the health visitor takes over
- delivering babies themselves, or in difficult situations assisting a doctor to deliver a baby.

### School nurses

The school nurse is an RGN. She gives advice on health matters in schools, and looks after the children, making regular screening checks and giving advice about such matters as immunisation.

## Professions allied to medicine

While the main, face-to-face delivery of care is from nurses and doctors, there is a large range of professions allied to medicine. They support the doctor and nurse in looking after and treating the patient.

### Radiographers

Radiographers use:

- X-rays and ultrasound to look at internal organs, for example the ultrasound, or 'scan', in pregnancy to look at the unborn baby
- X-rays and gamma rays to destroy tissues in illnesses such as cancer.

The radiographer is a technician, instructed by a radiologist – a specialist doctor who, for example, interprets X-ray pictures and produces reports for the doctor requesting the X-ray.

*Training:* Radiographers have to undertake a three-year course leading to a diploma or degree in radiography.

*Entry requirements*: 3 GCSEs at grades A–C, and 2 A levels or BTEC National Diploma in Health Studies.

## Physiotherapists

Physiotherapists help people to overcome problems caused by a wide range of illnesses and physical conditions. They treat people of all ages, either in hospital or in their own homes. They play an important role in the mobility of patients, using supportive and manipulative exercises to develop muscles for movement. For example, a person who has had a broken arm and has just had the plaster removed may need help to build up the muscles or loosen stiff joints. Physiotherapists also provide treatment to relieve pain.

Patients are usually referred to physiotherapists by doctors. The physiotherapists then work in co-operation with doctors in planning patients' physiotherapy programmes, and also discuss treatment with patients.

*Training:* Physiotherapists have to undertake a three-year degree course in physiotherapy.

*Entry requirements*: 5 GCSEs at grades A–C, including English and two science subjects, plus 2 A levels or a BTEC National Diploma in Health Studies. Three A-levels are required for entry to many courses.

Academic requirements are important, but a physiotherapist should also have:

* an interest in people
* compassion
* patience
* fitness
* confidence
* the ability to work in a team.

There are approximately 9,500 physiotherapists working in the NHS. Some have private practices.

## Occupational therapists

Occupational therapists (OTs) treat physical and mental illness with activity. They help people to overcome the effects of illness, disability or severe injury by first assessing their capabilities and then helping them to overcome difficulties and learn to carry out tasks by themselves. They advise on aids and adaptations that might help a client to manage better in their home.

A large part of their work is with people suffering from physical or learning difficulties. They work both on a one-to-one basis and with groups. Their work requires a great deal of tact, sympathy and understanding.

Many OTs work in the community and in Social Services Departments. In the community their job is to visit clients in their own homes and assess with their carers how they manage daily tasks, such as washing, dressing, and getting in and out of bed.

*Training:* Occupational therapists have to undertake a three-year training course.

*Entry requirements:* Minimum of 2 A levels and 3 GCSEs at grade C or higher, which must include English Language and a science subject. A BTEC National Diploma in Health Studies or appropriate GNVQ qualification may also be accepted.

Nearly 5,000 occupational therapists (OTs) work in the NHS.

### Activity 2

Contact your local Social Services Department and find out if they employ occupational therapists. Make arrangements to visit the OT and talk to him or her about their job and the people they support.

*Occupational therapists assessing a client performing daily tasks*

### Speech therapists

Speech is an important part of everyday life. Speech therapists help people with speech disorders, ranging from children with delayed speech development to older people recovering from a stroke. Most of their work is with children. Many work in hospitals, but others work in schools and clinics.

The skills of the speech therapist are directed towards helping people gain some independence and intelligible communication. They use their practical skills to rehabilitate, educate and counsel patients and their families.

*Training:* A three- or four-year degree course, or a two-year postgraduate diploma.

*Entry requirements*: 5 GCSEs at grade A–C, including English Language, a biological science and sometimes a modern language, plus 2 A levels or BTEC National Diploma in Health Studies.

The personal qualities needed are:

- the ability to build a one-to-one relationship with people
- flexibility
- patience
- the ability to listen, explain and reassure people.

### Health care support workers

The **health care support worker** (or health care assistant – HCA) is someone who assists health care professionals in hospitals, clinics and community nursing. They:

- help maintain stock on the ward, and equipment and materials in their workplace
- help patients in and out of bed
- help patients to dress
- make beds
- prepare drinks for patients.

They may also take patients' temperatures, perform simple urine tests and change simple dressings.

*Training:* Training is on-the-job and many support workers complete Levels 2 and 3 **National Vocational Qualifications** in Care.

*Entry requirements:* There are no minimum entry requirements for this type of work. However, most hospitals set their own entrance tests.

### Dentists

Dentists in general practice carry out all types of dentistry:

- fillings
- fitting dentures
- putting crowns on teeth
- cleaning teeth
- advising people on dental hygiene and how to look after their teeth.

*Training:* A five-year degree course provides the basic training for the work.

*Entry requirements*: Usually 3 or 4 A levels and a number of GCSEs are necessary for entry to university.

*Dentists should be able to put people at ease*

To be an effective dentist you must:

- have a liking for people
- have an interest in their welfare
- be able to put tense and nervous people at ease.

Over 23,000 dentists work in the UK. Most do some work for the NHS.

### Opticians

Opticians measure people's eyesight, and advise whether glasses should be worn. They fit glasses and contact lenses. This is done in optician shops or sometimes in hospitals or clinics. Most people have to pay the full cost for testing, glasses or contact lenses. Full-time students and children obtain the service free or may pay some contribution towards the cost.

*Training:* A three-year degree course followed by further training for professional examinations and registration.

*Entry requirements:* 5 GCSEs and 2 A levels.

## Community and social services

Social Services Departments (SSDs) were set up by Local Authorities in the late 1960s to provide community-based services for people in their own homes. The service is available to everyone, but is particularly concerned with families.

The Social Services Committee of every Local Authority (council) oversees the four main responsibilities of its Social Services Department:

- to provide childcare as specified in the various Children's Acts and Adoption Acts, including the 1989 Children Act

- to provide and regulate residential accommodation for older people and people with disabilities, as specified in the 1948 National Assistance Act and the 1984 Registered Homes Act
- to provide welfare services for older people, people with disabilities and people who are chronically (long-term) ill and to act as set out in the various Mental Health Acts
- to refer clients to other organisations, such as voluntary organisations, for services.

*What do the initials SSD stand for?*

## Jobs in community services

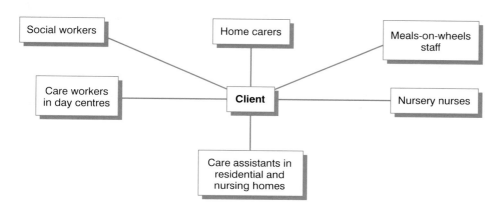

### *Social worker*

The first worker we think of in the social care field is the social worker. Social workers provide support for individuals and families in terms of social rehabilitation and community services. They work in the community or in hospitals (hospital social workers). They specialise in:

- childcare work
- helping elderly people
- working with people suffering from mental illness.

*Training:* Qualified social workers have obtained a qualification covering all areas of social work. They may specialise in one area later.

Most social workers obtain the Certificate of Qualification in Social Work (CQSW). Residential and day-care staff may have obtained the Certificate in Social Service (CSS). However, recent changes to training have involved the development of a new qualification to replace these – the **Diploma in Social Work** (Dip.SW).

The Diploma in Social Work is now the professional qualification for all social workers (field and residential). It involves two years of study and practice supervised by a qualified social worker.

*Entry requirements*: 2 A levels at grade A–E and 3 GCSE passes at grade A–C. A GNVQ at Advanced level or a BTEC National Diploma are also accepted.

### Home care staff

A number of staff provide the everyday emotional, social and practical support to clients living in their own homes. By law, Local Authorities must provide home care assistants (formerly called home helps). They carry out such tasks as:

- simple cleaning
- lighting fires
- shopping
- cooking
- basic personal tasks.

Most of their work is concerned with supporting elderly people, but they do also work with people with physical disabilities and families with young children.

*Training:* Short training courses are offered by employers.

*A home carer*

### Meals-on-wheels

This service is becoming increasingly important as more and more elderly dependent people choose to carry on living in their own homes. About 33 million meals are provided every year to people in their own homes in England. This service is provided by the Local Authority in many areas but it is still also offered by voluntary agencies such as the Women's Royal Voluntary Service (WRVS) or Women's Institute (WI) in rural areas.

*Meals-on-wheels*

### Nursery nurses

The Children Act 1989 made it law that Local Authorities should provide day care for children in need aged under 5 years. Day nurseries for children between 6 weeks and 5 years old are staffed by workers with qualifications in childcare. There are also privately run day nurseries. The tasks of a nursery nurse involve all aspects of routine care, such as:

- feeding
- washing
- toilet training
- play activities.

A nursery nurse is both supervisor and friend to the children in his or her care.

*Training:* The special skills required for this type of care are recognised and nursery nurses have either National Nursery Examinations Board (NNEB) Diploma, a BTEC National Diploma or a Certificate in Caring Services (Nursery Nursing). Courses leading to these qualifications are still available in colleges in the UK. However, since 1994 many courses have been organised so that a student can obtain all or part of an NVQ.

NVQs in Early Years and Education at levels 2 and 3 are also available for these workers.

Most of these qualifications can only be obtained by on-the-job training, which is more relevant than learning from books or in college without work experience placements.

*Entry requirements:* No formal requirements, but a good level of education, such as 3 GCSEs or a GNVQ Intermediate in Health and Social Care.

*What do the initials NVQ stand for?*

## Key Skills

You can use Activity 3 to provide evidence for Key Skills Communication Key Skills C1.1.

### Activity 3

Talk to the manager of your college nursery (if there is one) or a local nursery or playgroup. Arrange to visit the manager and discuss with him or her the type of work that is available locally in the childcare field. Make notes and compare them with those of your classmates.

### National Vocational Qualifications (NVQs) in Care

In the past many areas of social care were staffed with untrained, unqualified staff, but now there are qualifications that recognise the skills of these people. In recent years the government in the UK has encouraged a new form of training, National Vocational Qualifications (NVQs). At the moment these qualifications are for people employed in hospitals, residential, day or home care situations.

To obtain an NVQ in Care, students have to show that they are competent (able) to do the job for which they are being assessed. NVQs measure what you can do, as well as how much you know and understand about the job.

If you want to know more about NVQs, talk to your tutor or careers adviser.

## Other jobs in health and social care

There are many other people who have an important role to play in supporting the people who work face-to-face with clients. Some, like receptionists, have direct contact with clients or patients, while others work in the background, for example maintenance staff and catering staff. These jobs can be described as indirect care.

### Receptionists and clerical jobs

Receptionists are often the first health and social care workers that people come into contact with. Receptionists work in hospitals, clinics, day centres, GP practices and health centres. They keep records, look after waiting lists and make appointments. As they are dealing with people under stress, they need tact and understanding to do the job properly. Clerical staff also keep and up-date patient and client records.

### Administrators and managers

Managers are responsible for planning, developing and monitoring services. The manager of a hospital usually has a degree in management. However, there are some doctors and nurses who have become hospital directors, and no longer practise medicine.

### Domestic and maintenance staff

Domestic staff work in hospital wards, residential care and day centres. They support the care staff by cleaning, washing up and also talking to clients and patients. Maintenance staff look after equipment, keeping such things as lifts and lights in working order. In care settings they also keep clients' aids and equipment in order.

### *Voluntary services*

Some services are provided by voluntary organisations. This means that some, or all, of their workers are volunteers – they are not paid. Many of them are charities and have to raise money to enable them to provide their services.

WRVS is a voluntary organisation that provides a wide range of services to people of all ages, for example toy libraries, clubs for elderly people, Meals on-Wheels, shops in prisons and hospitals.

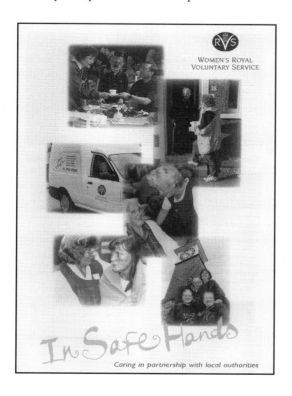

*Private services*

Some patients and clients prefer to pay for their health and social care. They may take out insurance to help pay for these services. Many services provided by the NHS and Local Authorities may also be provided by private organisations, such as:

- private day nurseries
- private specialist clinics
- private hospitals
- private nursing homes.

# 8.2 How to choose a job or training that suits you

## Some more jobs in health and social care

The assignment at the end of this unit will give you the opportunity to identify some jobs in the health and social care field that might suit your skills, experience and ambitions. You will be asked to look at two jobs, one which you might like to go into when you finish this course or the GNVQ Intermediate course, and a second job that you might progress to after you have gained more experience and qualifications.

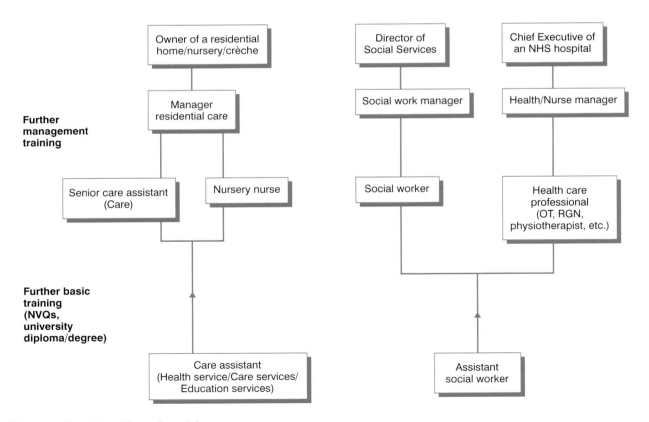

*Career paths in health and social care*

To give you some help with this task we will look at two jobs in more detail:

- the care assistant
- the nursery nurse.

We will consider the tasks and responsibilities of each job, and the skills and qualifications needed. In the final section of this unit we will look at how you might apply for such jobs.

## The care assistant

The job of a basic grade care assistant looking after children, adults or elderly people is the first rung on the ladder of a career in health and social care.

**You can use this opportunity to provide evidence for Key Skills Communication C1.2 and C1.3.**

### Case study: Mary Jackson

Mary Jackson works as a care assistant in a home for elderly people. She spent two years at college. In her first year she completed a one-year preparation for vocational work (CPVE) course, and in her second a BTEC First Diploma in Social Care.

The CPVE course was something like the course you are now completing and the BTEC First Diploma is the equivalent to the GNVQ Intermediate qualification. When she had left school she was determined not to do her A levels. She wanted to go to a large college where she could have a wide choice of courses. She chose the CPVE course because, like the GNVQ Foundation course, it allowed her to gain experience of care and also gave her the opportunity to find out about other subjects, such as leisure and tourism, the performing arts or art and design.

Mary had at first wanted to work with children. However, after work experience in a home for elderly people, she changed her mind. Many students come to college or schools thinking they know exactly what they want to do. However, one of the main characteristics of a good care worker is flexibility and a willingness to learn from experience. This Mary had obviously done.

As she said: "The Foundation course allowed me to test out a number of care situations. I knew from the start that I didn't want to gain experience in art or acting. At first, I had wanted to work with children. I obtained work experience in a children's playgroup, a nursery, an old people's home and a casualty department. It was during this work experience that I found that I wanted a job helping old people, and not children as I had originally thought.

"I enjoyed working with children but I got great satisfaction from working in the old people's home. I felt at home with old people and

▶▶

I think they liked me. During my work experience I found that many of the care assistants had BTEC or City and Guilds qualifications. I was lucky to be able to progress to the BTEC First course in Care at the college where I did the Foundation course. The tutors were very nice. Because I had a number of work experiences on the Foundation course, they allowed me to spend most of my BTEC work experience working with elderly people at day centres and residential homes."

She had also kept her ears and eyes open during her work experience. When she found out that many of the care staff had either BTEC or City and Guilds qualifications, she was determined to get on to such a course if she could. She applied for the BTEC course and was lucky to obtain a place.

Once Mary had completed the BTEC First Diploma course, she applied for a job as a care assistant at an establishment near her home. She was told later that she was successful in getting the job because she had submitted an excellent application form and had impressed the selection panel by her confidence and her obvious love of working with elderly people. A good reference from her tutor was also helpful, but more important was the references she had obtained from the people in charge of the establishments where she had her work experience.

She said: "The job suits me. My manager has told me that she will put me forward for more training when I get some experience. I think it is important to get as much training as you can. It helps you to do the job properly and you owe it to the clients to be as skilled as possible.

"At the moment I work under a senior care assistant who helps me when I have problems or when I want to know something. I mostly help the residents with dressing and undressing, bathing, and I help those with mobility problems to get around. I also change beds and empty commodes. What I like best is talking to the elderly people and their visitors and going on outings with the residents. They are such interesting people and have lived such varied lives."

ⓠ *Visit the careers library in your college or school. Make a list of courses and training programmes that would be suitable for Mary to further her career.*

Mary has a varied work routine and no two days are quite the same, but there is a routine. She is always aware of the fact that the residents come first and that she must never impose her ideas or views on them. If she is worried because someone doesn't take their pills or eat their meals, she always tells a senior member of staff. She is aware that the establishment is the residents' home, and she treats them as she would if she was in their own home.

"I get to work about 7 o'clock in the morning. The staff who have been working during the night tell us of any problems that may have happened during the night. My first job is to lay the tables for breakfast. Residents can come for breakfast at any time during the morning up to about 11.30 when we have to get ready for lunch.

"We work in teams. Each team is responsible for looking after about 10 residents. That way you get to know them really well. It doesn't mean that we don't talk to or help the others. It just means that we concentrate on our residents. I help get anyone up out of bed if they ask. We always knock on the door of their room before entering. One or two residents, if they are not too well, may have their meals in bed.

"When breakfast is finished, I help clear away the tables and help those who ask for support to go to their own rooms, to the TV or to the activities room. I have plenty of time to talk to and listen to residents. I like doing this. I also like going out to the library, pub or shops with the residents.

I make drinks for residents and visitors. At lunchtime I help to feed any residents who may have difficulty feeding themselves. After lunch I help clear up and find out what the residents want to do after lunch. I finish work at 1 o'clock.

"Some days we have meetings at which we discuss how the residents are getting on and the best way to help them. Sometimes a resident's GP is present, together with the district nurse. I am expected to write any unusual happenings in a reporting book, such as a resident not taking their tablets, not eating or perhaps if they had an accident. I also see one of the senior managers once a week for supervision sessions. We talk about how I am getting on and how I do things. I also discuss how I could do things better. I look forward to these sessions and am disappointed if they have to be cancelled because of an emergency in the home. We also report if the resident has had a visit from relatives or friends. This is not to check on the residents. If we know that a person doesn't get visits, we can make sure that they don't feel lonely."

We can see from what Mary has said that she has the qualities necessary to do this job. She is pleasant, caring, willing to talk to people and, most importantly, she listens to them. She respects other people's views, does not impose her views on others and tries to find out what people really want. She is willing to work as part of a team and to be flexible. Importantly, she realises that you do not stop learning when you get a job. She likes supervision sessions when she can discuss her job and how to do it better. She is also aware that she needs further training to become better at her job.

"I feel positive about the idea of further training. However, I would like to wait a few years. I am not sure that I want to become a manager of a residential establishment. I might like to work with elderly people in their own homes. If I stay in residential care work I shall do my NVQ qualification in care. I don't have to leave work to do this and there are no exams. I am assessed by my supervisor as to how competently I am doing my job. After looking at me doing certain tasks a number of times, and me telling her why I did certain tasks in a certain way, I become competent and can be awarded the NVQ in Care at level 2. I can go on to take levels 3 or 4 later."

So Mary has a number of options open to her. She can stay working in residential care and gain NVQ qualifications. She may wish to leave residential care and work in the community as a social worker. If she does this she will need further training and to obtain the Diploma in Social Work at a local college or university. What would you do?

*What are the personal qualities you think are necessary for an individual to be able to carry out the role of care assistant in a nursery school?*

## The nursery nurse

### Case study: John Sheffield

Nursery nurses play an important role in the early years of many children's lives. Nursery nurse training, like that for social work or for teachers, offers training that allows them to take responsibility for the overall care of children in many situations. Nursery nurses work in a variety of situations:

*   schools
*   day nurseries
*   crèches
*   residential nurseries
*   hospitals
*   private homes.

John Sheffield said: "I always wanted to be a nursery nurse, ever since I left school at 16 with 6 GCSEs. I attended my local college to do my two-year full-time childcare training. I felt strange at first being only one of two lads in a class of 22 girls. However the teaching staff made me feel very welcome and supported me through the two years."

Fewer males than females do nursery nurse training, but it is by no means uncommon, as it is now recognised that they have the qualities to do the job. John had more than the usual entry qualifications for the childcare course. The usual entry requirements were 3 GCSEs at A–C, but in parts of the UK where competition for places is high you may also need A levels.

"The two days a week that I spent gaining practical work experience in different childcare situations helped me to make up my mind that I wanted to work in a day nursery. I liked working with children from all kinds of backgrounds. Some parents paid the full cost of the child's place, while other parents got the place free – paid for by social services. Some children had behaviour problems and we had to plan how to help them when they were at the nursery."

The childcare course gave John the chance to experience different childcare work experiences. It allowed him to make his mind up about what area he would like to work in. He chose a day nursery, thus giving himself much choice. Day nurseries can be either private or run by Local Authorities.

As he said: "The nursery I work in at the moment is run by a local college and is open to children of students and staff. Some places are also available to children from the local community. We open at 8 o'clock in the morning and close at 5 o'clock in the evening. We are open all the year around, taking more children from the local community during the school holidays.

"I am involved in the routine care of children at the nursery. This involves feeding, washing, dressing and toileting them. First thing in the morning I help set the play equipment and play activities. I am able to play with the children and I become a friend to many of them. I sometimes give first aid to those children who have minor cuts and bruises.

"One of the aspects of the job I like best is monitoring the development of a child during his or her stay at the nursery. I have to be very observant and try to identify any problems either before they arise or as they occur. This requires a responsible and caring attitude, as well as sound judgement. I also like the teaching part of the job. I teach children to do up their shoes, life and social skills and table manners. I also do some pre-reading and number work.

"I like the job very much as every day is different. Some days I spend most of the time outside overseeing the children's play. Other days I assist with meals. I see myself staying at this job for some time to come. I hope one day to own and run my own day nursery."

# 8.3 How to write a job or training application

The main stages of **recruitment** (finding someone to fill a vacancy) are the same for any job:

- the employer advertises the job
- the applicants apply for the job
- the employer selects the most suitable applicants to interview
- the applicants attend for interviews
- the employer decides which applicant to employ and offers them the job.

## The job advertisement

Organisations use the following methods to advertise and recruit people for health and care jobs:

- The press:
  - national newspapers
  - local newspapers, especially for basic grade health and social care jobs.
- Specialist journals and magazines, such as:
  - *Nursing Mirror* for nursing jobs
  - *Community Care* and *Care Weekly* for social care jobs
  - *British Medical Journal* for doctors.

- Publications for minority groups, such as *The Afro-Caribbean Times*, and specialist newspapers aimed at people with disabilities.
- Job centres.
- Youth training or adult training schemes.
- Careers offices.
- Employment agencies (both for permanent and temporary posts) – see the back pages of *Community Care* for examples of employment agencies for social care staff.
- Specialist recruitment agencies.
- Visits to schools, colleges and universities.
- Job clubs.
- Careers conventions.
- The Placing, Assessment and Counselling Team based at the local job centre or employment service who deal with workers with disabilities.

Job **advertisements** should at least show the following information:

- the organisation's name and address
- an outline of the major duties
- qualifications and experience required
- salary
- benefits, such as pension, car allowance etc.

---

## Qualified Social Worker

### £16,000 – £24,398

Required to join a busy children's duty team, providing a service of assessment, support and child protection investigation to local families. You will divide your time between the Duty Service and carry your own small case load of mixed short- and long-term work. This area office serves a small inner-city area with a high level of social need indicators. A high proportion of the population belong to ethnic minority communities.

We would particularly welcome applications from social workers with Asian or Afro-Caribbean origins, as these groups are under-represented in our teams serving the inner-city multi-cultural community.

For further information contact: J. Anderson, Team Manager, on 998 567893.

Applications forms are available from Personnel Section, Central Area Office, on 998 567894 quoting reference NWR176.

Closing date 15 February 2001. Interview dates 28 and 29 March 2001

---

## Primrose Residential Home For the Elderly

### Care Assistant
### Salary £7000-£10500

A vacancy has arisen for a care assistant with the promotion of the present postholder. We are looking for a hard-working person, willing to work unsociable hours. Must have a caring nature and be willing to work as part of a team. A willingness to undergo training would be an advantage.

Further particulars from: Mrs Willis, Manager, Primrose Residential Home, West Street.
Please write for application form to be returned within two weeks of the date of this advertisement

**Activity 4**

**a** Visit your college, school or local library. Ask the librarian for a number of journals that advertise job vacancies. Make a list of the kind of vacancies that are advertised in each journal.

**b** Read the situations vacant section of a social care or health journal. Make a note of all the details of four or five advertisements. Do they provide sufficient information to give you everything you need to know? Do you think more details are needed?

**c** Discuss your views with your class colleagues.

## Finding out more about a job

Before you decide to make an application for a post that you may be interested in, it is important to gather as much information about the job as possible. How can you do this?

Most employers will supply written information about the job and conditions of employment. Your first task is to write for that information and also ask for an application form. The information will describe the skills required for the job, the knowledge, education and qualifications needed. The employer will also explain any other special requirements necessary, such as age, health, physical characteristics, locality and availability to start work.

The job description describes as closely as possible the actual work to be done.

### Job description

**Post: Care Assistant, Primrose House**
**Responsible to: Manager of home (through assistant managers)**

Main responsibilities:

* Assist residents with dressing, undressing, bathing and toilet as required
* Care for residents who are sick and needing minor dressings or bed nursing
* Support residents who have problems with mobility
* Help residents with the use of and care of aids and personal equipment
* Make and change beds, empty commodes and tidy room
* At meal times, set tables and trays, serve meals, feed those who need help, clear and tidy dining room
* Greet visitors, answer doorbell, telephone and emergency bell
* Read and write reports, take part in training activities as required
* Take part in residents' meetings and managers' meetings as required
* Support residents by talking to them, taking part in their activities, taking them out, participating in their hobbies etc.
* Such other duties that may be required by the manager as are reasonable.

**Activity 5**

**a** From a local newspaper, select an appropriate job advertisement and obtain information about the advertised post from the employer.

**b** Discuss the information you have obtained with your colleagues. Was there enough information to let you know what the job is and what qualifications and experience the employer is looking for?

You can use Activity 5 to provide evidence for Key Skills Communication C.1.1 and C1.2.

## Applying for a job

When you have found out as much as you can about the job it is time to make an application. This requires very careful thought and preparation. You will not get a second chance if the application does not result in you being invited for interview.

The job advertisement will often say how you should apply, usually in one of the following ways:

*What is a job description?*

- by sending a **curriculum vitae** (CV) – a summary of the relevant information that the employer needs to know. You write the CV yourself and send it with a **covering letter**
- by completing an **application form** supplied by the employer.

### Why send a CV?

The purpose of a CV is to let the employer know your personal details and experience. It is your chance to sell yourself to a prospective employer. One of the good points about a CV is that you can design it yourself and tailor it to suit each job you apply for. A standard CV is not the most effective means of selling yourself for a specific job.

If you are writing to someone to see if they have any vacancies, a CV with a covering letter is essential.

To create a good impression your CV should:

- be easy to read, concise and well designed (a clear layout)
- give details of your experience that are relevant to the specific job that you are applying for
- include actual facts and figures, such as grades achieved in examinations and relevant voluntary work or work experience that you have done.
- be typed.

*What is the purpose of a CV?*

Your main aim should be to encourage the person making the selection to read your CV rather than putting it in the wastepaper bin.

## What should you put in your CV?

What you put in your CV will depend on the job that you are applying for. For example, a CV for the post of kitchen cleaner will have a different emphasis from that for a care assistant or a nursery nurse, where you would need to put greater emphasis on your caring experience.

## Writing your CV

The first stage of producing a CV is to write a draft. You may have to do a number of drafts before you are happy with what you have done.

The length of your CV should be no more than two sides of A4. There will be many CVs sent in for any one job and the employer needs to be able to read them quickly and gain an impression of your suitability for the post.

Your style of writing should be concise and to the point. Use words that suggest you are keen and willing to do things. Verbs such as 'produced', 'arranged', 'wrote', 'contributed' and 'accomplished' should be used. They suggest that you are a person who has done things. Just include facts.

The tone of your writing should be positive and optimistic. The different sections should be well-spaced and you should also leave wide margins.

> **Remember**
>
> A CV is not your complete life story. It is a summary of the relevant things you wish the prospective employer to know.

---

### Curriculum Vitae

**Personal details**

| | |
|---|---|
| Name | Ann Mary Jones |
| Date of birth | 16 May 1978 |
| Home address | 26 West Hill, Derby DB66 7JJ |
| Telephone no. | 0189 123456 |

**Education and qualifications**

| | |
|---|---|
| 1989–1994 | Queensway School, Crewe |
| | GCSEs: English (E), Mathematics (E), |
| | Childcare (C), History (D) |
| 1994–to date | Ashton College |
| | GNVQ Foundation Health and Social Care |
| | GCSE: Sociology – Welfare in Society |

**Work experience**

| | |
|---|---|
| 1992 | Two weeks working in Westcott Old People's Home |
| 1993 | One week on Geriatric Ward of St Thomas's Hospital |
| 1994/5 | I have had a number of placements: |
| | Apple Day Centre |
| | Bush House Residential Home |
| | Beacon School |

**Other skills**

I have done baby-sitting for my sister and neighbours for the past three years. I also help out at a club for mentally handicapped children on Saturdays. I like horse-riding and going to dances. On Sunday I work for a few hours at a local store.

---

When you have produced a draft of your CV, ask another person, perhaps your teacher or a classmate, to read it through. Ask them to tell you if it is appropriate and whether it creates a good impression.

When you are satisfied that you have produced a good CV, either type it yourself or ask someone else to do it for you. Never send a handwritten CV to a prospective employer. (Sometimes, however, employers will request that the application form or the covering letter is completed in your own handwriting.)

Post the CV to the employer with a covering letter. The letter will introduce you to the employer and it will encourage him or her to read your CV.

## *What should you put in the covering letter?*

- The job for which you are applying
- The reference number (this will be found in the advertisement)
- The reason why you are applying for the job
- Where you saw the job advertised
- Relevant details related to your work experience, skills or qualifications – important facts that will catch the eye and make the person want to read your CV.

---

26 West Hill
Derby
DB66 7JJ

26 January 2001

Ms J. W. Harris
Manager
St Vincent's Residential Home for the Elderly
88 Leafy Glade
Coventry
CB66 2HH

Dear Ms Harris

Care Assistant Post – Reference No. 12345
I read with interest the information about the above vacancy in *The Star* newspaper last Monday. I would like to be considered for the post and I enclose my curriculum vitae.

As you will see from my CV, I am just about to finish my Foundation GNVQ course in Health and Social Care. This is an introductory course to social care. The work experience that I have had over the past year has only served to increase my interest in wanting to work in the care field.

The job you have advertised appeals to me because I have always wanted to work with the elderly and it is also within easy travelling distance from my home.

I look forward to hearing from you soon.

Yours sincerely

*Ann Jones*

Ann Jones (Miss)

---

*An example of a covering letter*

### Remember

- Draft out what you want to say in rough first.
- Write clearly, using plain paper, pen and ink or a ballpoint pen – do not use pencil.
- Type the letter if you can, especially if your handwriting is not tidy.
- Keep the letter short and to the point.
- Check your spelling, punctuation and grammar.
- Say which job you are interested in and where you saw it advertised.
- Make the information you give relevant to the position. So read the advertisement again carefully.
- State why you are interested in the job and what skills and experience you have.
- Print your name clearly under your signature.

## Key Skills

You can use Activity 6 to provide evidence for Key Skills Communication C1.1, C1.2 and C1.3 and Information Technology IT1.1 and IT1.2.

### Activity 6

**a** Read and give very careful consideration to the advertisement for a nursing assistant below. Write a CV, giving the relevant information that you think would get you an interview for the post.

---

**North Area Hospital**
**Johnson Ward**

**Nursing Assistant**
**Salary £8,000 – £9,500 p.a. inc.**
**38 hrs per week on a shift basis**

Johnson Ward is based in a new Community Unit. At present it has 16 male and 8 female clients with long-term mental health needs. The duties of the nursing assistant will include the daily support and the personal care of the clients. Previous experience of caring for people would be desirable but it is not essential. However, you will need to have an interest in working with people with long-term mental health needs. You will need to be flexible and willing to work as part of a team. It is essential that you possess good communication skills and a positive caring attitude.

Telephone Mrs H. Maloney for an informal chat about the job on 888 98000 ext. 1234

Application is by CV to:
Personnel Officer, 24 Jackson Road, Doncaster DN56 8MF
Please quote ref. BN 678

Closing date 26 January 2001

---

**b** Discuss and compare your completed CV with your class colleagues.

## 8.4 How to prepare yourself for interview

### Filling in an application form

Employers use application forms to make decisions about who to call for interview. They can find out more about an applicant from an application form than from a CV. This is because they can ask for the precise information they need to know.

Many employers still ask questions about marital status, number of children and ethnic origin. Do you think this is necessary? Does it matter if a person has three children, is married or what their ethnic group is? Would any of these things stop someone from carrying out the job? Personal information like this can lead to employers making subjective and inaccurate impressions of candidates. This can lead to prejudice and discrimination. A person should be selected for interview for the job on their ability to do the job.

Oldcastle Social Services Department
Civic Offices
Downtown SC56 2TR

**APPLICATION FOR EMPLOYMENT**
*Please print clearly*
Position: Care assistant
Post no.: 123

Personal details
Surname ................................................    Forenames ...................................
Address ................................................    Date of birth ...............................
................................................    Telephone no ...............................
........................ Post code ....................

Do you have a full driving licence YES/NO

Present employment
Name and address of employer          From          Salary
................................................    .....................  ................................
Job title ................................................

Previous employment
List below your past employment, beginning with the most recent.
Name and address of employer          From     To     Salary
................................................    .....................  ................................
................................................    .....................
Job title ................................................    Reason for leaving ...........................

Name and address of employer          From     To     Salary
................................................    .....................  ................................
................................................    .....................
Job title ................................................    Reason for leaving ...........................

Name and address of employer          From     To     Salary
................................................    .....................  ................................
................................................    .....................
Job title ................................................    Reason for leaving ...........................

Education
Secondary School          From     To     Examinations/Results
................................................    .....................  ................................

Further/Higher Education          From     To     Courses/Results
................................................    .....................  ................................

Other courses and training          From     To     Results
................................................    .....................  ................................

Membership of professional organisations


Interests/Experience and skills
Outline your experience, either paid or voluntary, which is relevant to this application.


References
Name ................................................    Name ...................................
Occupation ................................................    Occupation ...................................
Address ................................................    Address ...................................
Telephone ................................................    Telephone ...................................

May we contact your referees before an offer of interview? YES/NO

Signed ................................................    Date ...................................

*An example of an application form*

Note: Employers can request special permission to advertise for a man or a woman or someone of a particular ethnic origin. For example, if a playgroup only admits black children, the employer could make a case for looking for a black worker.

## The job specification

Before an employer advertises a job, he or she will have drawn up a job specification. This will include not only details of the actual work to be done (the job description, see page 294), but also the sorts of things they would like to see in the applicant – the ideal type of person for the job. The specification will detail the knowledge, skills, experience and qualifications required, and also any other requirements such as age, sex, ethnic group and physical characteristics.

The employer will compare the information in your CV or application form with the specification. If your application meets the specification, you may be invited for interview. You will be notified of:

* the date and time of the interview
* how long the interview will last
* the place where the interview will be held
* the name of the person to report to
* whether you will be told of the outcome of the interview on the day.

The interview has a number of aims:

* to help the employer decide if you are a suitable person for the job
* to give you the chance to see if you could do the job
* to give you an opportunity to decide if you want the job or not.

## Preparing for the interview

The more you can find out about the job and the employer's business before the interview, the more prepared you will be. You will need to think about:

* why you have applied for the post
* your ambitions
* the skills you can offer the employer
* why you would find the job interesting
* your previous achievements.

Make sure you know exactly when the interview will be held, how you are going to get there, who you are going to see and the time of the interview.

### What should you wear?

You should give careful thought to the clothes you will wear for the interview. You should think about the following:

* Do your clothes need dry cleaning?
* What would be appropriate clothing for the interview?

- Your footwear?
- Your hair?

Appearance and grooming are important because they help to create that vital first impression the interviewer will get of you. Use your common sense about appearance.

*Appearance and grooming create that vital first impression*

## What questions might you be asked?

Be prepared. It is useful to have some idea of the kinds of question that you may be asked in the interview. Show a genuine interest in the work of the organisation to which you have applied – find out what you can about it beforehand. This will help you prepare so that you will not be taken by surprise. It will also boost your confidence.

If you were the interviewer, what questions would you ask? Imagine that you are interviewing an applicant for a job as an assistant in a nursery. What questions would you ask?

Tell me about yourself.

- Why are you applying for this post?
- Why do you want to work at this nursery?
- What experience have you had of working with children?
- How would you make sure that you treated boys and girls equally?
- What skills do you have that make you think you can do the job?
- What do you do in your spare time?
- What is your ultimate ambition?

What questions do you think that the person applying for such a post might like to ask?

- What are the normal hours of work?
- Are there any unsociable working hours?
- What is the pay? Will I be paid weekly or monthly?
- What are the holiday arrangements?
- What are the promotion prospects?
- Will I be offered training opportunities?

## How can you make a good impression during the interview?

- Be pleasant and polite.
- Don't sit down until offered a chair.
- Don't smoke.
- Relax and sit upright in the chair. Don't fidget.
- Try to be positive and optimistic when replying to questions.
- Always look at the interviewer and members of the panel.
- If you do not understand a question, ask for it to be repeated.
- Don't be flippant. Don't make any silly remarks to hide your nerves.
- Try to hide your nerves by controlling your voice. Use pauses in speech to stress important points.
- Be honest. Don't invent answers. If you cannot answer a question, say so.
- Make sure you know the names of the interviewers.
- At the end of the interview you should always ask two or three questions. When the interview ends, always shake the hand of the interviewers and thank them.

## National Record of Achievement

We have already discussed how to present information in the form of a curriculum vitae or application form. You can also take your National Record of Achievement to the interview and ask if you can show it to the interviewer. Make sure that is it neat and tidy and has all the relevant information in it, such as:

- certificates
- sports achievement
- letter of recommendation from work experience
- school reports.

### Activity 7

The aim of this activity is to investigate two jobs in health and social care that might suit you.

a  Choose two jobs that might be suitable for you:
  – a job that you might like to do when you have finished this course

▶▶

- a job that you might like to do in some years' time after further training and experience.
**b** Write a description of each job's main purpose. One way to do this is to get information from books, job descriptions and discussions with people already in similar jobs. Use a word processor for your work, wherever possible.
**c** For both jobs, list the main skills that you would need to carry out the jobs. Use the following headings:
  - Practical skills
  - Emotional skills
  - Communication skills.
**d** List the qualifications and training needed for both jobs.
**e** Describe how you would gain the skills, training and qualifications appropriate to each of the jobs you have chosen.

## Key terms

After reading this unit, you should be able to understand the following words and phrases. If you do not, go back through the unit and find out, or look them up in the Glossary.

*Registered General Nurse (RGN)*
*Project 2000*
*Monitoring the person's ability*
*Health care support worker*
*Diploma in Social Work*
*National Vocational Qualifications (NVQs)*

*Advertisements*
*Curriculum vitae*
*Covering letter*
*Application form*
*Recruitment*

## Test yourself

1  What basic qualification do you need to begin training for social work?
2  What do the letters NVQ stand for?
3  What should be in a letter of application for a job?
4  What kinds of information would you expect to find in a job advertisement?
5  Describe the main stages in the recruitment process.
6  List six places where you could find out about jobs in health and social care.
7  What five main pieces of information should a job advertisement give?
8  What is a curriculum vitae?
9  When you are invited for interview, what five main things should you be notified of?
10  What is an application form?

# Assignment for Unit Eight

*Produce an employment folder containing information about the main ways to find a job, information about jobs that interest you, an application for a job and a record of your performance at a mock interview.*

*Tasks*

1 Use information to find out about a job or training vacancy that interests you – information sources could include newspapers, journals, libraries, job centres, school careers officers.

2 Complete an application form or CV (which should include personal information, your skills and qualifications, and interests and hobbies) and a letter for the job or training position that you have selected.

3 Take part in a mock interview for a job or training.

4 Use at least three information sources that you have found yourself about jobs or training.

5 Explain clearly in your written application why you are suitable for the job you have chosen.

6 In the mock interview use appropriate non-verbal and verbal skills to communicate your interest in the job to the person interviewing you.

7 Make sure that your information in the application shows clearly that it is linked to your chosen job. This information should be detailed and the content and presentation should be of a high standard.

8 Review your information, search, application and interview. Give information on ways to improve your job-seeking skills.

## Get the grade

To achieve a **PASS** you must complete tasks 1–3.

To achieve a **MERIT** you must complete tasks 1–6.

To achieve a **DISTINCTION** you must complete tasks 1–8.

## Key Skills — Opportunity

| | You can use this opportunity to provide evidence for the following key skills |
|---|---|
| Information Technology IT1.1 | Find information about jobs/training (when you use a database). |
| Information Technology IT1.2 | Produce a job application – CV etc. |
| Communication C1.1 | Answer an interviewer's questions and ask questions. |
| Communication C1.2 | Find out about opportunities. |
| Communication C1.3 | Produce a written CV or application form or letter |

# Working as part of a team

## What is covered in this unit

9.1 *How to choose an activity and set out your aims*
9.2 *Plan the activity as a team and identify roles and responsibilities of all the team members*
9.3 *How to carry out the activity*
9.4 *How to review the activity to find out how you and the team worked*

---

At the end of this unit you will be asked to produce a written or oral report on your chosen activity. If you would like to see further details of the tasks you are likely to need to carry out for assessment, please refer to the end of the unit where an assignment has been set (see pages 332–333). This unit will guide you through what you need to know in order to successfully put together this report. You will be assessed on this work and awarded a grade. This grade will contribute to the overall grade you will get for Unit Nine.

### Materials you will need to complete this unit

- Plan of the activity
- Review of the activity.

### Introduction

This unit focuses on developing your skills in working with others in a team and carrying out a specific activity. The activity that you and your colleagues decide to carry out must be related to caring for people. Some suggestions are given below.

When carrying out the activity you should use the knowledge you have gained from the other Foundation units you have completed.

Your tutor or teacher will help you with the team activity by meeting with you as a team on a regular basis and reviewing with you individually how you have undertaken the activities. This will enable the tutor to assess what you have learned from the activity and why you contributed what you did in team discussions. Either you or the tutor will keep a written record of these discussions.

## 9.1 How to choose an activity and set out your aims

When you have got to know and trust the rest of your team, you are ready to decide what activity you would like to do. There are many activities that you can choose from:

- organising a party or a day out for a group of children or elderly people
- producing a booklet containing a list of voluntary care organisations in your locality
- organising a fund-raising event
- planning and organising a playgroup for children during half-term at your college
- preparing and printing a newspaper for your school or college
- producing a booklet giving healthy-living advice for a specific group of people.

These are just a few ideas. Use them to prompt other suggestions among your team.

### How can you decide what activity to carry out?

To help the team decide what activity to carry out, you can have a **brainstorming** session. This simply means that all the members of your team individually write down as many ideas as they can think of. Then you discuss the ideas in the group and select one activity that you are all happy with.

Brainstorming helps to overcome the problems of making decisions too quickly or doing things in a certain way just because that is the way we always do it. Brainstorming helps you to look at things in a new and imaginative way – try it out in Activity 1 below.

*You might decide to organise a playgroup outing, as in this photograph*

### Activity 1

**a** Write down the answer to the following question: What possible uses can metal paper clips be put to? Do not worry how silly or unusual some of the uses are.

**b** Discuss what you have written down with the rest of your team. As a team you may have written down a few uses, such as, clipping two pieces of paper together or use as a pipe cleaner. As a group, choose the most original idea.

Did your list include any of the following possible uses:

- made into chains?
- hooks?
- unlocking car doors?
- their sharp ends can punch holes in paper?
- cocktail stick?
- toothpick?

*A brainstorming session*

Brainstorming can be used effectively in small teams. Each member can shout out possible solutions to the problem. One member of the team should write each suggestion on a flip chart. Only when all the team members' ideas are exhausted, should a full discussion of the suggestions take place. The team can then make a final decision on the best solution or idea to follow up.

### Remember

Never put down, ridicule, criticise, tease or embarrass other members of the team or their ideas.

The team should now be in a position to select an activity that will allow each member to play an individual as well as a team role.

## Time management: how to organise the team's activity

Planning is an important part of carrying out any task or activity. When the team has selected an activity, you will need to consider how long you have been given to carry it out and whether you can fit in all the tasks to complete the activity. This is called **time management**. Ask yourselves the following questions:

- How long do we have to carry out the activity?
- How available are the resources – the things we might need to complete the activity (people, money, accommodation, transport etc.)? How easy is it to get the information we might want (cost etc.)?
- Can we do all we want to do in the time given?
- Do the team members have the individual skills to complete the activity (people who can organise, manage money, write letters etc.)?

As a example, let us suppose you are going to organise a party for a group of children who attend a school for children with learning difficulties. Your time plan might look like this:

### An example of team management

| Task | Estimated time needed to carry out task (weeks) |
|------|------|
| Discussion within team and agreement of activity | 1 |
| Agreeing the team action plan | 1 |
| Agreeing your individual action plans | 1 |
| Discussion and agreement with school | 2 |
| Organisation of party | 4 |
| Review of activity, team and individual | 2 |
| Preparation of evidence for report | 2 |
| *Total* | *13 weeks* |

You can see from the list of tasks in the above example that for an activity such as organising a party you may need to think in terms of at least 13 weeks. Planning your time is a very important aspect of carrying out an activity.

---

**Activity 2**

As a team you have been given the task of producing an information leaflet about your course for new students. You have to design the leaflet and decide what it should include.

List the tasks that you might have to do complete the activity and the time that you might take to do them. Use a table like the example below:

| Task | Estimated time needed to carry out task (weeks) |
|------|------------------------------------------------|
| ................................... | ..................................... |
| ................................... | ..................................... |
| ................................... | ..................................... |
| Total | ......................... *weeks* |

---

Did you include any of the following tasks:

- Gather information on course?
- Decide on the layout?
- Decide on the lettering
- Time to print the leaflet?
- Time to review the activity?

## Contacting people

To complete an activity you will need to contact other people with expertise or access to resources. These people may be individuals or they may represent organisations, for example a social worker may represent the local Social Services Department.

There are a number of different ways that you can contact people:

The method you choose will depend on a number of things:

- the distance from you that the person lives
- how busy they are
- whether they are on the telephone, email or have a fax machine.

Whatever method you choose you must keep in mind the following:

- Whom do you need to contact? If you wish to invite a group of children from a school to a party perhaps you should contact the head of the school.
- How do you make arrangements to contact people? You can telephone people on the off-chance that they may have time to talk to you. But it is better to telephone to agree a specific time to telephone again. By doing this, you will be sure of speaking to the correct person. Never visit without making an appointment. Make an appointment by letter or telephone, telling the person:
  - who you are
  - the organisation you represent
  - why you wish to see them.
- If you are writing to people, do not forget to enclose a stamped, addressed envelope. If you do this, they are more likely to reply to your letter.
- What is it you want them to do? You must be clear in your own mind what you want them to do. Remember that they are busy people. They will be more likely to help you if you know exactly what it is you want them to do. Make a list of the things you want to say or know before you see or ring them.

The example below makes it clear to whom the letter is written and what it is you want the person to do.

---

Best College
Circle Road

12 December 2000
Mrs Jackson
Head of St Ann's Centre
Straight Street
Any Town S1 0TY

Dear Mrs Jackson

Party for Elderly People February 2001

I am a student on a GNVQ Foundation Course at Best College. My class has decided that we would like to organise a party for the elderly people who attend your day centre. Could I please make an appointment to visit you so that I can discuss this with you?

I am free every Wednesday afternoon and Friday mornings. Would either of these days suit you? Please let me know which date and time you could see me.

I enclose a stamped addressed envelope for your reply.

Yours sincerely

*Mary Thorn*

---

> ### Remember
>
> Each member of the team will need to write their own copy of a letter, not to send to the individual or organisation, but to keep as evidence that you are capable of writing such a letter. You must keep a copy of this letter in your portfolio as evidence. A copy of the actual letter sent will not do, unless of course you actually wrote it.

### Activity 3

The team has asked you to write a letter to the head of the local youth club requesting the following:

* permission to use a room in the club for a meeting
* the cost of hiring the room
* dates when a room would be available.

Write the letter, taking into account the points above. *Remember to use capital letters and full stops in the appropriate places.*

## 9.2 Plan the activity as a team and identify roles and responsibilities of all the team members

### Working as a team or group

We all have a need to belong to one sort of group or another. We form groups:

* for security – people are naturally sociable and want to be with others, sharing common ideas, values and pleasures
* to help others – this could be a voluntary group or charity
* to get things done – we can often achieve things we want to do as part of a group that would not otherwise be possible on our own.

Membership of a group or team can have the following benefits:

* pleasure and satisfaction from sharing a common interest
* security, which can give you confidence
* learning opportunities – you can learn skills in the group that can be practised in your personal life
* opportunities to develop leadership skills
* experience the democratic processes.

*A group at work*

When you have completed this team activity you should:

- be able to understand and accept other members of the team
- have improved your communication skills as a result of working together, sharing ideas and discussing how to do things
- be more able to take responsibility for your own learning and behaviour
- co-operate with one another in planning, carrying out and reviewing tasks and activities
- understand the need to have a process for making decisions
- feel free within the team to discuss problems and resolve conflicts constructively.

These things will not just happen; your tutor or teacher will help you to set targets, plan activities and review them.

## *Getting to know other members of the team*

Before you decide what team activity to do, the members of the team need to be able to trust one another. To do this, you have to get to know each other well. You have to reveal things about yourself to the other members of the team. When you have done this, they will be more willing to reveal something of themselves.

This **mutual exchange** of personal information leads to better understanding and acceptance of each other. When you have reached this stage you will feel more comfortable with each other. As a result, you will not be afraid to make suggestions and contributions to the team action plan.

/ **Activity 4** /

**a** Fill in as many of these incomplete statements as you wish. You do not have to answer them all:

My name is:

My age is:

I live in:

I was born in:

My marital status is:

My friends:

My hobbies:

I want to get a job as:

At this very minute, I feel:

My ambition:

Things I find difficult:

My religious beliefs:

To me, being black/white means:

**b** Read your completed statements out to the rest of the team. Anyone in the team can comment on any of the statements. (You will get the chance to do the same when the rest of the team read out their statements.) You can stop discussing your statements whenever you like. There must be no compulsion for anyone to discuss something they do not wish to.

**c** When you have finished this activity, ask yourself:
  – How do you feel?
  – How honest were you in revealing your feelings?
  – Were you more open about some things than others?

Telling the team about yourself will involve you in exchanging facts, feelings and opinions with other members. This sharing of details allows you to discover things that you have in common with each other. It will help you to develop trust and make members of the team more open and communicative with each other.

## Preparing your team action plan

When you have permission from the organisation or individual to carry out the activity, the team is in a position to draw up a **team action plan**. Ask yourselves:

• Can we carry out our plans?
• How long do we have to complete the activity?
• Has each member of the team the ability to carry out their individual action plan as agreed originally?
• Is the team in a position to prepare a team action plan?

## What is action planning?

Planning is an essential part of the process of learning, doing or accomplishing something. With small tasks or problems, it is often an automatic process. For example, after travelling to a distant town by bus or train, you may use this experience automatically next time you want to plan a journey. You do not have to find out again where to buy a ticket or catch the bus. With new or big activities, this system may not work. What we need is a plan to help us organise what to do – an action plan.

Action plans can be developed by individuals or teams. When we work as part of a team action planning is a must. It helps to co-ordinate what each individual member and the team itself will do. When developing an action plan you must record and agree each member's task, for example: 'Mary will contact the head of the school by a certain date and Jack will write the invitations to the children.' This is a form of agreement, or contract, between the people involved in carrying out the activity.

*What is an action plan?*

The essential parts of an action plan are:

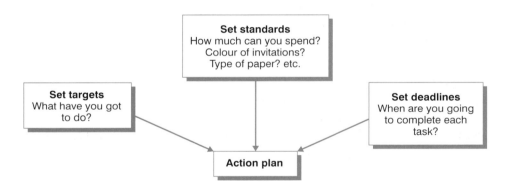

For example, below you will find a list of some of the tasks you might have to do both as a team and as individuals to organise and plan a party for a group of elderly people. Each of the tasks has to be agreed by the team members and some of the tasks allocated to individual members of the team.

To help you plan either an individual or team action plan, you must list all the things to be done. Then you need to decide who is to do them and how long they will take to finish the task.

The team will need to draw up a team action plan like the one on page 315. Each individual member of the team will also have to make an individual action plan.

## Action plan

*Time and day of party*
When are you going to have the party?
What day is best for the party?
At what time of day will you have the party?

*Premises*
Where will the party be held?
What facilities will be needed?
How many plates, cups, etc. will be needed?
What facilities are needed for storage of food, etc.?
Will the team have to pay for premises? If so, how much can the team afford to pay?
Types of premises to think about: community centres, youth clubs, college refectories, scout halls or church halls

*Collection of elderly people from their own homes*
Who will decide who is to be invited?
How will those attending the party be transported?
Types of transport: private cars, college mini-bus, hired bus

*Timing of the party*
When should the party take place?
What day is most suitable?
What time during the day best suits the participants?
Things to consider: age of people attending, time of year

*Publicity*
What kinds of invitation will you use?
How will they be delivered?
How will those invited let you know that they accept the invitation?
Consider: letter, cards, postal delivery, hand delivery

*Money*
How will you pay for food, transport, the venue, invitations?
What kind of accounting system will you need to let people see how you are spending the money?
Where will you keep the money?

*Food*
Who is going to prepare the food?
Who is going to pay for the food?
Who will serve the food?
Who is going to wash up?

*Finishing up*
Who is going to clear away?
Who is going to write thank-you letters?
Who is going to find out if the elderly people enjoyed the party?
The tasks that are necessary to organise a party for a group of elderly people ▶▶

| Team action plan schedule<br>Tasks to be carried out<br>(Goals) | Date to be<br>completed | Person to carry<br>out task |
|---|---|---|
| *Collection of elderly people<br>from their own homes*<br>Who will decide who is to be<br>invited? | 10.12.00 | Mary |
| How will those attending the<br>party be transported? | 10.2.01 | Team |
| *Publicity*<br>What kinds of invitation will<br>you use? | 14.12.00 | Team |
| Who will design them? | | Susan |
| Who will get them printed? | 4.1.01 | Susan |
| How will they be delivered? | 6.1.01 | Team |
| Who will deliver them? | | John/Mary/Helen |
| How will those invited let<br>you know they accept the<br>invitation? | | Team |
| *Money*<br>How will you pay for food,<br>transport, the venue,<br>invitations? | 10.12.00 | Team |
| Who will look after the money? | | Jack |
| What kind of accounting system<br>will you need to let people<br>see how you are spending the<br>money? | | Team |
| Where will you keep the money? | | Team |
| *Food*<br>Who is going to prepare the<br>food? | 25.1.01 | Team |
| Who is going to pay for the<br>food? | | Team |
| Who will serve the food? | | All |
| Who is going to wash up? | | Team |
| *Finishing up*<br>Who is going to clear away? | | Team |
| Who is going to write thank-<br>you letters? | | Michelle |
| Who is going to find out if<br>the elderly people enjoyed<br>the party? | 1.3.01 | Joanne |

**Key Skills**

| Activity 5 |

The team has decided to paint the room in the college used by a voluntary playgroup. They will need to consider:

- how long they have to carry out the task
- how much it will cost
- how much money they have
- what colours to use
- who will do the painting
- who will clear up afterwards
- who will liaise with the playgroup organiser.

Use the schedule below to draw up a team action plan:

**Team action plan schedule**

| Tasks to be carried out (Goals) | Date to be completed | Person to carry out task |
|---|---|---|

## Undertaking a role in a team activity

Before you begin to undertake any role as an individual member of the team, you must draw up an individual action plan. This looks very similar to the team action plan, except that it only relates to the job or jobs that you have agreed to do. It should indicate:

- the job you will do
- when you hope to finish it
- the resources you will need to complete successfully.

See the example below.

| Name: **John Kendall** | | Class or group **1a** |
|---|---|---|
| Tutor: **Helen Sullivan** | | |

Activity   **Organising an outing for children in the college nursery**

| Individual tasks | Date to be done by | Resources needed |
|---|---|---|
| **Telephone head of nursery** | **3.6.00** | **Telephone** |
| **Get list of children** | **6.6.00** | **From teacher** |
| **Find out if any children have medication** | **10.6.00** | **List from teacher** |
| **Arrange transport** | **16.6.00** | **Minibus** |
| **Report back to team** | **20.6.00** | **Written report** |

*An example of an individual action plan*

## Making the best use of available resources

How do you make the best use of available resources? Let us look at an example from the individual action plan above – deciding which form of transport to use to take children from the college nursery on an outing. What kind of questions should you ask yourself?

- How many children are going on the outing?
- What health and safety considerations do I need to take account of?
- How many staff will be needed to escort the children?
- Do any of them use a wheelchair?
- What kind of transport will be able to accommodate a wheelchair?
- How many seats are in a mini-bus?
- How many children will a mini-bus carry?
- What is the cost of a mini-bus?
- What is the cost of a 50+ seater bus? Can it accommodate a wheelchair?
- How much money do I have to spend on transport?
- Would it be cheaper to use the college mini-bus?

### Activity 6

You have been allocated the individual task of arranging for the design and printing of invitations to a party for elderly people. You have limited money and cannot go to a professional printers. You are a student in a college with a large number of students doing art and design courses.

What questions would you need to ask yourself to make the best use of the resources available to you?

Did your list of questions include any of the following:

- Who is the best group or person to do the printing? College reprographics? Art/design students? Private printers?
- Which is the best group or person to design the invitation? Myself? Art students?

It would possibly be the cheapest and best use of available resources if the art and design students designed and printed the invitation cards.

## Note-taking to give feedback to the team

Remember to take notes of any conversations you may have or agreements that you may make with any individual or organisation. You can use notes you have taken when reporting back on your actions to the team.

**Note-taking** is a very important aspect of your work. If you are going to work in health or social care, it is a skill that you must practise and develop. Note-taking provides a written record of what you have been studying or the information that you have been collecting. To be useful the notes must be accurately taken and, later, accurately presented.

You should take notes in a consistent format:

- In class a loose-leaf binder is better than an exercise book because you can rearrange your notes for discussions, tutorials or revision.
- If you are observing a situation and taking notes, or interviewing someone, then a less obvious method is best – perhaps use a small notebook or tape-recorder. Remember to ask permission before you tape record anyone or any situation.

## Preparation of interview notes

### *Make a note of key points*
When recording any conversation, or when note-taking in class, you should take clear, brief notes that will allow you to recall the important points later. You need to capture the important points of agreement, or the important line of argument. When interviewing anyone, concentrate on following the flow of argument and just jot down any key points with a structure that you can understand later.

### *Be sure you know what you want to talk to the other person about*
Before you interview anyone you should be very clear in your mind what it is you wish to get out of the interview, what is it you want to find out or get agreement for. Plan the interview and the questions you will ask. Work out what notes you will want to make.

*Plan the questions you will ask*

### Make notes in your own words

The process of converting the ideas or conversation of the person you are interviewing into your own language will also ensure that you understand the content – what you write down. Add your own comments where appropriate.

---

**Activity 7**

**a** Read the first four pages of Unit One. Make notes of the main points that are made in the text.

**b** Compare and check what you have written with the other team members. Discuss the different way each of you took notes and what you have written.

---

## Review of the team action plan

Before the team moves on to allocating and agreeing individual action plans, it is useful to sit down and look at everything you have done so far. There are two parts to this review.

### 1. What have you done so far?

- Have you a written record of the team's activities?
- Have you all agreed on the activity to be undertaken?
- Is the plan going as you would have hoped?
- Has everyone in the team made a contribution?
- Have your tutors helped you? Is there any way they could help you in the future?

### 2. *What needs to be done to put the team plan into action?*

- How can you overcome any problems that you have identified in part 1 above?
- Do you want to make any changes to the plan?
- What resources will you need to continue?

| Tasks to be carried out (Goals) | Task completed Yes | No | What needs to be done? |
|---|---|---|---|
| Have you agreed: | | | |
| on a party? | / | | – |
| on transport? | / | | – |
| who is attending? | / | | – |
| the kinds of invitation you will use? | | / | Agree design |
| printers for the invitations? | / | | – |
| how to deliver the invitations? | | / | Post or by hand |
| how activity will be paid for? | | | – |
| the accounting system to be used? | | / | Advice from tutor |
| where the money will be kept? | / | | – |
| who will prepare the food? | / | | – |
| who is going to buy the food? | | / | Advice from catering students |
| who will serve the food? | / | | – |
| who is going to clear away? | / | | – |
| who is going to write thank-you letters? | / | | – |
| who is going to find out if the elderly people enjoyed the party? | | / | Further discussion |
| Did all members take part in decision-making? | / | | – |
| Have you considered health and safety factors? | | / | Read Unit Four and talk to tutor |

*An example of a review of a team action plan*

Use a review sheet like the one above to help you review the team action plan. As you can see, there are still one or two activities to be decided upon. The team should either decide upon these issues themselves or ask their tutor for advice.

# 9.3 How to carry out the activity

## Recording what you do as a team

Remember that you must provide evidence in your portfolio of your ability:

- to work as a member of a team
- to work on an individual basis, on your own.

It is, therefore, very important that you devise a method of **recording** individual contributions in the team. You will need to provide evidence that the team can:

- identify the resources that are available
- identify which member of the team is going to carry out which task.

This will be shown in the team action plan discussed above.

## Recording what individuals do within a team

However, you must also provide evidence that you contributed to team discussions and in making decisions within the team. Your tutor can watch what you do in the team, but you yourselves can also record who made contributions, decisions and identified resources.

The activity below describes one method that you can use to show who did what in the team.

### Activity 8

The aim of this activity is for half the team to observe the other half performing a team task.

**a** As a team, decide on a task. This may be something as simple as a topic for discussion. The members who are to carry out the task sit in a circle or around a table. The observers place themselves where they can see what the others in the team are doing. See the example below.

**Key**

Members who perform tasks

Members who observe and record

**b** Begin the task. The observers should observe and record what they see. They should look for:
- Who speaks to whom?
- Who identifies resources that are available?
- Who agrees to carry out different activities?
- Who contributes to the development of the team action plan? ▶▶

To record what goes on within the team (the interactions between the members), use a table like the one below, perhaps allocating an initial letter to each member.

| | | | | |
|---|---|---|---|---|
| Who identifies resources that are available? | A C H I B | | | |
| Who agrees to carry out different activities? | B D C H K | | | |
| Who contributes to the development of the team action plan? | B I H K C | | | |

c At the end of the task, the observers and participants in the task can swap roles, so that everyone has a chance to provide evidence for their portfolio.

You may have noticed that certain members of the group say very little, while others say a lot. Some may be intimidated by those who are aggressive or say a lot. Why does this happen? Communication between people is called **interpersonal communication**.

## What stops people from communicating?

Although everyone communicates, it is true to say that good communicators are made. Most of us will have learnt communication skills from the people that we lived with (starting with our families) and went to school with.

Communication is not always easy. There are a number of factors that can create barriers between ourselves and other members of the team. We may not want to, or may be unable to, communicate with colleagues for many reasons. Colleagues may be confused, tired, shy or embarrassed, disabled, in pain or emotionally distressed. Difficulties could arise because colleagues may:

- be from a different ethnic background
- be from a different social class
- have different cultural or religious beliefs
- have different social values
- even be of the opposite sex.

## *Health and safety considerations*

When working in the health and social care services, we must always make sure that what we do does not make it hazardous for either the client or ourselves. You must, therefore, take into consideration any health and safety factors of the activity you are organising. Read Unit Four again before you start the activity. It will give you a basic understanding of health and safety procedures.

When planning the activity, remember to examine and identify any common hazards that could occur, such as:

- the danger of fire
- unsafe equipment
- problems caused by the possibility of infections.

*quick fire*

*What is meant by the term interpersonal communication?*

Is the environment safe? Make sure that any equipment or accommodation you use is safe. In particular, consider:

- first aid equipment
- safety precautions (fire or evacuation procedures etc.)
- safe working practices (fire guards etc.)
- alarms and emergency systems, such as fire alarms.

The benefits of this will be:

- the prevention of accidents
- improved and safer working conditions
- improved and safer services for clients.

## 9.4 How to review the activity to find out how you and the team worked

When you have completed the activity, you will need to review the team's and your own individual performance against the tasks that the team and you agreed to undertake in the action plans. To review the activity you will first need to look at whether you carried out the agreed tasks as a team and as an individual. You should look at:

- whether or not resources were used effectively
- whether you dealt with any problems effectively
- whether you maintained the health and safety of those you were looking after and also your colleagues.

Your tutor will also observe your performance in the team and review your individual performance on a one-to-one basis.

### Review of the team's performance

To do this, you will need to look back at your original team action plan. For example, if the team activity was to design and print a health promotion booklet to give advice on the effects of smoking, the review could consider some of the following points:

- Were there any spelling or grammatical errors?
- Did the contents make sense to those who were intended to read it?
- Was the paper it was printed on the most appropriate type?
- Were the illustrations appropriate?
- Was the print size the most appropriate for your audience?
- Was the whole activity carried out within the time scale that was given to you?
- Did you raise enough money to pay for the booklet?
- Did it cost what the team agreed upon?

Answers to the above questions should be recorded only after a thorough discussion and agreement between all the team members. See the example below.

---

### Review of illustrations: Were the illustrations appropriate?

We decided to illustrate the booklet with drawings – some colour and some black-and-white line drawings. As the booklet was aimed at teenagers we thought that some colour drawings would catch their attention. Jack was given the job of asking students on the art course to do some drawings illustrating some of our ideas. When this was done we selected the ones we thought would be best. We had a lot of discussion on this and it took a long time for us to come to an agreement. When Mary talked to some of the teenagers that we had given the booklet to, they said that the illustrations were very good and made them think of the dangers of smoking.

We all agreed that the illustrations were appropriate.

---

When reviewing what you have done, it often a very good idea to ask the people you did the activity for what they thought about it. In the example above, the teenagers were asked about the illustrations. If you had organised a party you could ask the people you organised it for what they thought of it. One way of doing this could be by asking them to fill in a questionnaire or you could ask members of the team to interview some of those attending the party. For example:

---

### An example of a questionnaire

Party for people over 65 years of age

| *Questions* | *Yes* | *No* |
|---|---|---|
| 1. Was the time suitable for you? | | |
| 2. Was the transport suitable? | | |
| 3. Was the venue appropriate? | | |
| 4. Did you like the food? | | |
| 5. Was there enough food? | | |

---

The information, or data, that you collect in the questionnaires can be presented in a number of ways. One way is to present it in the form of a chart, for example:

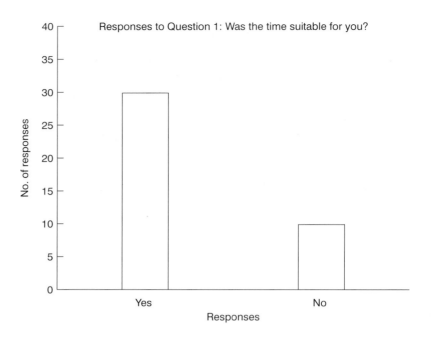

## Review of an individual's performance

You can use the same methods to review your individual performance. You can ask people what they thought about what you did. However, you must also evaluate your individual action plan yourself, such as any letters you may have written.

---

*"The team agreed that I should write a letter to the local leisure centre asking if we could book a swimming session for a group of children with physical disabilities."*

Seaforth College
Seaforth
SF1 2PP

16 January 2001

Manager
Seaforth Leisure Centre
Seaforth

Dear Mrs Atkinson

Me and my friends want to organise a swimming session for some people with physical disabilities. how much would it cost?
Can you let me know as soon as possible because we want to bring the people along next week.

Yours sincerely

*mark smith*

---

## Activity 9

Read the letter that Mark has written to the manager of the local leisure centre on page 326. Do you think this is a good letter?

**a** Is it clear what Mark wants the centre manager to do?
**b** Does the centre manager know which days Mark wants the use of the swimming pool and for how many people?
**c** Is it clear whether Mark wants to pay for the session or is he asking for a free session?
**d** If you were the manager, would you know how to answer Mark's letter?
**e** Is it a courteous letter?
**f** Are the grammar and punctuation correct?
**g** Has Mark used capital letters in the appropriate places?

### This is Mark's own review of his letter:

I can see now that I did not write a very clear letter. I did not enclose a stamped, addressed envelope, my English was not so good and I did not use capital letters to start all my sentences or when I signed my name. I feel that I should also have made it clearer when I wanted to use the centre.

Can you think of any other suggestions you might offer to Mark to help him write a more appropriate letter?

## Health and safety

Health and safety is a very important aspect of any activity that we carry out. Reviewing the health and safety factors of what you have done may prove a little more difficult than some of the other tasks that the team or you as an individual carried out. Read Unit Four again before you review the health and safety factors of your activity.

## Activity 10

The team agreed to organise a summer playgroup for children on a housing estate. The local housing department has agreed to let the team have the use of a ground floor flat with a garden to use for the summer months.

What basic health and safety factors would the team need to consider before it could open the playgroup?

**Key Skills**

You can use Activity 10 to provide evidence for Key Skills Communication C1.2.

Did your answers include any of the following:

- safe electrical plugs and wires?
- appropriate door locks?
- no access to kitchen for children?
- toilet and washing facilities?
- is the garden safe?
- can the children get out of the garden?
- are the toys safe?
- appropriate number of staff and volunteers?
- number of children?

Can you think of any more things that the team should consider as far as health and safety is concerned?

## Feedback

It is important to provide clear and **constructive feedback** to your colleagues on their performance and respond appropriately to feedback from others.

**What do we mean by constructive feedback?**

To help people in a sensitive and caring manner, we have to pay constant attention to the effectiveness of our communication skills. You will need to develop your communication skills and this team activity will help you to begin to do this.

All caring work involves good interpersonal skills. Telling people what you are doing will put them at ease. By explaining things, people will understand what you are doing and the reasons for your actions:

- Always maintain a friendly, welcoming approach.
- Always show an interest and understanding of other people's needs.
- Try to be helpful and supportive.
- Be ready to respond to others' conversation with a laugh, a smile or a word of support.

Providing feedback to people is also an important interpersonal skill that you will need to develop. But, before you can provide feedback to your colleagues, you must listen to what they are saying.

## How do you listen?

- The person speaking should be the focus of your attention.
- Listen to what has been said even if you do not agree with the other person.
- Do not disrupt the speaker by talking to others.
- Do not move around or fiddle with paper or pencils etc.
- Ask questions of the speaker and react to them.
- Encourage your colleagues to talk and explain their ideas and feelings. Find out what are the main threads of their argument or ideas.
- Keep eye contact with the person who is speaking.

When you have listened to other people in the team and you understand what they are talking about, then you may be in a position provide positive (fair) feedback. Positive feedback means that you should:

- acknowledge what people say or do
- praise them as appropriate and compliment them
- let them know how they are getting on – how clearly they have expressed their ideas, whether you think, for example, their suggestion or ideas could work.

Giving feedback is not just talking; it can also be done non-verbally (without talking). You can let others know what you think or feel about them by the expression on your face. You can have a bored expression or a happy one. By keeping eye contact with others, you also show that you are interested in what they are saying.

## Activity 11

Work in pairs.

**a** Sit opposite each other. One person should talk to the other. You can say anything, perhaps how you arrived at college this morning or the last film you saw. The person listening should not look at the face of the person speaking (do not make eye contact). Change roles after about five minutes.

**b** Each of you should explain what your feelings were when you were talking to the person who was not keeping eye contact. For example, did it make you feel uncomfortable? Did you feel angry?

*The person speaking should be the focus of your attention. By keeping eye contact, you show that you are interested in what they are saying*

People like to work with those who give positive or good feedback. Such people are usually cheerful, friendly and helpful. However, you do not have to agree with everything everyone says. Responding to feedback positively does not mean always agreeing with the other person. It means giving them a fair hearing and not reacting angrily to their suggestions or ideas. You may not agree with the feedback that a member of the team gives you, and they may not agree with your ideas. However, the important thing is that you can listen to each other and discuss your ideas without getting angry with each other.

You must show that you value your team members as people and you do this by:

- listening to them
- allowing them to put their ideas forward without fear of undue criticism.

*List two things you can do that show that you value people.*

## Aim to:

- Listen and respond to communications from other team members.
- Use good eye contact and keep smiling.
- Be sincere, sympathetic and understanding.
- Be kind, gentle and tactful.
- Be willing to allow other members of the group to do as much as possible for themselves. Encourage others to be as independent as possible.

## Writing up the report of the team activity

Although you will have done many tasks as part of the team, each member will have to write a report describing:

- what the team has done
- what you have done individually – your individual contribution to the activity.

Your report must include all of the following:

- Team performance
  - Why you chose the specific activity
  - Why as a team you agreed to do particular things
  - Why you made the contributions you did
- Team action plan
  - The aims of the activity – what you intended to do
  - The actions the team and individual members took
  - A list of available resources
  - The resources used and why
  - Any problems the team encountered and what you did about them
- Your individual action plan
  - How you followed the individual action plan
  - How you made the best use of available resources
- How you maintained health and safety
- How you co-operated with your team members
- Review of the activity
  - The resources used
  - Your responses to any problems encountered
  - Health and safety
  - Your feedback to colleagues and how you responded to any feedback from other team members
- Your suggestions for improvements in the way you would tackle a similar activity in the future
- Evidence of core skills you obtained while doing the activity.

## Key terms

After reading this unit you should be able to understand the following words and phrases. If you do not, go back through the unit and find out, or look them up in the Glossary.

| | |
|---|---|
| *Mutual exchange* | *Team action plan* |
| *Brainstorming* | *Recording* |
| *Time management* | *Interpersonal communication* |
| *Note-taking* | *Constructive feedback* |

## Test yourself

1 Why do people form groups?
2 What does it mean for a group to brainstorm?
3 What is time management?
4 What should you consider before you contact people?
5 What is the purpose of note-taking?
6 What is a team action plan?
7 What things may stop people from communicating?
8 What are the two parts of reviewing team activity?
9 What does it mean to provide feedback to your team members?
10 What does non-verbal communication mean?

# Assignment For Unit Nine

*Produce a written or oral report of a chosen team activity.*

### Tasks

1 Describe the activity that you have chosen, identify the client group and give three aims of the activity. One of the aims must indicate what benefit the activity is to the client. You should also say how the group selected the activity.

2 Draw up a plan as a group and show the individual roles or jobs that the group has decided for each member. Also, list the resources needed. These must include:
   – finance
   – people
   – equipment
   – tasks to be done.

**You must carry out and record tasks 1 and 2 before you start the activity.**

3 Describe what you and the other team members did during the activity. You can record this in the form of a diary or log of events. You must make it clear what you did as an individual.

4 Demonstrate that you have negotiated and listened to others and their ideas. You must also show that you worked with your team members to solve any problems or disagreements.

5 Write a review of the activity to show
   – what went well and what did not
   – how well you carried out your role
   – how well your team members worked
   – how important team work is.

### Get the grade

To achieve a **PASS** you must complete tasks 1–3.

To achieve a **MERIT** you must complete tasks 1–5.

To achieve a **DISTINCTION** you must complete tasks 1–7.

6 Clearly communicate your ideas about the activity. You should show how you communicated ideas and listened to others, how you identified potential problems and any work you undertook towards their solution.

7 Demonstrate fluent skills of communication throughout the activity.

## Key Skills

### Opportunity

| | **You can use this opportunity to provide evidence for the following key skills** |
|---|---|
| CommunicationC1.1 | Plan and review the activity with your team. |
| Communication C1.2 | Find out about resources for the activity. |
| Communication C1.3 | Write a plan for the activity and write the review of the activity. |
| Application of Number N1.2 | Use money – carry out straightforward calculations. |

# Glossary

**Adolescence**

The years between the onset of puberty and the beginning of adult life, approximately between the ages of 11 and 18

**Advertisements**

An item on television or in magazines and newspapers that communicates a particular message or informs people. Advertisements might be used to advertise jobs or to promote healthy eating

**Application form**

A form used by employers, and completed by people applying for jobs, to make decisions about who to call for interview. Employers can often find out more about an applicant from an application form than from a CV because they can ask for the precise information they need to know

**Assistive equipment**

Items such as wheelchairs, walking frames, hoists, specially designed knives, spoons and forks, etc. that help people with disabilities to perform daily tasks for themselves or help their carers to care for them

**Balanced diet**

A diet that provides you with enough of the various types of nutrients required to meet the needs of your body (i.e. the correct amount of carbohydrate, protein, fat, vitamins and minerals)

**Basic physical needs**

Needs that humans have that need to be fulfilled in order to stay alive. These include the need to satisfy hunger, thirst and sexual desire, to maintain temperature, and the need for oxygen, sleep and sensory pleasures

**Body language**

A non-verbal form of communication. For example, if you smile you communicate that you are happy without needing to say 'I'm feeling happy' but if you cross your arms you look defensive and unapproachable. A significant amount of communication is done without speaking

**Brainstorming**

When the members of a team quickly write down as many ideas about the subject as they can think of, when they think of them. It helps you to look at things in a new and imaginative way

**Carbohydrates**

A group of chemicals found in food that are made up of simple sugars (e.g. glucose and sucrose). These are filling and provide a lot of energy. Carbohydrates can be found in bread, potatoes and pasta

**Care value base**
Care values are principles, standards and qualities that are considered worthwhile or desirable by people who care for others. It is important that people working in health and social care (e.g. nurses, home helps, teachers, etc.) hold these values and apply them in their work. They are working from the care value base

**Confidentiality**
The right of a client to have any information about him or herself kept private. So, if a client tells you a secret, you should not tell anyone else unless this would mean you breaking the law, or the information makes you think the client might harm themselves or others

**Constructive feedback**
Giving someone information about their performance, for example, how well they have completed a task and how they could improve

**Covering letter**
A letter to accompany your CV that introduces you to the employer and will encourage him or her to read your CV

**Curriculum vitae (CV)**
A written document designed to let employers know your personal details, qualifications and experience

**Daily living activities**
Everyday activities such as eating, walking and getting dressed

**Degenerative disease**
A disease which gradually worsens over time

**Diagnosis**
When a doctor examines a patient, discusses their symptoms, runs tests and then decides what is wrong, they have made a diagnosis

**Diet**
Any food we eat. A balanced diet (the correct proportions of carbohydrates, protein, fats, vitamins and minerals) is essential for good health

**Diploma in Social Work**
The professional qualification for all social workers (field and residential). It involves two years of study and practice supervised by a qualified social worker

**Directed thinking**
The ability to concentrate on one thing

**Discrimination**
How a person can treat another person or group of people unfairly, based on their prejudice

**Empower**

To give power to someone. For example, giving clients choice and allowing them to make decisions that affect their own lives is empowering

**Fat**

A macro nutrient found in food and needed to provide energy for all body activity. Also needed to maintain cell structures as cell membranes are largely fat. Fat is found in margarine, milk, chips, chocolate, etc.

**Fibre**

An indigestible material found in food, mainly in vegetables, cereals and brown bread

**First Aider**

A person who has attended training and gained a first aid certificate that enables them to give basic first aid in an emergency. The certificate has to be renewed every three years

**Health Action Zones**

Designed to bring local health organisations together with local authorities, community groups, voluntary groups and local businesses to promote improved health for local people

**Health care support worker**

Someone who assists health care professionals in hospitals, clinics and community nursing

**Indirect carers**

People who work in the health service and provide indirect care to clients (e.g. porters in hospitals who wheel clients around) rather than the direct services provided by social workers or nurses

**Intellectual recreational activity**

A mentally stimulating and relaxing form of recreation. These types of activity often involve problem solving, for example chess

**Interpersonal communication**

Communication between people

**Language**

An organised system of symbols which humans use to communicate and establish relationships with one another (e.g. the written or spoken word and sign language)

**Life expectancy**

The length of time a person can expect to live

**Macro nutrients**

These are simply large nutrients. There are three macro nutrients: protein, fat and carbohydrate

**Major life changes**

Alterations that are sometimes planned but more often are unexpected which change our lives significantly. Examples are the death of a family member, the breakdown of a relationship and the loss of a job. These can be sources of stress

**Menopause**

This involves a series of changes in female hormones which eventually means the end of a woman's ability to have children. Women begin to experience the menopause or the 'change of life' any time after 40 years of age

**Microbes**

Small living organisms or micro-organisms

**Micro nutrients**

These are simply small nutrients. There are two important classes of micro nutrients: vitamins and minerals

**Minerals**

Chemicals that are found in food, not produced by the body, but needed to stay healthy (e.g. calcium and iron)

**Monogamy**

When a person is married to only one other person (e.g. a man has only one wife)

**Moving and handling techniques**

The European Handling Regulations came into effect on 1 January 1993. They place the responsibility for the safety of workers on the management of the organisation. All employers must ensure the safety of their workers by making sure these techniques are used

**Mutual exchange**

The passing of personal information between individuals which leads to better understanding and acceptance of each other

**National Health Service**

An organisation formed in 1948 by the National Health Service Act to plan and distribute health care funded with public money

**National Vocational Qualifications (NVQs)**

A new form of qualification that is gained through vocationally based learning. Students train for jobs in the environment in which they will be working

**NHS Direct**

A public service that gives advice and immediate information on what to do and not to do in an emergency. The public can telephone NHS Direct for advice at any time of day or night

**NHS Trusts**

Self-governing health care organisations, such as hospitals, with responsibility for managing their own money and employing their

own staff. They compete for contracts to provide health care
alongside private and voluntary sector providers

## Note-taking/Recording

Making a written record of what you have been studying,
information that you have been collecting or the items discussed in
a meeting for future reference

## Nutrients

The content of food is described in terms of the nutrients it
contains (i.e. protein, fat, carbohydrate, vitamins, minerals, etc.)

## Passive smoking

When non-smokers inhale tobacco smoke from the cigarettes of
smokers because they share the same space and breath the same air

## Physical recreational activities

Leisure activities that require physical exertion (e.g. swimming,
aerobics) and improve fitness. They contribute to greater strength,
stamina, suppleness, speed of reaction, heart and lung efficiency
and determination

## Plasma

A colourless fluid which forms most of the volume of the blood

## Polyandry

When a woman has several husbands

## Polygamy

When a man has several wives

## Pre-school child

A child between the ages of 3 and 5 who is not yet in formal
education

## Primary Health Groups (PHGs)

Made up of GPs and community nurses, primary health groups
work with NHS Trusts to plan the new services to deliver quick,
accessible, co-ordinated care of a high standard

## Private sector

Health care provided by the private sector is paid for by the patient
rather than with public money. Private health care is available
within NHS-owned institutions, with the patient paying for the
services, and within totally separate private health care facilities

## Project 2000

A three-year training programme for nurses. Most nurse training
takes place at university

## Protein

A nutrient found in food. Our bodies use it to build and repair
cells and tissues. Protein can be found in meat, fish, eggs, lentils,
etc.

### Psycho-social

Many of the issues associated with adolescence are psycho-social in nature, that is, dependent on the individual's level of maturation and also on the demands of the society in which they live. For example, spots are physical but they may cause problems such as depression, shyness and embarrassment because society tends to make fun of teenagers with spots

### Puberty

Term meaning 'age of manhood', when physical changes occur to the body because of the increased production of sex hormones (oestrogens in girls and testosterone in boys)

### Purchasers and providers

Purchasers are individuals and organisations (GPs or Primary Care Groups) who buy services for their clients, for example operations in hospital. Providers are the organisations (for example, hospitals) who provide these services

### Recruitment

The process to find someone to fill a job vacancy. The main stages of recruitment are: the employer advertises the job, applicants apply for the job, the employer selects the most suitable applicants to interview, these applicants attend an interview, the employer decides which applicant to employ and offers them the job

### Reference nutrient intake

The daily requirements of nutrients for different groups of people

### Registered General Nurse (RGN)

Qualified nurses who mainly work in hospitals, carrying out practical tasks like giving injections, dressing wounds, administering drugs and washing and feeding patients

### Regional Health Authorities (RHAs)

There are eight Regional Health Authorities in England. They are responsible for regional planning and allocating money to other health authorities

### Remedial treatment

A course of action to correct something, for example a brace to straighten or exercises to strengthen a muscle

### Risks to health

Anything that may have negative effects on health is a risk. These things can be physical, social, emotional or intellectual and include poor diet, changing jobs or schools, loss or bereavement or stress.

### Safety hazards

Something that has the potential to cause harm, including ill health and injury. The hazard presented by a substance (e.g. poisons and chemicals) is its potential to cause harm

**Self-esteem**

How much a person values him or herself

**Socialisation**

The process by which people are taught the 'correct' way to behave in society

**Social recreational activities**

Leisure activities that involve contact with others. For example, playing football on a Saturday

**Social services**

In 1970 the Local Authority Social Services Act set up local authority social services departments in England and Wales. The aim was to form an effective, family-oriented, community-based service that was available to all who needed it

**Stereotyping**

Saying that people who belong to a particular social group are 'all the same' on the basis of little evidence. Particularly applied to minority groups and closely linked to prejudice

**Team action plan**

A plan that outlines what each team member needs to do and how each person's work slots together to complete a task given to the team

**Therapeutic community**

An environment where health care is provided (e.g. at home, in hospital, in a day care etc.) and people receive treatment for their illness

**Time management**

Defining how much time you have to complete tasks and organising your time effectively

**Toxic effects**

The harmful effects of poisonous chemicals. These include skin disorders, headaches, sickness, chest problems, heart, lung and liver disease and cancer

**Vegetarian**

A person who does not eat meat

**Vitamins**

Chemicals produced by living organisms that are needed to help your body to function properly

**Voluntary sector**

This term refers to all non-statutory organisations that contribute to social care, for example the WRVS

# Index

Page references in *italics* indicate tables or diagrams

A B C rule (first aid) 162
abdominal thrusts 170, *170*
access to services
    cost considerations 32–5
    information sources 30–1,
      35–6
    physical access 31
    referrals 28–30
    to recreational activities
      230–1
accidents 69
action plans
    individual 317, *317*
    review of 320–1
    team 313–16, *314*
administrators 284
adolescents
    basic needs *49*
    diet 51, 52, 192
    emotional development 95
    intellectual development 95
    and parents 118
    and peer groups 118
    personal hygiene 70
    puberty 93–4
    recreation 217, 221
    social development 94–5
adoption 18–19
adrenaline 73
adults 96
    18 to 25 years 96–7
    25 to 40 years 98
    40 to 64 years 98
    basic needs *49*
    diet 52, 192–3
    exercise risks 58–9
    height and weight *79*
    relationships 96–7, 98, 118
    *see also* elderly people
advertisements, job 292–4
aerobic exercise 55
age
    and recreation 215
    *see also* adolescents; adults;
      children; elderly people
AIDS 65, 68
aids *see* assistive equipment
airways 162, 163–4
alcohol 62–4, *64*, 187
allergic conditions 167
amino acids 177, 178, 179
amphetamines *66*

anabolic steroids *66*
anaemia 52, 185
anaerobic exercise 55
anorexia nervosa 190
application forms, job 295,
    298–300, *299*
artificial respiration 165, *165*
assistive equipment 240, *243*, 250
    dressing and undressing 252,
      *252*
    eating and drinking aids 252
    hoists and lifting equipment
      *137*, 250, *252*
    mobility aids 253, *253*
    personal care support 250,
      *251*
    reading and hearing aids 253
    safety and care of 264
    sources 254–6, *254*
asthma 167–8
atheroma 244, *244*

babies 87, *87*
    diet 51
    height and weight 78, *78*
back injuries 136, *137*
bacteria 139
balanced diet *see* diet
bleeding 151, 155–6
body language 259
body mass index 78, *79*
bones, broken 157–8
Braille 38
brain degeneration 244
brainstorming 306–8
breakfast 195
breathing 164, *164*, 167
broken bones 157–8
burns 152–3

calcium 52–3, *177*, *182*, 185, 193,
    201
cancer 244
cannabis *66*
carbohydrates 175, *176*, 180–1,
    187
cardio-pulmonary resuscitation
    (CPR) 165–6, *166*
care assistants 287–90
carers
    attitudes of 23, 240–1
    and client's informed

      decisions 247
    and confidentiality 23,
      121–2, 263
    and health and safety 146–9
    relationships with clients
      119–20
    support for 248
care value base 22–3
    confidentiality 23
    and discrimination 25–7
    non-judgemental attitude 25
    people as individuals 23
    and stereotyping 24–5
cellulose 180
change 71–2, *72*
    coping with 75–6
    emotional changes 74
    loss and grieving 72
    social effects 73–4
    and stress 73, *73*, 74, 75
charities 11
charters 36
chemicals, safe use of 130–1
chest massage 165–6, *166*
childminders 19, 21
children
    basic needs *49*
    development to 3 years 86–7,
      *88–9*
    development 3 to 5 years
      90–1
    development 5 to 10 years
      91–3
    diet 51, 192
    early years services 21–2
    exercise risks 58
    height and weight 78–9, *78*
    and language 117
    learning 109, 116–17
    personal hygiene 70
    position in family 109
    recreation 215, 217, 218–20
    relationships 91, 92–3, 115,
      117
    residential care 18–19
    *see also* adolescents
choking 169–70
cholesterol 187
Chronically Sick and Disabled
    Persons Act 1971 255
clerical staff 284
clients

and confidentiality 121–2, 263–4
as individuals 12, 23, 122–4, 261–3
lifting or moving 136, 139, 264–6
needs 28, *28*, 103–5, *104*
and physical care services 246–9, *246*, *247*
relationships with carers 119–20, 247
closed fractures 157, *157*
cocaine *66*
communication
contacting people 309–10
difficulties 323
information about services 30–1, 35–9
interpersonal 323
non-verbal 259–61
skills 328–30
community (district) nurses 8, 15, 275
community psychiatric nurses 15, 273
compulsory referrals 29
concussion 150–2
confidentiality 23, 121–2, 263–4
consciousness, levels of 163
contraception 67
Control of Substances Hazardous to Health Regulations 1988 (COSHH) 130
convulsions 168
costs and funding
health and social care 4, 32–5
recreational activities 217–18, 232–3
Council for Voluntary Services (CVS) 11–12
covering letters (job applications) 297, *297*
CPR (cardio-pulmonary resuscitation) 165–6, *166*
crack cocaine *66*
cross-contamination, avoiding 203
Cross-roads 248
cultural needs 107
culture
and diet 198
and recreation 216
cuts 155–6
CV (curriculum vitae) 295–7, *296*
CVS (Council for Voluntary Services) 11–12

daily living activities 239
day-care workers 19
day centres 19, 226, 249
day nurseries 19, 21, 283
deficiency diseases *176*, *177*, 184, 185
degenerative diseases 244, 245
dementia 60
dentists 15–16, 279–80
depression 74
development *see* personal development
DHAs (District Health Authorities) 4, 5
diabetes, diet and 200
diagnosis 14
diet 45
and anaemia 52
average energy requirements *191*
balanced 174
balanced diet benefits 183
calcium and vitamin D imbalance 52–3
and change 75
control of food eaten 51–2
dietary patterns 194–7, *194*
for different groups of people 190–3
hygienic food preparation 202–4
importance of 188
and income 114
influences on diet choice 197–9
NACNE Report 186–7
nutrients 174–83, *175*, *176*, *177*, *182*
overweight problems 189–90, *190*
special diets 199–201
unbalanced diet effects 184–6, *184*, 188, 190
underweight problems 190
dietary fibre 180–1, 184–5, 187
dignity, maintaining client's 257–8
Diploma in Social Work (Dip.SW) 281
directed thinking 91
disabilities, people with 241
assistive equipment 250–6
elderly people 244
empowerment 257–8
recreation 224
residential care 19
and stereotyping 24–5

Disabled Living Foundation 254
discrimination 24, 25–6
behaviours indicating 26
sexual 26–7
District Health Authorities (DHAs) 4, 5
district (community) nurses 8, 15, 275
doctors 271–2
*see also* GPs
domestic staff 284
dreaming 46
dressing aids 252, *252*
drinking aids 252
drugs 62, 63, 65, *66*

early years services 7–9, 21–2
eating aids 252
eating patterns 195–7
economic factors 114
and diet 198
and health risks 60, 61
and personal development 114–15, *114*
and recreation 217–18, 232–3
ecstasy *66*
education 109–10
elderly people 99, 241, *241*, 257
assistive equipment 250–6
basic needs *49*
degenerative diseases 244–5
diet 52, 193
eating patterns 196–7
health risks 59, 60
independence and dignity 257–8
and physical care services 246–9, *246*, *247*
physical changes 100–1
psychological changes 101
recreation 215, 217, 221–2, 226–7
residential care 18
social aspects of ageing 101–2
and stereotyping 24
electric shock 153–4
emergencies *see* health emergencies
emotional development *85*
adolescents 95
children 90–1, 93
and families 109
infancy *88–9*
emotional needs *48*, *49*, 106
employees
and health and safety 146–9
*see also* staff

employers and health and safety 144–5
employment
    sheltered workshops 19–20
    *see also* jobs; staff
empowerment 257–8
epilepsy 168–9
European Handling Regulations 1993 136, 265
exercise 53
    aerobic and anaerobic 54–5
    benefits 55, *56*
    and coping with change 75
    how to 53–4
    and overweight 189
    risk and 58–9
    starting a regime 57
    *see also* physical recreation
eye contact 260

facial expressions 259
families
    changes in old age 102
    and emotional security 109
    individual's position within 109
    recreation 217, 222
    and relationships 117
    size 108
    structure 107–8
family centres 22
Family Health Service Authorities (FHSAs) 6
fats 175, *176*, 179–80, 186–7, 190
feedback, constructive 328–30
feet 70–1
FHSAs (Family Health Service Authorities) 6
fibre, dietary 180–1, 184–5, 187
fire extinguishers 133, *133*
Fire Precautions Act 1971 132
fire safety 132–3, 148–9
    on discovering a fire 134
first aid 135, 161–2
    A B C rule 162
    how to get help 162
first aid boxes 135
first aiders 135
fitness
    and recreation 210, 215
    *see also* exercise
fits 168–9
folic acid *182*
food
    availability 197–8
    hygienic preparation 202–3, 203–4

prices 198
storage 203
tables 182
*see also* diet
foster care 18
fractures 157–8, *157*
fungi 139

gangs 118, 221
gender
    and discrimination 26–7
    and recreation 215–16
general practitioners *see* GPs
germs 139–40
good health *see* health and well-being
GPs (general practitioners) 6, 13–14, 272
    and Primary Health Care Groups 8
    referrals 29
'grand mal' 168
greenstick fractures 157, *157*
grieving 72
groups
    membership of 112–13, 118, 221, 311
    support 20
    *see also* teams and teamwork
growth 85
    *see also* personal development

hair 70
handling *see* lifting
hazards 129, 141
    *see also* health and safety
HCA (health care assistants) 17, 279
head injuries 150–2
health and safety 129–30
    assistive equipment 264
    common hazards in care settings 141–3
    considerations for teams 323–4, 327–8
    employees and 146–9
    employers and 144–5
    fire 132–4, 148–9
    first aid 135, 161–3
    hazardous substances 129–32
    in the home 69
    infectious disease 139–41
    lifting 136–8, *138*
    lifting or moving clients 136, 139, 264–6
    passive smoking 132
    recreational activities 233–4

safety needs 104
safety signs *146*
*see also* health emergencies
Health and Safety at Work Act 1974 144
health and well-being 43–4, *44*
    accidents 69
    and alcohol 62–4
    basic needs 48, *48*, *49*
    and breakdown in normal daily activities 60–1
    and diet 45, 50–3, 190
    and drugs 65, *66*
    effects of change 71–6
    and exercise 53–7, 58–9
    health plans 47–8
    health risks 49–50, *50*, 71
    indicators of 76–80
    personal hygiene 59–60, 69–71
    and recreation 45
    and relaxation and sleep 46–7
    and sexual practice 67–8
    and smoking 62
Health Act 1999 6, 7–8
Health Action Zones 9
Health Authorities 4, 5, 8, 9
health care assistants (HCAs) 17, 279
health care services
    career paths *286*
    costs and funding 32–3, 34–5
    the future 7–9
    information about 30–1, 35–9
    organisation 2–7, *3*
    physical access to 31–2
    physical care 246–7, *246*, *247*
    private 12–13
    referrals 28–9
    staff 13–17, 21, 271–80, *271*, 284
health care support workers 17, 279
health centres 14–15
health emergencies
    airways 163–4
    asthma 167–8
    broken bones 157–8
    burns and scalds 152–3
    choking 169–70
    consciousness and unconsciousness 163
    cuts and bleeding 155–6
    electric shock 153–4
    epileptic fits 168–9
    first aid 161–3

head injuries 150–2
heart attack 158–60
poisoning 160–1
resuscitation 164–6
shock 150
Health Improvement Programmes 8
health plans 47–8
health risks *see* risks to health and well-being
health visitors 15, 275
hearing aids 253
heart attacks 158–60
heart massage 165–6, *166*
height 77–8, 78, *78*, *79*
height when communicating 260
heroin *66*
HIV (Human Immunodeficiency Virus) 65, 68
hoists 250, *252*
home care assistants 19, 282
home helps 19, 282
homelessness 61, 70
hospitals 2, 16, 271
staff 16–17, 271–2, 276–7
housing 110
and personal development 111, 115
sheltered 18, 112
human development *see* personal developmenmt
Human Immunodeficiency Virus (HIV) 65, 68
hygiene
in care setting 145
food preparation 202–3
*see also* personal hygiene

identity 93, 94
ill-health *see* risks to health and well-being
income 114, *114*, 198, 217
independence, maintaining client's 257–8
indirect care 21, 284
individuals
needs 28, *28*
people as 23, 122–4, 261–3
*see also* clients
infancy 86–7, *88–9*
*see also* children
infections 139–40
preventing spread of 140–1
information 30, 35
about assistive equipment 254

adapting to meet client needs 37–8
charters 36
location of publicity 39
mutual exchange of in teams 312
sources 31, 35–6
intellectual development *85*
adolescents 95, 110
children 90, 91–2, 109
elderly people 101
infancy *88–9*
intellectual needs 48, *49*, 106, 109
intellectual recreation 208, *208*
benefits 211
children 218, 219, 220
elderly people 227
intelligence in old age 101
interpersonal communication 323
interpersonal skills 328–9
interviews
job 300–2
note-making 319
iron 52, *177*, *182*, 185, 193

jobs
advertisements for 292–4
application forms 298–300, *299*
applying for 295
career paths *286*
CVs 295–7
information about 294
interviews 300–2
specifications 300
*see also* staff

language 109, 117
learning 116
leisure
income and 114–15
*see also* recreational activities
life events 72, 76
stress scale *75*
*see also* change
life expectancy 99, *100*
lifting 136–8, *138*
equipment *137*, 250, *252*
or moving clients 136, 139, 264–6
listening skills 261, 329
loneliness in old age 102
LSD *66*

macronutrients 175, *176*
carbohydrates 180–1, 187

fats 179–80, 186–7, 190
proteins 177–9, *182*, 187, 192
maintenance staff 284
managers 284
Maslow's theory of human needs 103–5, *104*
meals 195–6
*see also* diet
meals-on-wheels 282
memory and old age 101
menopause 52–3, 98, 185
mental handicap nurses 15, 273
microbes 139–40
micronutrients 175, *176*
minerals *177*, 185, 192, 193
and vegan diet 139–40
vitamins 185, 192, 193
middle age 98
midwives 15, 275–6
minerals 175, *176*, 177
adolescent's diet 192
deficiencies *177*, 185
and pregnancy 193
mobility 47, 239
aids 253, *253*
monogamy 108
mothers 117
*see also* parents
mouth-to-mouth resuscitation 164–5, *165*
moving *see* lifting

NACNE (National Advisory Committee on Nutrition Education) Report 186–7
nails 70
National Health Service (NHS) 2–7, 270
the future 7–9, *9*
staff 13–17, 21, 271–80, 284
structure to 1999 *4*
supply of assistive equipment 256
National Record of Achievement 302
National Vocational Qualifications (NVQs) in Care 284
needs 28, *28*, 103
'activities of daily living' model 105
basic 48, *48*, *49*, 85–6
Maslow's theory 103–5, *104*
meeting 106–7
NHS *see* National Health Service
NHS and Community Care Act 1990 4, 6, 9, 10, 35
NHS Direct 8

NHS Trusts 6, 8
non-discriminatory attitude 25
non-judgemental attitude 25
non-verbal communication 259
    eye contact 260
    facial expressions 259
    feeling threatened 261
    height 260
Northern Ireland 4, 10
note-taking 318–20
NSPCC 11
nursery nurses 283, 290–2
nurses 273–4
    community (district) 8, 15,
        275
    hospital 17
    mental handicap 15, 273
    nursery 283, 290–2
    practice 14, 274–5
    psychiatric 15, 273
    school 276
nursing homes 18, 33
nutrients 174, 174–5, *176*, 181
    carbohydrates 180–1, 187
    fats 179–80, 186–7, 190
    minerals 175, *177*, 185–6,
        192, 193
    proteins 177–9, *182*, 187,
        192, 193
    reference nutrient intakes
        181–2, *182*
    in seasonal foods 197–8
    vitamins 175, *176*, 185–6,
        192, 193
NVQs in Care 284

occupational therapists (OTs) 17,
    277–8
oestrogen 93
old age *see* elderly people
open fractures 157, *157*
opticians 6, 280
osteo-arthritis 244
osteoporosis 52, 185
OTs (occupational therapists) 17,
    277–8
out of school clubs 22
overweight 78, 189–90, 190,
    225–6
Oxfam 20

parents
    and adolescents 118
    adoptive 18–19
    and education 110
    family relationships 117
    foster 18

passive smoking 132
patients
    records 263, 264
    *see also* clients
Patient's Charter *36*, 122
peer groups 113, 118, 221
personal care support 250, *251*
personal development 85, *85*, *107*
    basic needs 85–6, 103–5,
        106–7
    economic factors 114–15,
        *114*
    and families 107–9
    and housing 111, 115
    and relationships 112–13,
        115–18
    and socialisation 109, 110
    stages
        adolescence 93–5
        adulthood 96–8
        childhood 90–3
        infancy 86–7, *88–9*
        old age 99–102
personal hygiene 59–60
    assistive equipment 250, *251*
    and coping with change 75
    feet 70–1
    hair 70
    nails 70
    skin 69–70
    teeth 70
personality
    development 94
    in old age 101
'petit mal' 168
pharmacists 6
physical aids *see* assistive
    equipment
physical care 239–40
    attitude of carer 240–1
    maintaining client's
        independence and dignity
        257–8
    those involved with 246–9,
        *246*, *247*
    *see also* assistive equipment
physical development *85*
    adolescents 93–4
    children 90, 91
    elderly people 100–1
    infancy *88–9*
physical needs *48*, *49*, 104, 106
physical recreation 208, *208*
    and age 215
    benefits 210
    children 218, 219, 220
    elderly people 221–2

physiotherapists 17, 277
plants, poisonous 69
plasma 152
play 218
playgroups 21
poisoning 160–1
    food poisoning 203
    poisonous plants 69
polyandry 108
polygamy 108
polyunsaturated fats 179, 187
poverty 114
    and health risks 60, 61
    and rickets 185
    *see also* economic factors
practice nurses 14, 274–5
pregnancy 67
    and diet 193
prejudice 25
pre-school children 90–1
Primary Care Groups 8, 9
primary groups 112
Primary Health Care Groups 8
private sector care 12–13, 286
    paying for 33–4
    supply of assistive equipment
        256
Project 2000 273–4
prone position 163
proteins 175, *176*, 177–9, *182*,
    187
    adolescent's diet 192
    children's diet 192
protozoa 139
providers and purchasers 6–7
psychiatric nurses 15, 273
psycho-social issues and
    adolescents 94
puberty 93–4
pulse rates 80
purchasers and providers 6–7

racial discrimination 25
radiographers 17, 276–7
reading 211, 215, 220, 222
    aids 253
receptionists 284
records
    patient 263, 264
    of teamwork 321–2
recovery position 151, *152*, 164
recreational activities 45, 208–10,
    *208*
    adolescents 221
    and attitudes 231, 233
    availability 228–30
    benefits 210–12

children 218–20
cost 217–18, 232–3
elderly people 221–2, 226–7
families 222
health and safety 233–4
and income 114
people with physical
    disabilities 224
people with specific health-
    related problems 225–6
people with specific needs
    222–3, 228
physical access 230–1
suitability of *214*, 215–18
surveying local 213–14
recruitment 292
referrals 28
compulsory 29
self-referral 28
through a professional 29
Regional Health Authorities
    (RHAs) 4, 5
registered general nurses (RGNs)
    273
registered mental nurses (RMNs)
    15, 273
registered nurses for the mentally
    handicapped (RNMHs) 15,
    273
relationships 115
adolescents 118
adults 96–7, 98, 118
barriers to good 122–4
childhood 91, 92–3, 115,
    117
client and carer 119–20
and confidentiality 121–2
group membership 112–13
and language 117–18
and socialisation 115–17
relaxation 46, 75
religion and diet 198
reports of teamwork 331
residential care 17
care assistants 287–90
children 18–19
elderly people 18
paying for 33–4
people with disabilities 19
residential homes 18, 33, 226
respect for clients 261–3
respiration 164, *164*, 167
resuscitation
cardio-pulmonary 165–6,
    *166*
mouth-to-mouth 164–5,
    *165*

retirement 101, 241
RGNs (registered general nurses)
    273
RHAs (Regional Health
    Authorities) 4, 5
rickets 185
rights, individual 23
risks to health and well-being 48,
    49–50, *50*, 71
accidents 69
alcohol 62–4
breakdown of normal daily
    activities 60–1
diet 50–3, 190
drug abuse 65, *66*
exercise 58–9
poor personal hygiene 59–60
sexual practice 67–8
smoking 62
RMNs (registered mental nurses)
    15, 273
RNMHs (registered nurses for
    the mentally handicapped)
    15, 273

safety *see* health and safety
salt 187
saturated fats 179, 190
scalds 152–3
school nurses 276
schools 91, 109–10
Scotland 5
secondary groups 113
self-esteem 47, 74, 105, 118
    and recreation 225–6
self-help groups and elderly
    people 248
self-image 91
    and overweight 189–90
self-referral 28
self-respect 105
sexual activity and health risks
    67–8
sexual discrimination 26–7
sexually transmitted diseases
    (STDs) 68, *68*
sheltered accomodation 18, 112
sheltered workshops 19–20
shock 150, 156
shock, electric 153–4
sign language 38
skin 69–70
skull fractures 150, *151*
sleep 46
    amount required 46–7
smoking 62
    passive smoking 132

snacks 195, 196
social care services 9–10, 280–1
career paths *286*
community-based 19–20
costs and funding 33–5
the future 7–8
information about 30–1,
    35–9
organisation 2, *3*, 7, *10*
physical access to 31–2
physical care 246–7, *246*, *247*
private 12
referrals to 28–9
residential care 17–19
staff 17–20, 21, 281–4, *281*,
    284, 287–92
voluntary 11–12, 20, 247–9
social development *85*
adolescents 94–5
and change 73–4
children 90–1, 92–3
elderly people 101–2
infancy *88–9*
*see also* relationships
socialisation 109, 110, 115–17
social needs 48, *49*, 104, 107
social recreation 208, *208*
adolescents 221
availability 229
benefits 212
children 218, 219, 220
elderly people 227
people with physical
    disabilities 224
social services departments (SSDs)
    10, *10*, 280–1
supply of assistive equipment
    54–5
social workers 19, 281
society 109
solvents *66*
speech therapists 17, 278–9
SSDs *see* social services
    departments
staff
health care services 13–17,
    21, 271–80, *271*, 284
social care services 17–20,
    21, 281–4, *281*, 287–92
voluntary sector 285
starches 180
statutory services 2
STDs (sexually transmitted
    diseases) 68, *68*
stereotyping 24–5, 110,
    122–4, 215–16
stress 46, 73

effects *73, 74*
scale of life events *75*
sucrose 180, 187
sugars 180, 187, 190
supervisory workers 19–20
support
coping with change 75
for elderly people 247–9
support groups 20, 248
swimming 226

teams and teamwork 306, 311–12
action plan review 320–1, *321*
action plans 313–16, *314*
action plans for individuals 317, *317*
best use of resources 318
brainstorming 306–8
communication within 323
contacting people 309–10
feedback 328–30
getting to know other members 312–13
and health and safety 323–4, 327–8
note-taking 318–20
performance review 324–8

records 321–3
report writing 331
time management 308–9, *308*
teenagers *see* adolescents
teeth 70
testosterone 93, 193
therapeutic communities 19
thiamin *176, 182*
time management 308–9, *308*
toxic substances 130–1
tuberculosis 61

unconsciousness 163
underweight 190

values *see* care value base
vegans 201
vegetarians 51, 185, 201
viruses 139
vitamins 175, *176*
children's diet 192
deficiencies *176*, 185
and pregnancy 193
vitamin B12 201
vitamin D 52–3, 185, 192
voluntary care sector 11–12, 20, 285

and elderly people 247–9
supply of assistive equipment 256

Wales 4
water in the diet 175, *176*
weight 77–8, *78, 79*
overweight problems 78, 189–90, 190
underweight problems 190
weight-reduction diets 199–200
well-being *see* health and well-being
women
diet 52–3, 185, 193
*see also* gender
work
health and safety *see* health and safety
*see also* jobs
workshops, sheltered 19–20
wounds, dressing 155–6
W position 159, *159*
WRVS 285

zinc *177, 182*